The Computer Industry: An Economic-Legal
Analysis of its Technology and Growth

The Computer Industry

An Economic – Legal Analysis of its Technology and Growth

John T. Soma

Lexington Books

D.C. Heath and Company
Lexington, Massachusetts
Toronto

Publishers Note: On November 11, 1975 Mr. Soma inquired as to possible publication of his manuscript on the computer industry. We requested a copy of the work on November 17, 1975, and subsequently agreed to publish the manuscript.

Library of Congress Cataloging in Publication Data

Soma, John T
    The computer industry.

    Bibliography: p. 173
    Includes index.
    1. Computer industry—United States. 2. Computers—Law and legislation—United States. 3. Computers. I. Title.
HD9696.C63U584   338.4'7'001640973   76-2989
ISBN 0-669-00643-2

Published simultaneously in Canada

Printed in the United States of America

International Standard Book Number: 0-669-00643-2

Library of Congress Catalog Card Number: 76-2989

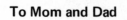

To Mom and Dad

Contents

List of Figures

Preface

Little has been written on the U.S. computer industry integrating the economic conditions of the industry with computer technology and the legal environment of the industry.[1] These three factors must be considered to obtain a comprehensive view of the industry. Therefore, this book focuses on the interaction of the economic, technological, and legal factors existing within the U.S. computer industry. After exploring the interaction of these three factors, the underlying causes of the rapid technological growth in the industry are examined, and a technological forecast is made based on the interaction of these three underlying factors. One of the central tasks faced by the U.S. computer industry is that of maintaining its present rapid technological growth rate, and therefore, its world dominance. To sustain its rapid growth and continued world dominance, the U.S. computer industry must remain at the frontiers of computer technology. Therefore, policy measures that will insure the continued advancement of computer technology are discussed.

This book concentrates on the U.S. computer industry and focuses on general purpose digital computers.[2] Although analogue and hybrid computers are currently manufactured, the overwhelming majority of computers built since the 1940s have been digital computers.[3]

The Economic Development of the U.S. Computer Industry

The electronic digital computer emerged after the successful integration of several diverse scientific disciplines. The process of integrating these scientific

---

[1] Many books ranging from nontechnical to highly technical have been written on computers in general, *See e.g.*, S. Thomas, *Computers: Their History, Present Applications, and Future* (1965).

[2] A digital computer operates with numbers expressed directly as digits and counts discretely, whereas an analogue computer operates on data represented by variable physical quantitites such as voltages, and measures continuously. A hybrid computer is composed of both digital and analogue components. *See generally* Serrel, *et al.,* "The Evolution of Computing Machinery and Systems," 49 *Proceedings of the Institute of Radio Engineers* 1039 (1961).

[3] Computer privacy is an important issue in the industry, but it is beyond the scope of this book. *See* A. Miller, *The Assault on Privacy. Computers, Databanks, and Dossiers* (1971); A. Weston, *Privacy and Freedom* (1967). *See also* A. Brier and I. Robinson, *Computers and the Social Sciences* (1974); D. Loth and M. Ernst, *The Taming of Technology* (1972); M. Martin and A. Norman, *The Computerized Society: An Appraisal of the Impact of Computers on Society over the Next 15 Years* (1970).

disciplines evolved through a repetitive series of events.[4]   This series of events began with a large underlying demand for information processing. The Federal Government then funded advanced computer development projects, many of which were at academic institutions. Finally, commercial development occurred in which the various technologies were molded into economically viable products to satisfy the underlying demand for information processing. Chapter 1 examines this development cycle in greater detail.

The Legal Environment

The computer industry has been greatly influenced in its development by the legal environment surrounding it. The legal environment can be expected to be a major factor influencing the future development of the industry. The major legal areas affecting the computer industry include antitrust regulation, proprietary ownership matters (patent, copyright, and trade secret protection of software), data communications, taxation, import-export regulations, and government procurement policies. Each of these areas is briefly analyzed in Chapter 2 to determine the interaction between the legal environment and advancing computer technology.

Computer Technology

Computer technology was defined by Turn as "the totality of means, devices, processes, and techniques employed in the construction and operation of digital computers."[5]   Since the emergence of the computer in the late 1940s, computer technology has rapidly advanced causing the ratio of computer cost-to-performance to decline dramatically. As a result, data processing costs have continuously decreased. Consequently, any study of the growth of the industry must include an analysis of the technology involved.

The study of technology is an important area of economics. Rosenberg states that if the:

studies of such people as Abramovitz and Solow are even approximately correct with respect to orders of magnitude, then the contributions of technological

---

[4] *See generally* Rosenberg, "Technological Change in the Machine Tool Industry, 1840-1910," 23 *J. Econ. His.* 414 (Dec. 1963) (Discussion of technological convergence explaining the development of the machine tool industry from its origins in the firearms industry in the 1700s to its full development in the early 1900s in the auto industry).

[5] R. Turn, *Computers in the 1980's* 6 (1974).

change to rising per capita incomes absolutely dwarfs the contribution from a rising but qualitatively unchanging stock of capital.[6]

Several studies on technology have been made.[7] Unfortunately, no complete theory of technological growth is available to explain in quantifiable terms how economic, technical, and social factors interrelate to cause technological growth.

Underlying this entire study of the computer industry is the fact that the computer industry is inherently a high-technology industry as compared with more technologically stable industries. Scherer concluded after examining the differences in research and development expenditures, patenting, and related activity in several industries, that the:

> most important determinant (for industrial innovation) is undoubtedly the richness of opportunities opened by advances in science and technical knowledge. . . . The richness of technological opportunity varies widely from one product area to another, giving rise to extensive inter-industry variation in R and D spending, patenting, and the like.[8]

Therefore, at least part of the reason for the rapid technological growth in the computer industry must be attributed to the fact that at present the industry is inherently a high technology industry. This must be taken into account in any attempt to predict the future course of the industry, as will be seen in the technological forecast in Chapter 3.

Technological Forecast

Jantsch defined technological forecasting as "the probabilistic assessment, on relatively high confidence level, of future technology transfer."[9] First attempted in the middle of the 1940s, technological forecasting emerged as a recognized management discipline in the early 1960s. Numerous techniques exist to forecast future social, political, and economic conditions.[10]

---

[6] Rosenberg, "Technical Change in the Machine Tool Industry, 1840-1910," 23 *J. Econ. Hist.* 414 (Dec. 1963). *See also* Abramovitz, "Resource and Output Trends in the U.S. Since 1900." 40 *Am. Econ. Rev. Papers and Proceedings* 1 (May 1956); Solow, "Technical Change and the Aggregate Production Function." 39 *Rev. Econ. Stat.* 312 (Aug. 1957).

[7] *See* E. Mansfield, *The Economics of Technological Change* (1968)

[8] F. Scherer, *Industrial Market Structure and Economic Performance* 371 (1970).

[9] E. Jantsch, *Technological Forecasting in Perspective* 7 (1967).

[10] *See generally* Lien, Anton, and Duncan, "Technological Forecasting: Tool, Techniques, and Applications," *American Management Association—Management Bulletin* No. 115 (1968).

Field interviews were used to supplement available library information concerning new technologies and products that are expected to affect the computer industry. The field interviews established a panel of experts whose views were pooled to draw a scenario of the future structure of the computer industry. The Bureau of Labor Statistics relied heavily on field interviews in its 1966 study of *Technological Trends in Major American Industries.*[11] The U.S. Department of Commerce also relied heavily on field interviews in its *Global Market Survey—Computer Equipment.*[12] In addition, private forecasting firms such as Predicasts use the field interview technique as an effective method of obtaining additional information concerning emerging technologies.[13]

Concluding Overview

A thorough understanding of the economic origins and development of the computer industry is obtained in Chapter 1. Next, the legal environment of the industry is analyzed in Chapter 2 to determine the effect this legal environment will have on future technological developments. A technological forecast is made in Chapter 3 based on an understanding of the economic origins and development of the industry as well as the legal environment surrounding the industry. Chapter 4 concludes with policy recommendations based on the interaction of the economic, technological, and legal factors existing within the computer industry.

[11] U.S. Department of Labor, Bureau of Labor Statistics, *Technological Trends in Major American Industries,* Bulletin No. 1474 (1966).

[12] U.S. Department of Commerce, Domestic and International Business Administration, *Global Market Survey—Computer Equipment* (1973).

[13] Predicasts, Inc., *Basebook* (1973).

Acknowledgments

The basis of this book was researched and written during the 1974-75 academic year at the University of Illinois. Minor, but very helpful, reorganizations of the text were subsequently made based on the recommendations of my editor, Philip W. Mason, and the D.C. Heath-Lexington Books staff.

At the University of Illinois, the author wishes to acknowledge the support of several individuals in the preparation of the manuscript. The writer is deeply indebted to Professor Hugh Folk for providing the necessary guidance, personal encouragement, and assistance both during the course of this study and during my earlier graduate work. Professor Folk has contributed more to my development as a research economist than any other individual. The author is also indebted to Professor Peter Maggs who provided assistance and support both during law school and during research on this work. His numerous hours of reading and commenting on various drafts greatly aided the author. Thanks are also due to Professors Paul Uselding and Frederick Gottheil.

The writer is also indebted to the interviewees listed in Appendix B, all of whom gave freely of their valuable time. In numerous instances, their thoughts and ideas provided critical insight into understanding various concepts within the computer industry. Although IBM did not permit any of their employees at Poughkeepsie or Yorktown Heights to be interviewed for the technological forecast made in Chapter 3 the author wishes to thank IBM for providing a complimentary photocopier for reproducing a limited number of copies of the manuscript.

Several individuals at the Center for Advanced Computation (CAC), University of Illinois also deserve mention. Gregory Chesson and Jody Kravitz not only read and commented on several parts of the work, but also served as reliable sounding boards for new concepts and ideas. Numerous other members of the CAC staff including James Gast, Steven Holmgren, Delbert Knecht, John McMillan, Thomas Milke, and Frederick Segovich provided technical assistance in many areas. This study also relied heavily on library resources. The author wishes to acknowledge the constant support and assistance provided by Carol Boast and Robert Berring at the University of Illinois Law Library, and Madhabarao Balachandran and Jean Koch at the University of Illinois Commerce Library. Their tireless efforts provided the foundation for this study. The author also wishes to thank Mathew Morey for reading parts of the manuscript. In addition, the writer thanks Stephen Bell, Linda Petzold, and numerous other University of Illinois Sherman Hall graduate students for their helpful suggestions in many areas of the manuscript's preparation.

Any book also requires the constant attention to administrative and procedural matters. The author was extremely fortunate to have Cynthia Gray as chief computer-text-editor teacher and typist. Cindy also provided the requisite editing support needed to produce the book. Thanks are also due to Cheryl Roe for her assistance in writing the bibliography, Gregory Ives for his assistance in drafting, and Joyce Fasnacht for her assistance in assembling and binding copies. The writer is also deeply indebted to Frieda Anderson who not only provided the ever necessary administrative support for the successful completion of the manuscript, but who also served as personal advisor and supporter throughout my entire graduate career.

Most of all, I am indebted to my parents for their continual support and encouragement during the entire course of my professional and graduate work.

The Computer Industry: An Economic-Legal
Analysis of its Technology and Growth

1

The Economic Development of the U.S. Computer Industry

The history of the computer industry actually began in the 1800s with the work of Charles Babbage. His work, however, was so technologically advanced for his time that it was soon lost after his death, and was not "rediscovered" by modern computer developers until the late 1940s.[1] Therefore, although Babbage is considered the founder of the computer, sadly, his work did not have a major impact on the development of modern computers. In fact, many of his key ideas had to be "rediscovered" during the 1940s before the electronic modern computer emerged.[2]

In the middle of the 1940s, the United States computer industry began to develop. During this development, a repetitive cycle of events occurred. This cycle began with an underlying demand for information processing followed by government funding of computer development projects aided by active participation of academic institutions, and finally commercial development of the technology to satisfy this underlying demand.[3] This cycle of events will first be analyzed. Several long term trends within the industry will then be examined, and, based on this analysis of the economic development of the industry, governmental policy recommendations aiding continued technological innovation will be discussed.

Computer Development Cycle

Underlying Demand. In the 1940s, the demand for information processing existed in many areas of society. In the government sector, the military had a huge demand for computational power for the development of ballistic firing

---

[1] *See generally* J. Berstein, *The Analytical Engine: Computers, Past, Present, and Future* (1964); P. Morrison and E. Morrison, *Charles Babbage and His Calculating Engines* (1961).

[2] According to John Pasta, members of the Electronic Numerical Integrator and Calculator (ENIAC) staff at the University of Pennsylvania were not aware of Babbage. Interview, John Pasta, National Science Foundation, Office of Computing Activities, Washington, D.C. (July 1975).

[3] *See generally* K. Pavitt, *The Conditions for Success in Technological Innovation* 22 (1971) (Organization for Economic Co-operation and Development).

1

tables. This demand was intensified by the occurrence of World War II.[4] In the civilian side of the government, enactment of the Social Security Act in 1935 meant that greater computational power was needed. In addition, since the late 1800s the federal census each decade was becoming more complex, and thus additional computational power was needed to compile the census.[5] In academic and scientific areas, there was also a great demand for information processing. For example, the Leontief input-output economic analysis needed a large amount of information processing power as well as scientific calculations for astronomy.[6] Finally, in the business sector, there existed a latent demand for information processing.[7] As the size of corporations from the early 1900s increased, corporations needed ever-increasing amounts of computational power. With the steady rise in wages since World War II, there has also been a trend to substitute capital for labor wherever capital proved cost effective.[8] Computers were easily adapted to accounting with its many repetitive tasks. Consequently, an enormous underlying demand for information processing existed in government, scientific research, and business.

Federal Research Funding. The second critical factor in the development cycle is government sponsorship to prove the technical feasibility of computer projects. The Federal Government has a long history of active participation in many scientific areas.[9] Hattery has stated:

Although the tangled skein of computer history reveals a mix of participation and contribution by the universities, government and industry, unquestionably the Federal Government has been a principal support to both investigation and innovation.[10]

---

[4] *See* J. Baxter, *Scientists Against Time*, (1968) (Discussion of the Organization of the Office of Scientific Research and Development during World War II by Vannevar Bush).

[5] *See* C. Eames, *A Computer Perspective* (1973).

[6] It is interesting to note that the need for astronomic computations was a major factor influencing several of the key developers of the first computers to enter the computer development field.

[7] *See generally* T. Whisler, *The Impact of Computers on Organizations* (1970).

[8] *See* J. Hicks, *The Theory of Wages* 124 (1932 edition). (Hicks states that a "change in the relative prices of factors of production is itself a spur to invention, and to invention of a particular kind—directed to econominizing the use of a factor which has become relatively expensive.")

[9] *See, e.g.,* A. Dupree, *Science in the Federal Government:* A *History of Policies and Activities to 1940* (1957).

[10] L. Hattery, "Federal Development and Application of the Electronic Computer," *Federal Contributions to Management: Efforts on the Public and Private Sectors* 248 (1971) (D. Brown ed.)

Federal support has had a double effect on the computer industry. Not only has it provided the necessary funds for research, but the technologies developed have had a ready market due to federal procurement of computers. In addition, this support has continued from the development of early computers down to the present. Wofsey has stated:

(n)ot only have Federal agencies played an important role in the early life of the computer, but the development of the second, third, and fourth generations of computers is being encouraged—and also funded—to a large degree by the Government.[11]

Federal computer development funding levels are relatively low. The National Science Foundation estimated that federal computer development funding for fiscal years 1972-1974 was $37.8 million (1972), $35.5 million (1973), and $30.7 million (1974). These totals include funding from the Atomic Energy Commission (AEC), Department of Defense (DOD) (including Advanced Research Projects Agency—ARPA), Department of Health Education and Welfare (HEW), National Aeronautical and Space Administration (NASA), and National Science Foundation (NSF) (Division of Computing Resources).[12]

From an economic perspective, federal support of computer development projects is necessary because of the resulting large positive externalities that result from these expenditures. In a broad sense, a positive externality occurs whenever the output from one firm enters as an input into the production function of another firm, without the second firm paying for the output of the first firm.[13] In addition, Barr and Knight tentatively concluded that private firms in the computer industry did not capture all the value from their own internally financed development projects.[14] Rather, much of the value of privately financed development escaped from the individual firm in the form of positive externalities. As a result, private firms are naturally hesitant to embark on large development projects that are only designed to prove the technical feasibility of a new computer technology. Therefore, it is wise for the Federal Government to

---

[11] M. Wofsey, "The Management of Computer Systems," *Federal Contributions to Management: Effects on the Public and Private Sectors* 277 (1971) (ed. D. Brown). *See also* M. Rose, *Computers, Managers, and Society* 16 (1969).

[12] Interview, Edward Romani, National Science Foundation, Washington, D.C. (July 1975).

[13] J. Due and A. Friedlander, *Government Finance: Economics of the Public Sector* 80 (1973). *See also* E. Mishan, *Economics for Social Decisions: Elements of Cost-Benefit Analysis* 85 (1973); Bator, "The Anatomy of Market Failure," 72 *Q. J. Econ.* 351 (Aug. 1958).

[14] Barr and Knight, "Technological Change and Learning in the Computer Industry," 14 *Management Science* 661 (July 1968) (No. 11).

bear the initial expense in proving the technical feasibility of development projects where huge positive externalities exist.[15]

The mere governmental financing of computer development projects, however, is not the answer. Rather, the timing of the funding is the critical factor. An Organization for Economic Co-operation and Development (OECD) report concluded that computer research projects need government support at an early period.[16] Due to the existing positive externalities, private venture capital is scarce in early stages of development, and thus early governmental support is extremely critical to the success of a development project. Related to the question of government support is the concept of development time versus project cost. Scherer found an inverse relationship to exist between development time and project cost in many research projects.[17] Figure 1-1 is an explanation of this tradeoff between time and cost. The horizontal axis in Figure 1-1 represents development cost, whereas the vertical axis represents time. Although there is an inverse relationship between the two variables, development time cannot be reduced below a minimum value, regardless of the funding level. The same is also true with a minimum funding level regardless of the project development time.[18]

Dollar figures of aggregate federal research and development funding (and for that matter private business funding) are impossible to determine accurately. The National Science Foundation has attempted to estimate both public and private research and development expenditures on a yearly basis.[19] Until recently, however, the computer industry was not listed separately, and also the electronic industry was aggregated to a two-digit Standard Industrial Classification (SIC) number. Thus the actual amount of research and development funding by both government and business is not available. No other figures have been compiled, and therefore the exact annual research and expenditure levels by the Federal Government and private enterprise are simply not known.[20]

---

[15] See W. Nordhaus, *Invention, Growth, and Welfare: A Theoretical Treatment of Technical Change* 39 (1969) (Theoretical discussion of the external economies of invention in general).

[16] Organisation for Economic Co-operation and Development, *Electronic Computers* (Gaps in Technology) (1969).

[17] F. Scherer, *Industrial Market Structure and Economic Performance* 369 (1970).

[18] See E. Mansfield, *The Economics of Technological Change* 72 (1968 1st ed.).

[19] National Science Foundation, *Research and Development in Industry—Surveys of Science Resources Series* (1973) (NSF No. 73-305).

[20] Governmental projects also need to be aimed at specific goals. In commenting on the need for specific project goals, Grosch stated that the annual 25 million dollars spent by the Department of Defense Advanced Research Project Agency (ARPA) was worth more in computer development than the computer technology spinoff resulting from the 2 or 3 billion dollars per year spent by NASA. Sperry Rand Corporation—Univac Division, *Technology and Change in the 70s: A Basis for Perspective and a Better Understanding of Some of the Forces*

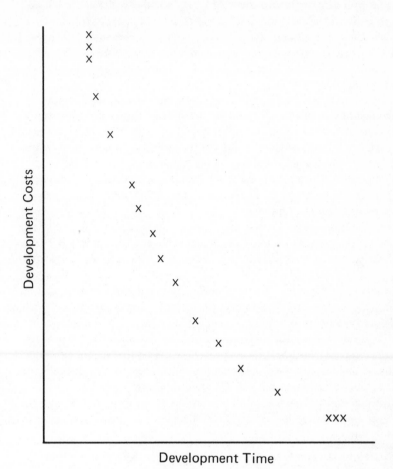

Figure 1-1. Development Time and Project Cost.

Source: Scherer, "Government Research and Development Programs," (in R. Dorfman, ed.,) *Measuring Benefits of Government Expenditures* 35 (1965) © 1965 by the Brookings Institution, Washington, D.C.

Which Influence Industrial, Economic, and Social Change in the Years Ahead 18 (1970) (Conference sponsored by Sperry Rand Corporation). In fiscal year 1971, the Advanced Research Projects Agency of the Defense Department (ARPA) spent 28 million dollars on computer projects such as ILLIAC IV, design of modular program for computer architecture, MULTICS at M.I.T., study of planning processes in computers, development of low cost graphic terminals, and plasma display terminal research. *Senate Hearings Before the Committee on Appropriations, Department of Defense Appropriations,* 91st. Cong., 2nd Sess., Fiscal Year 1971, Part 1, at 775. *See also* Organisation for Economic Cooperation and Development, *Problems and Prospects of Fundamental Research in Multi-Disciplinary Fields: Computer Science* 146 (1972).

The Role of Academic Institutions. Although not always directly involved in each technological development in the electronic component and computer field, academic institutions have played a large role in computer development. Mechanical calculator technology was historically very advanced. Academic institutions were a major force bridging the technological gap from calculators to computers.[21]

In numerous instances, the Federal Government has funded computer development at various universities. By this procedure, academic institutions have played a dual role of providing an environment for technological development and computer manpower training.[22] In addition, the university environment has successfully aided in bridging the gap between government funding of development projects to show the feasibility of the projects and commercial development of the projects. There has always existed a close relationship between universities and business.[23]

Finally, it is mandatory that a free flow of ideas exists between all parties involved in the research. A free flow of ideas between government, academic institutions, and business will insure that research is not needlessly repeated.[24]

Commerical Development. The final evolutionary stage of any computer innovation is the commercial development of the idea. Much economic research has been done on how firms acquire and apply technology.[25] For example, Nordhaus has developed a theoretical model in which firms view research and development effort as a capital investment.[26] It is generally agreed that the profit motive is the underlying force in the development of technology, or at least the fear of losses if new technology is successfully applied by competitors.[27]

Interwoven with the fear of losses due to successful application of technology by competitors is the concept of lead time developed by Schmookler. Lead

---

[21] Interview with Maynard J. Brichford, University of Illinois Archivist (Oct. 1974).

[22] *See* J. Pasta, *The Role of the University in the Computer Age* (May 20, 1969) (University of Illinois, D.C.L. Rep No. 330).

[23] *See* C. Eames, *A Computer Perspective* (1973).

[24] Weiner, "How the Transistor Emerged," 10 *I.E.E.E. Spectrum* 24 (Jan 1973). *See also Technology Transfer Hearings Before the Subcommittee on Science and Technology of the Select Committee on Small Business of the U.S. Senate,* 90th Cong., 1st Sess. (Sept. and Oct. 1967).

[25] *See generally* Kamien and Schwartz, "Market Structure and Innovation: A Survey," 13 *J. of Econ. Lit.* 1 (March 1975).

[26] W. Nordhaus, *Invention, Growth, and Welfare: A Theoretical Treatment of Technical Change* (1969) (Chapter 2 has a theoretical model in which a firm treats the acquisition of research and development as any other product).

[27] Rosenberg, "The Direction of Technological Change: Inducement Mechanisms and Focussing Devices," 18 *Economic Development and Cultural Change* 22 (Oct. 1969).

time can be defined as the period between the first introduction of an innovation and the successful imitation by other competing firms. The longer the lead time, the more profitable is the innovation for the lead firm. Schmookler emphasized the importance of lead time by stating that leadtime:

is both a necessary and usually a sufficient condition for a large part of present day corporate research. In its absence, any one firm would be better off to engage in no research at all . . . . One may surmise that it is either the advantage of being first or the necessity of catching up which motivates corporate invention.[28]

Within the computer industry, this drive for profits results in a constant stress among technical characteristics such as capacity, cost, and speed.[29] A firm is constantly evaluating these competing technical features. As a result, each firm has a multitude of technical possibilities to consider as it modifies existing products and develops new products.

Schmookler has stated that a clearly defined cycle of industrial inventive activity exists.[30] In studying several major industries he found that as industrial activity increased, the rate of inventive activity as measured by patent applications also increased. According to Schmookler, the key is the underlying demand for the products in the industry. This demand begins the industrial innovative cycle. Applied to the computer industry, historically there has been (and still is) a large demand for information processing. Through the development cycle, this demand has been transformed from the initial governmental projects—proving technological feasibility—to final commercial products.

Although agreeing with Schmookler on the importance of demand in industrial invention, Rosenberg also stresses the need to consider the supply of technological knowledge.[31] To Rosenberg, the existence of a huge demand is not enough unless there is an adequate supporting base of technical and scientific knowledge. Once this technical base is adequately developed, the cost of commercial development and marketing becomes economically viable.[32]

---

[28] J. Schmookler, *Invention and Economic Growth* 61 (1966).

[29] A Zwllweger, *Five Year Computer Technology Forecast* 67 (1972) (Department of Transportation Report No. DOT-TSC-OST-72-23).

[30] J. Schmookler, *Invention and Economic Growth* 180 (1966).

[31] Rosenberg, "Science Invention and Economic Growth," 84 *Econ. J.* 90 (Mar. 1974).

[32] Bernard Cohen states that three themes merged in the 1940s to form the scientific basis of the development of the computer. The three themes were logical machines (self-controlling and self-regulating devices), statistical machines (devices capable of sorting or processing information), and calculators (instruments which could perform mathematical operations). E. Eames, *A Computer Perspective* (1973) (Introduction by Cohen).

Thus, for the commercial development of advanced technology, there must not only be a demand for the end products, but also, there must be a sufficient base of scientific knowledge to make the commercial marketing of the end products economically viable.[33]

Once the first individual firm has successfully bridged the gap between a new technology and a commercially viable product, the last stage in the development cycle is the diffusion of this technology through the remaining firms in the industry. The diffusion rate is important because the invention will not have its full economic impact until the imitation process by competing firms is well under way. Mansfield has called the process whereby firms adopt new technologies the "bandwagon effect." That is:

research by one segment of an industry tends to bring forth research in other segments of the same and other industries, both because it creates competitive pressures and makes additional research profitable, and because firms, like people, tend to follow the leader.[34]

The rate of diffusion or the bandwagon effect is controlled by several factors. The extent of economic advantage that the innovation has over older products is the first factor. In the case of the computer industry, the progress in both electrical component technology as well as computer technology has quickly antiquated older computers. The uncertainty involved in first using the new technology is the second factor, and the third is the aggregate investment in the innovation needed to bring the new technology through product development into initial marketing. Finally, the rate of uncertainty decreases as the innovation is taken from product development to initial marketing. For example, if a new computer system requires a billion dollar investment before commercial acceptance is achieved, the diffusion speed of this innovation will be slower than an innovation such as a new software technique which might only require a few thousand dollars investment.[35]

---

[33] E. Mansfield, *The Economics of Technological Change* 7 (1968).

[34] E. Mansfield, *The Economics of Technological Change* 123 (1968).

[35] E. Mansfield, *The Economics of Technological Change* 119 (1968). Sharpe adds that the timing of introduction of the innovation into a new computer design is critical. If a specific innovation is incorporated into a new computer design at an early stage, then the diffusion rate will be relatively fast. On the other hand, if the innovation is added to a computer system at a later date (and probably at greater expense), then the diffusion rate will be slower. W. Sharpe, *The Economics of Computers* (1969).

Computer System Generations

Once computer development passed the early experimental stages, its growth can be viewed from the perspective of a series of electrical component developments. These successive electrical component developments have been used as popular focal points in loosely categorizing the computer development into several computer generations. In addition to these hardware developments, however, software innovations have also greatly influenced computer development.[36] Much has been written about computer generations; however, confusion on the subject still exists.[37] The cost-to-performance ratio of computers has steadily declined over time, with no distinct break points.[38] Consequently, from a purely economic perspective it is difficult to talk about computer generations because cost-to-performance ratios can not be used to classify computer generations.[39]

Rosen stated that "from the time it was invented in 1948, the transistor was expected to become the key to revolutionary advances in computer technology."[40] The concept of computer system generations is closely interwoven with component development. Although it is not the purpose of this book to study extensively the electrical industry, a brief inquiry into the development of the transistor, integrated circuits, and large scale integration is appropriate.[41]

---

[36] See generally Withington, "The Next (and Last) Generation," 18 Datamation 71 (May 1972).

[37] See 13 Datamation (Jan. 1967) (Entire issue devoted to the question of computer generations).

[38] W. Sharpe, The Economics of Computers 344 (1969).

[39] This gradual decline in the cost-to-performance ratio can also be seen in the famous Grosch's law. According to Grosch, computer equipment average cost decreases substantially as computer size measured in million instructions per second (MIPS) or memory capacity increases. In equation form, the famous Grosch's law holds that:

$$C / E = K / E^{1/2}$$

where C denotes the cost of a computer system, E denotes the effectiveness of the computer system measured in speed or throughput, and K is some constant. See W. Sharpe, The Economics of Computers 315 (1969). In estimating the change in the cost-to-performance ratio between 1944 and 1963, Knight found a close parallel to Grosch's law in commercial computers. Knight, "Evolving Computer Performance," 14 Datamation (Jan. 1968). Since the advent of minicomputers in the late 1960s, however, this relationship may not hold for minicomputers and microprocessors using large-scale integration. See Hayes, "Europe's Computer Industry: Closer to the Brink," 9 Columbia J. World Bus. 113 (Summer 1974).

[40] Rosen, "Electronic Computers: A Historical Survey," 1 Computing Surveys 1 (March 1969).

[41] See generally J. Tilton International Diffusion of Technology: The Case of Semiconductors (1971); Hirsch, "The United States Electronics Industry in International Trade," National Institute Economic Review 92 (Nov. 1965) (No. 34); Rudenberg, "Large Scale Integration: Promises Versus Accomplishments, The Dilemma of Our Industry," 35 A.F.I.P.S. Conference

The interaction of electrical components and computer technology can best be seen with the aid of a two-dimension time graph. In Figure 1-2 the upper horizontal line shows the development of electrical component technology, whereas the lower level denotes the development of computer technology. As one can see, there is a trend toward shorter adaptation periods from the development of components to their use in computer systems. At this point, brief analysis will be made of each of these component developments. The vacuum tube was quickly replaced by the transistor, and thus the disucssion will begin with transistors.

Transistor Development. Although a major innovation, the development of the transistor did not occur in a scientific void. Rather, there was a long history of

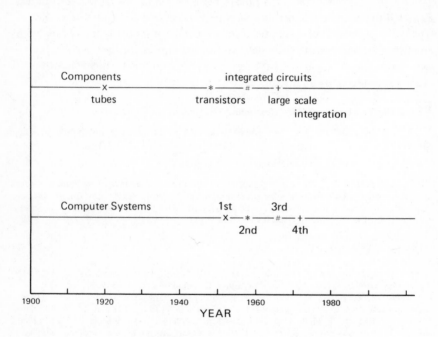

Source: Adapted from Organisation for Economic Co-operation and Development, *Electronic Computers* (Gaps in Technology) 144 (1969).

Figure 1-2. First Commercial Production of Electrical Components and Computer System Generations

Proceedings 359 (Nov. 1969). Roesti, "The American Semiconductor Industry in World Trade," 3 *Q. J. Econ.* 49 (1963).

scientific research leading up to the discovery of the transistor.[42] In late 1945, Bell Laboratories authorized a research project to make "fundamental investigation of conductors, semiconductors, dielectrics, insulators, piezoelectric and magnetic materials."[43] Although this included a broad area of research, the goal was to increase understanding of semiconductors so that this knowledge could be applied to communications technology. After two and a half years of intensive work, the transistor effect was discovered by the joint efforts of Bardeen, Brattain, and Shockley.[44] Difficulties in mass producing high-purity silicon had to be mastered as well as the ability to separate electrical elements by very small tolerances. Rapid development occurred, and by 1951 Western Electric began commercial production of transistors.

Integrated Circuits. Early research was done on printed circuits in conjunction with radar development during World War II.[45] With the development of transistors, active elements could be placed on a circuit board. Thus rapid progress was made in the 1950s on the development of integrated circuits.[46] By 1961 integrated circuits were commercially available.

The economic reasons for the rapid success of integrated circuits were their: small size, low power consumption, increased speed, reduced cost, and improved reliability due to fewer external interconnections.[47] In the 1950s the Federal Government invested large sums of money for research in integrated circuits for military applications and the space program. In addition, the large usage of integrated circuits by the military and the space program assured volume production needed to achieve sizable economies of scale.[48]

---

[42] *See generally* Gosling, "Pre-History of the Transistor," 43 *Radio and Electronic Engineer* 10 (Jan.-Feb. 1973); Hogarth, "Transistor—Its Invention and Current Prospects," 4 *Physics in Technology* 173 (1973).

[43] Weiner, "How the Transistor Emerged," 10 *I.E.E.E. Spectrum* 25 (1973).

[44] *See generally*, H. Bridges, ed., *Transistor Technology* (1958).

[45] An integrated circuit is defined as a group of electrical components (*i.e.* transistors, resistors, *etc.*) that are all manufactured on a substrate (most often silicon) and act together as a single device.

[46] S. Herwald, "Appraising the Efforts of the Technological State of the Art on the Corporate Future," *Technological Planning on the Corporate Level* 53 (1961) (J. Bright, ed.) (Proceedings of a Conference sponsored by the Associates of Harvard Business School).

[47] Light travels at approximately 1 foot per billionth of a second. Thus, as cycle times of a billionth of a second and faster are used, distances between electrical components become more important. Hittinger and Sparks, "Microelectronics," 215 *Scientific American* 56 (Nov. 1965). *See generally* L. Stern, *Fundamentals of Integrated Circuits* (1968).

[48] Brothers, "Integrated Circuit Development," 43 *Radio and Electronic Engineer* 39 (Jan.-Feb. 1973).

Large Scale Integration. The present state of the evolutionary process from
transistors through integrated circuits is large scale integration (LSI).[49] The
advent of LSI, whereby hundreds of transistors and other electrical elements
can be placed on a single silicon chip a few millimeters in diameter, has created
tremendous opportunities for developments in computer design. LSI has
further increased external reliability due to fewer external interconnections, as
well as increasing speeds due to shorter distances between electrical elements.
In addition, weight and size have been further reduced from initial integrated
circuits.[50] As a result, very low fabrication costs per component have been
achieved.

From the discovery of the transistor in 1948, through the development of
integrated circuits, to the existing large scale integration, the computer industry
has successfully used these developments in the design of computers to produce
dramatic decreases in cost-to-performance ratios. The absorption time of
electrical component technology into computer development has been shortened
from several years in the case of the transistor, to only two or three years in the
case of large scale integration.

The effect electrical component technology has had on the development of
the computer industry can be seen in Figure 1-3. In Figure 1-3, the vertical axis
is the logarithmic representation of the bit rate per dollar of switching circuit.
Over time, performance has dramatically increased. Although many different
technologies have been used—from vacuum tubes through large scale integration—
the increased performance has been steady but gradual.[51]

An accurate description of computer generations must consider both computer development and component technology. As Rosenberg noted, after a
major innovation is first introduced (such as a new electrical component), there
are many complementary innovations (in both software and hardware) that also
occur to bring the entire product to its technological limit.[52] A matrix of
electrical component and computer technology will aid in the understanding of
computer system generations. It is also useful to think of each generation as a
system of advancing component and computer technology.

The horizontal axis in Figure 1-4 describes component technology and
shows the development of components beginning at generation zero. On the
vertical axis, computer technology is shown. The two vectors constantly

[49] A. Khambata, *Introduction to Large Scale Integration* (1969).

[50] *See generally* S. Weber, *Large and Medium Scale Integration: Devices and Applications*
(1974) (Technical aspects of integrated circuits and LSI); Hockman and Hogman, "Technological Advances in Large-Scale Integration," 7 *I.E.E.E. Spectrum* 50 (May 1970).

[51] *See also* Withington, "Five Generations of Computers and Their Evolution," 52 *Harv.
Bus. Rev.* 99 (July 1974) (Withington views computer generations from the perspective of
firms using data processing techniques).

[52] Rosenberg, "Factors Affecting the Diffusion of Technology," 10 *Explorations in Economic
History* 3 (1972).

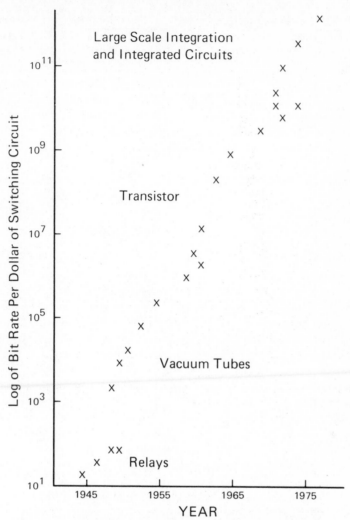

Source: Rudenberg, "Large Scale Integration: Promises versus accomplishments–The dilemma of our industry," 35 *A.F.I.P.S. Conference Proceedings* 359 (Nov. 18-20, 1969).

Figure 1-3. Electrical Component Technology.

interact, resulting in a diverse mix of system generations. The component industry leads the development cycle, but simultaneously, a backward diffusion of demand occurs from the computer industry to the component industry.[53] As noted in Figure 1-4, software advances such as higher level languages and

---

[53] *See generally* Brozen, "Determinants of the Direction of Technological Change," 43 *Am. Econ. Rev.* 297 (May 1953).

	1900's to 1957		1956	1961	1962	after 1967
component technology ********* computer technology	system generation 0 relays, others	system generation 1 tubes	system generation 2 transistors	system generation 3 hybrid circuits	system generation 3 integrated "ic's"	system generation 4 ISI circuits
1940's system generation 0 [no stored program]	ZUSE Z3 ASCC [MARKI]	ENIAC				
early 1950's system generation 1 [stored program] machine language		EDSAC EDVAC UNIVAC 1 IBM700 series				
1955-1961 system generation 2 higher level languages			IBM7090 IBM1401 RCA 300 PHILCO 212			
1961-1968 system generation 3 multiple programming [families of computers]			GE 625 CDC 6000 series	IBM 360 series	RCA SPECTRA BUR-ROUGHS 6500	
1969 to date telecommunications time sharing			CDC7600		BUR-ROUGHS 7500 UNIVAC 1109 IBM 370 DEC 10	BURROUGHS-ILLIAC IV CDC-STAR100 GOODYEAR-STARAN-IV

Source: Adapted from Organisation for Economic Co-operation and Development, *Electronic Computers* (Gaps in Technology) 71 (1969)

Figure 1-4. Computer and Component Generations.

multiple programming techniques have also occurred during each system generation. Therefore, one should view computer generations as a loosely knit combination of many different software and hardware technologies that group together to form a series of system generations.

The development cycle is thus multidimensional in nature due to the intermix of technology, competition, and end user demand. Although lacking clear boundaries, the concept of computer system generations is useful in tracing the development of the computer industry. The interesting fact is the constant repetition of events from the requisite computational demand, through government financing of development projects (mainly at academic institutions), then further business development of the technology by private firms, and finally commercial production. Due to their overlapping nature, system generations zero and one are grouped together in this discussion, whereas system generations two through four will be analyzed separately.

System Generations Zero and One[54]

Several different computer projects were funded by the Federal Government at various universities in the 1940s.[55] Each of the major federally funded projects will now be examined.

ENIAC. During World War II, the Army needed great computational capacity for the calculation of ballistic tables at the Ballistic Research Laboratory in Aberdeen, Maryland. Consequently, in 1943 the Ordnance Division of the War Department contracted with the University of Pennsylvania to build the Electronic Numerical Intergrator and Computer (ENIAC).[56] Containing 18,000

---

[54] The invention and production of equipment in the United States to solve computational problems is not new. By the late 1800s, the U.S. census was becoming increasingly difficult to tabulate in a timely fashion. C. Eames, *A Computer Perspective* (1973). As a result of this demand for more advanced computational equipment, Hollerith invented a system using punched cards to tabulate the census. By the early 1900s, the U.S. had a strong computational equipment industry. It is interesting to briefly speculate on why computer development did not occur during World War I rather than World War II. Many of the scientific and technical factors upon which modern computers are based were present by the early 1900s. The only apparent reason for the lack of computer development during World War I is the lack of massive governmental funding in World War I for computer research as compared to the funding level of computer development during World War II. *See generally* R. Casey, *Punched Cards: Their Applications to Science and Industry* (1958); H. Goldstine, *The Computer From Pascal to vonNeumann* (1972); B. Randell, ed., *Origins of Digital Computers: Selected Papers* (1973).

[55] In 1967, the Smithsonian Institute began to collect oral histories on the early development of the computer industry from 1935 to 1955. This study was done in cooperation with the American Federation of Information Processing Societies (AFIPS). Unfortunately, sufficient funding for the project was not obtained, and thus the project was only partially completed. *See Computerworld* (May 24, 1972) p. 40. The interesting fact of this early computer history, however, is that much is simply not known about early events in the development of the computer industry. In commenting on this situation, John R. Pasta, Department of Computer Science, University of Illinois, stated "(p)erhaps the Smithsonian can unravel the true story (of the early development of the Computer industry) but more than likely what is being written will, in fact, *become* the true story," (Letter to Maynard J. Brichford, University of Illinois Archivist, June 20, 1969.)

[56] H. Goldstine, *The Computer From Pascal to von Neumann* 152 (1972); Mauchly, "Mauchly on the Trial of Building of ENIAC," 12 *I.E.E.E. Spectrum* 70 (April 1975); A Goldstine, "Report of the ENIAC," U.S. Army–Ordnance Department Contract No. W-670-ORD-4926.

vacuum tubes, ENIAC was completed in 1946. ENIAC could perform approximately seven instructions per second. A standard measure of computer performance today is million instructions per second (MIPS). In those units, ENIAC could perform approximately .00007 MIPS.[57] Its weakness, however, was the lack of stored programming capability. As much as a full day was required to reprogram the computer before a new problem could be analyzed.[58] Before ENIAC was completed, however, Burks, Goldstine, and vonNeumann wrote the draft proposal for a second computer called the Electronic Discrete Variable Automatic Computer (EDVAC). This paper entitled the "Preliminary Discussion of the Logical Design of an Electrical Computing Instrument" became the cornerstone of modern computer theory.[59] Construction of EDVAC began in 1946 under another government contract with the Army, but was not completed until 1950.[60] With the concept of the internally stored program developed, the main elements of the modern computer were finally unified.[61]

In 1946, Eckert and Mauchly, the key developers of ENIAC at the University of Pennsylvania, left the University and set up their own company to produce a computer following the design of EDVAC. The computer, called the UNIVAC I (Universal Automatic Computer), was also heavily financed by the Federal Government. Three UNIVAC I's were originally ordered by the National Bureau of Standards, one each for the Bureau of Census, Army Map Service, and the Air Comptroller.[62] The first UNIVAC I was delivered in early 1951. All six of the first machines produced were eventually sold to governmental agencies, and the first commercial delivery finally occurred in 1954.

In 1950 Remington Rand Corporation bought the Eckert-Mauchly company. Two years later, Remington Rand also purchased Engineering Research Associates (ERA), a small Minnesota firm that developed the first computer

---

[57] See Figure 1-5.

[58] B. Randell, ed., *Origins of Digital Computers: Selected Papers* (1973).

[59] vonNeumann, Burks, and Goldstine, "Preliminary Discussion of the Logical Design of an Electronic Computing Instrument," 8 *Datamation* 24 (Sept. 1962).

[60] An internally stored program means that the computer has an internal logic control mechanism that is capable of operating at speeds that are fast enough to keep up with the calculation speed performed by the arithmetic unit in the computer.

[61] *See* C. Eames, *A Computer Perspective* (1973). Eames states that in "1945 the three lines of development that had grown from the early calculating machines, statistical machines, and logical automata were converging. New techniques for calculation had been combined with automatic control in gun directors, and with scientific data handling in punch card accounting machines. One more insight was needed to bring all the ideas and technologies together into the modern combputer: the vonNeumann concept of the stored program" (p. 136).

[62] Joint Economic Committee, Subcommittee on Economic Stabilization, *Hearings on Automation and Technological Change* 572 (Oct. 1955) (Testimony of Dr. A.V. Astin, Director of the National Bureau of Standards).

to use a magnetic drum memory. The nucleus of ERA consisted of a group of Navy engineers who actively worked in communications research during World War II. After the War they contracted with the Office of Naval Research to design the ERA 1101, which was the first computer to use a magnetic drum memory.

Thus from the original contract for ENIAC in 1943, the development cycle evolved from the initial government funding at an academic institution, through the development of ENIAC and EDVAC, and finally to the commercial development of UNIVAC I in 1954 for commercial sale. Due to the huge positive externalities existing at the beginning of the sequence in 1943, the first commercial computer would not have emerged as quickly without the Federal Government financing the early stages of the computer development.

Another critical factor that occurred during this sequence was the free flow of ideas between early computer developers. The critical paper by vonNeumann, Burks, and Goldstine was widely circulated to many people interested in the computer industry. In addition, during the summer of 1946, the Federal Government funded a course held at the University of Pennsylvania for twenty-eight American and British computer professionals. Thus the original ideas of ENIAC including the stored program concept from EDVAC were able to gain immediate and wide circulation after they were formulated.[63]

Harvard MARK I. Although the main line of computer development originated with ENIAC at the University of Pennsylvania, Harvard University also played a substantial role in the early development of computers. Construction of the Harvard MARK I (actually called the Automatic Sequence Controlled Calculator) began in 1939 by a joint team composed of Aiken and his associates at Harvard and IBM. Completed in 1944, the MARK I and later the improved model, the Selective Sequence Electronic Calculator (SSEC)—completed in 1947 by IBM—were both considered examples of IBM engineering talent and gifts to science and engineering.[64] The SSEC, however, was not offered for commercial sale, and indeed, Thomas J. Watson Sr., then president of IBM, did not believe that computers had any commercial applications.[65]

The MARK I was an electromechanical device 51 feet long by·8 feet high and could perform approximately .00000004 million instructions per second (MIPS) or .04 instructions per second.[66] After completion of the MARK I,

---

[63] *See generally* G. Patterson, ed., *Theory and Techniques for Design of Electronic Digital Computers* (1946) (University of Pennsylvania, Moore School of Electrical Engineering).

[64] *See* U.S. v. IBM Corp. (Defendant's Pretrial Brief, 1974) (p. 357) (Discussion of the MARK I).

[65] *See* Schussel, "IBM vs. Remrand," 74 *Datamation* 10 (May and June 1965).

[66] See Figure 1-5.

Aiken and his associates completed the MARK II, III, and IV under various governmental contracts.[67] Although IBM gained valuable experience in building the MARK I and SSEC, the electromechanical technology was basically a dead end.[68] Many of the SSEC staff including programmers, however, did go on to aid in the design of the IBM 701.[69]

In the late 1940s IBM concentrated on electromechanical calculators, because it did not believe that a commercial market existed for computers. According to Rodgers, IBM did not actively pursue computer development until UNIVAC I was first placed into operation in 1951 at the Census Bureau.[70] The Korean War caused a great expansion in defense-related industries, all of which required greater computational capabilities. In 1950, IBM announced its Defense Calculator, later known as the IBM 701.[71] The 700 series eventually evolved into a major IBM line of commercial computers.

Although it is not the purpose of this paper to trace the development of IBM from its initial 700 series of computers to its present dominance of the computer industry, it is interesting to note that its economic origins can be traced back to an early computer model developed at a university. In addition, its first commercial series of computers had indirect government backing.[72] Therefore, although not a clear line of events as seen in the ENIAC-UNIVAC I development cycle, one can still detect the close interaction of early government funding at an academic institution, and finally commercial development of the computer. Harvard University did sponsor several seminars on computers in the late 1940s, many of which were financed by government contract.[73]

---

[67] H. Goldstine, *The Computer From Pascal to vonNeumann* 118 (1972).

[68] The funding of research that later reveals a deadend technology is one of the risks of research and development. Because technology has this inherent risk, to assume reasonable success in research and development of new technologies, several competing technologies should be simultaneously funded.

[69] B. Randell, ed., *Origins of Digital Computers: Selected Papers* 189 (1973).

[70] W. Rodgers, *Think: A Biography of the Watsons and IBM* 199 (1969).

[71] Rosen, "Electronic Computers: A Historical Survey," 1 *Computing Surveys* 13 (March 1969).

[72] IBM also developed the Naval Ordnance Research Calculator (NORC) for the U.S. Naval Weapons Laboratory at Dahlgren. NORC was started in 1951, and was delivered to Dahlgren in June 1955, By 1955 industrial use of computers had advanced rapidly from the late 1940s and IBM development of the 704 was well under way. Consequently, NORC was never commercially produced. It should be noted, however, that the computer technology developed in NORC was undoubtedly used by IBM in the development of its commercial computers. *See* W. Eckert and R. Jones, *Faster, Faster: A Simple Description of a Giant Electronic Calculator and the Problems it Solves* (1955).

[73] Harvard University, "Symposium on Large-Scale Digital Calculating Machines," 16 *Annals of the Computation Laboratory* (1974) and 26 *Annals of the Computation Laboratory* (1949).

Additional Computer Projects. In addition to the ENIAC and MARK I projects, numerous other computer projects existed during the late 1940s and 1950s. Many computer development projects were sponsored by the Federal Government.[74] All the projects could not be adequately discussed. A few, however, warrant attention. The simultaneous funding of several development efforts is essential for rapid technological growth because it is impossible to predict the success of any individual development project.

IAS. As ENIAC was nearing completion in 1946, vonNeumann and his associates returned to the Institute for Advanced Studies (IAS) at Princeton and began development of the IAS computer.[75] A series of reports published by the IAS computer project were very instrumental in the early development of electronic computers. In 1952 the IAS computer was completed under a contract with the U.S. Army Ordnance Corps.[76] Several other computers similar to the IAS design were built including the ILLIAC series at the University of Illinois.[77]

MIT-WHIRLWIND. Supported jointly by the U.S. Air Force and the Office of Naval Research, Project WHIRLWIND was conducted at the Massachusetts Institute of Technology. Initial work was begun in 1947 and WHIRLWIND I was completed in 1952.[78] WHIRLWIND I was the first computer to successfully incorporate coincident-current magnetic core memory, which soon replaced the cathode-ray tube memory in the entire computer industry. The MIT-WHIRLWIND I could perform approximately .0001 million instructions per second (MIPS) or 100 instructions per second.[79] Radar research during World War II served as the foundation for the development of the coincident-current magnetic core memory.[80]

Several of the key elements in the development cycle can be seen in the MIT-WHIRLWIND project. First, early federal sponsorship established the

---

[74] *See generally* Rosen, "Electronic Computers: A Historical Survey," 1 *Computing Surveys* 1 (March 1969); Gruenberger, "Digital Computers: The History of the JOHNNIAC," (Oct. 1968) (Rand Corporation Report Rm 5654-PR) (JOHNNIAC was funded by the Air Force and named after vonNeumann for his help in designing JOHNNIAC).

[75] The IAS computer could perform approximately .0005 million instructions per second (MIPS), or 500 instructions per second. (See Figure 1-5.)

[76] Serrel, *et. al.,* "The Evolution of the Computing Machines and Systems" 50 *The Proceedings of the Institute of Radio Engineers* 1039 (May 1962).

[77] One can again see the early federal funding of the projects as well as emphasis on the free flow of communication in the reports that were published.

[78] A. Zellweger, *Five Year Computer Technology Forecast* 40 (1972) (Department of Transportation Report No. DOT-TSC-OST-72-23).

[79] See Figure 1-5.

[80] J. Baxter, *Scientists Against Time* 41 (1968).

technological feasibility of new memory technologies. Next, the project was goal-oriented to establish a computer capable of operating in real time environment. Finally, the resulting technology was further developed by industry and eventually introduced into commercial computers.[81]

EDSAC-ZUSE-ATANASOFF. The development of these three computers is included more as a comparison of what happened when early government funding was not provided in adequate amounts. First, in the case of the British Electronic Delay Storage Automatic Calculator (EDSAC), early government support did occur, and thus the British were on the same level of technical development as the U.S. during the early stages of computer development. The British, however, lacked sustained governmental support, and thus gradually dropped behind in the continuously advancing computer technology.[82] The ATLAS computer project, however, was later one of the leading projects in time sharing developments along with the MIT Project MAC.[83] Thus although the British have been influential in computer development, they have not remained abreast of U.S. computer technological developments.[84]

In the late 1930s Zuse began developing computers on his own in Germany. World War II interrupted his work, and in addition, he did not receive funding from the German Government for his research during World War II. Many have argued that the ZUSE computer in 1941 was the first electronic digital

---

[81] In 1937 Stibitz began experiments at Bell Laboratories with relays, and in 1939, MODEL I or the Complex Number Computer was produced. This calculator formed the basis of several models. MODEL II, the Relay Interpolator was built for the the National Defense Research Council and was designed to solve fire control problems. MODEL III, another relay calculator, called the Ballistic Computer was begun in 1942 and was completed in 1944. Finally, MODEL V was first delivered in 1946 to the National Advisory Committee on Aeronautics at Langley Field and a second MODEL V was delivered in 1947 to the Ballistics Research Laboratory at Aberdeen, Maryland. B. Randel, *Origins of Digital Computers: Selected Papers* 239 (1973). Bell Labs then emphasized development of switching equipment for telecommunications and thus drifted out of general digital computer development. Stibitz, "The Relay Computers at Bell Labs" 13 *Datamation* 35 (April 1967).

[82] Organisation for Economic Co-operation and Development, *Electronic Computers* (Gaps in Technology) 62 (1969); B. Randell, ed., *Origins of Digital Computers: Selected Papers* 353 (1973).

[83] Rosen, "Electronic Computers: A Historical Survey," 1 *Computing Surveys* 10 (March 1969).

[84] *See* Y. Hu, *The Impact of U.S. Investment In Europe: A Case Study of the Automotive and Computer Industries,* 75 (1973); M. Murphy, "The Computer Industry Itself," *Computers and the Year 2000* 181 (Lord Avebury, ed. 1974); *Hearings on S. 1167 Before the Subcommittee on Antitrust and Monopoly of the Senate Committee on the Judiciary,* 93rd Cong., 2d Sess., pt. 7, at 5317 (July 23-26, 1974) (The Industrial Reorganization Act—The Computer Industry) (Statement of Christopher Layton, Director Responsible for Data Processing, Commission of European Communities).

computer.[85]   After World War II, Zuse resumed his work, and formed the Zuse KG computer company in Germany.[86]

The final early computer development to be discussed was the work of Atanasoff at the Iowa State College (now Iowa State University). Begun in the late 1930s, work by Atanasoff and his associates made several important advances in the development of his ABC computer. Again due to the lack of funding, the project was abandoned in 1942.[87]

The lesson learned from these three computer projects was the essential role played by governmental funding in initial stages of development. In economic terms, the positive externalities are so huge that no individual firm can hope to receive all the benefits from the initial development investment. Thus not only is governmental funding necessary for successful development projects, but in addition, the funding must come at an early time when the technological feasibility of the project is determined.

System Generation Two

The second system generation was a period of diffusion within the computer industry as the technologies developed in the late 1940s and the early 1950s were applied to commercial computers. In addition, during this time period, the transistor was introduced into computer design. Demand for information processing continued, and the second generation of computers peaked in 1961.[88]

Many firms entered the industry, but IBM successfully transferred its dominance from commercial punched cards in the 1940s to the commercial computer industry in the 1950s. Although starting after Remington Rand (later Sperry Rand), IBM soon caught up in the commercial computer industry. One of the key factors to its success was its constant emphasis on service and support, a lesson undoubtedly learned from its commercial punched card business in the 1930s and 1940s.

Hardware was almost exclusively emphasized in the zero and first system generations, but by the second generation, software began to receive emphasis. Hopper had worked on the Harvard MARK I as a programmer and later worked on the programming of UNIVAC I and II. She was instrumental in the development of the first programming language for the UNIVAC series called

---

[85] B. Randell, ed., *Origins of Digital Computers: Selected Papers* 155 (1973).

[86] Desmonde and Berkling, "The ZUSE Z 3," 12 *Datamation* 30 (Sept. 1966).

[87] Gardner, "Will the Inventor of the First Digital Computer Please Stand Up," 20 *Datamation* 84 (Feb. 1974).

[88] A. Groppelli, *The Growth Process in the Computer Industry* 186 (1970) (Ph.D. Dissertation, N. Y. University).

Flow-Matic.[89] By the middle of the 1950s the Federal Government and in
particular, the Department of Defense (DOD), realized that its diverse inventory
of computers (each with its own unique software) was causing serious inefficiency
due to software duplication. Therefore, DOD initiated development of the
Common Business Oriented Language (COBOL) in 1959. In a few months a
standardized COBOL was developed.[90] DOD was successful in enforcing this
standardization by refusing to buy computers that did not have a COBOL
compiler. Software development, therefore, had a slow start as compared with
hardware. But it is important to note that one of the first attempts to standardize software was initiated through federal procurement policies.

As the second generation of computers was being commercially marketed,
third generation development was beginning. The third generation, however, did
not occur without heavy input from the Federal Government. In the middle of
the 1950s, the Atomic Energy Commission (AEC) financed two large computer
projects. The Livermore Atomic Research Computer (LARC) was built at the
Livermore Laboratory in conjunction with Remington Rand and was delivered
in 1960. The UNIVAC LARC could perform approximately 0.2 million instructions per second (MIPS).[91] The second major project also sponsored by the
AEC was in conjunction with IBM at the Los Alamos Laboratory and was called
the IBM STRETCH. The IBM STRETCH could execute approximately 0.4
million instructions per second (MIPS).[92] Although both computers were not
commercially produced, they did have a great impact on third generation computers by their use of advanced technologies. As Rosen stated, the "real
venture capital" for the third generation computers was provided by the Federal
Government.[93] Although the computer development for this second and half
generation did not precisely follow the government-sponsored development at
academic institutions and final commercial development pattern, the influence
in the third computer system generation of the federally sponsored development
aimed at specific projects was great.

---

[89] S. Woolridge, *Software Selection* 21 (1973) (Excellent history of software).

[90] Hopper, "Standardization and the Future of Computers," 8 *Data Management* 32
(April 1970).

[91] Eckert, "UNIVAC–LARC, The Next Step in Computer Design," *Proceedings of the
Eastern Joint Computer Conference* 16 (Dec. 1956). See Figure 1-5.

[92] W. Buchholz, *Planning a Computer System: Project STRETCH* (1962); Dunwell, "Design
Objectives For The IBM Computer," *Proceedings of the Eastern Joint Computer Conference*
20 (Dec. 1956). See Figure 1-5.

[93] Rosen, "Electronic Computers: A Historical Survey," 1 *Computing Surveys* 25 (March
1969).

System Generation Three

The Atomic Energy Commission continued to fund computer development after the LARC and the STRETCH projects with a project grant to Control Data Corporation (CDC). Formed in 1957, CDC originated from a group of Univac-Sperry Rand employees, some of whom were from the original Engineering Research Associates (ERA) group. The AEC contracted with CDC to build a computer three times faster than the IBM STRETCH. The CDC 6600 emerged, and most large AEC installations eventually acquired a CDC 6600.[94] Thus the economic origins of the third generation of computers began with heavy governmental support in development contracts through the Atomic Energy Commission.

The high point of system generation three was the IBM System 360, which was announced in 1964.[95] Development on the System 360 began in the late 1950s and as previously discussed, the information acquired in building STRETCH undoubtedly aided in the development of the 360 series. Total development cost of the 360 series was estimated at five billion dollars.[96] At the time of development, the IBM 1400 and 7000 series were huge revenue producers. IBM, however, saw the trend in technology toward integrated circuits and thus reacted with the 360 series.[97]

The original 360 models, however, used a hybrid integrated circuit design in which all transistors were separately wired apart from the integrated circuits.[98] The 360 series was a financial success.[99] The 360/195, the largest computer in the 360 family, could perform approximately 0.4 million instructions per second (MIPS).[100] Rosen stated that IBM chose hybrid integrated circuits rather

---

[94] Thornton, "Parallel Operation In the Control Data 6600," 26 *A.F.I.P.S. Proceedings* 33 (1964) (Part II).

[95] McGovern, "The Computer Field and the IBM 360," 16 *Computers and Automation* 16 (Jan. 1967).

[96] Wise, "IBM's $5,000,000,000 Gamble," 74 *Fortune* 118 (Sept. 1966).

[97] It can be argued that—due to the rapid technological diffusion rate—IBM knew that its lead in the computer industry would be lost if the 360 series was not developed and sold. Thus IBM was forced to develop and market the 360 series by competitive forces in the computer industry.

[98] Tolta, "IBM Reliability Experience With Hybrid Microcircuits," *I.E.E.E. International Reliability Physics Symposium—11th Annual Proceedings* 92 (March 1973) (Technical discussion of hybrid circuits).

[99] T. Billings and R. Hogan, *A Study of the Computer Manufacturing Industry in the U.S.* 49 (1970) (Masters Thesis-Naval Postgraduate School, Monterey California). (An estimated 15,000 360s were eventually installed).

[100] See Figure 1-5.

than monolithic integrated circuits (transistors are included in the monolithic integrated circuit) because IBM underestimated the speed monolithic integrated circuit technology would develop.[101] Wise, however, reported that IBM chose hybrid integrated circuits because the monolithic integrated circuit design technology was not economically viable in the early 1960s.[102]

From an economic perspective, the critical issue in the competition between hybrid and monolithic integrated circuit technology is the rapid acceptance of both technologies by the computer industry. Quite obviously, much of the integrated circuit research was done by computer manufacturers; however, the basic integrated circuit technology originated from the electrical industry. The gains in cost reduction and increased performance of integrated circuits were great enough to warrant rapid implementation of this technology. The acceptance by the computer industry of integrated circuit technology and the rapid diffusion of this technology throughout the industry can be viewed as the final stage in the development cycle of small-scale integrated circuit technology.

System Generation Four–Present Status

Computer development is presently in a period of consolidation. Many new technologies are in the early governmental funding stage, whereas other technologies are being applied within the computer industry, and finally, several others are in the commercial diffusion stage. Thus the development of a single technology as originally outlined during the ENIAC-UNIVAC I period no longer exists. Rather, many different computer-related innovations are in various stages of the development cycle. The pattern of development still exists for computer innovations as the innovations progress through each distinct developmental stage. Several relevant examples of present computer technology will be examined at this point.

Supercomputers and Computer Networks. A supercomputer is actually an entire computer system composed of many advanced technologies. Two examples are the ILLIAC IV and the Control Data STAR 100.[103] The development and construction of both computers were funded by the Advanced Research Projects Agency (ARPA) of the Department of Defense. The development of ILLIAC IV follows closely the development cycle. There existed a demand for massive but

---

[101] Rosen, "Electrical Computers: A Historical Survey," 1 *Computing Surveys* 30 (March 1969).

[102] Wise, "IBM's $5,000,000,000 Gamble," 74 *Fortune* 120 (Sept. 1966).

[103] Graham, "The Impact of Future Developments in Computer Technology," (June 1970) (Rand Corporation Report No. P-4401).

inexpensive information processing for projects such as weather forecasting. Development began at the University of Illinois, and subsequently ILLIAC IV was moved to NASA-Ames Research Laboratory in California. ILLIAC IV can perform over 100 million instructions per second (MPIS).[104] If the development cycle continues, Burroughs (which built the large computer) will use the technology acquired in the construction of ILLIAC IV in the development of its own large commercial computers. Due to the free flow of information, other computer manufacturers may also use the technology developed in ILLIAC IV in the development of large computers.[105] The CDC STAR 100 follows a slight variation from the typical funding-development-production cycle. Capable of performing slightly under 100 million instructions per second (MIPS), the STAR 100 was developed by CDC under a federal contract.[106]

A rough measure of the large increase in computer performance from the ENIAC and MARK I computers of the middle of the 1940s to the ILLIAC IV and STARAN IV computers of the early 1970s can be seen in Figure 1-5. The development and implementation of computer performance standards are extremely difficult. A commonly applied standard as an approximation of computing power is million instructions per second (MIPS). In Figure 1-5 the vertical axis represents MIPS and the horizontal axis denotes time from the middle of the 1940s to the middle of the 1970s. A few selected computer performances are shown. Using MIPS as a standard, in thirty years computer performance has increased by a factor of ten to the tenth! Development during this thirty-year period has been rapid but steady.

Networks. Related to the development of supercomputers is the concept of computer networks in which the development cycle is again followed. The Advanced Research Projects Agency of the Department of Defense (ARPA) realized that a large computer such as ILLIAC IV would have end users scattered over the United States, and thus an inexpensive means of access to the computer would be needed. Consequently, ARPA funded Bolt, Beranek and Newman, Inc., Cambridge, Massachusetts and several universities including the Stanford University's Research Institute (SRI) to develop the technology necessary to link heterogeneous computer installations located both in the

---

[104] See Figure 1-5.

[105] Bouknight, "ILLIAC IV System," 60 *Proceedings of the I.E.E.E.* 369 (April 1972). Slotnick, "The Fastest Computer," 224 *Scientific American* 76 (Feb. 1971).

[106] Holn and Jones, "Control Data STAR 100 Paging Station," 42 *A.F.I.P.S. Proceedings* 421 (1973). See Figure 1-5. Turn has an excellent discussion of other large computers. R. Turn, *Computer in the 1980's* 62 (1974). Seymour Cray, the key individual behind the CDC 6600 and 7600 series is presently developing a computer five times faster than the CDC 7600. The CDC 7600 is the biggest computer CDC is presently selling. *See* "Seymour Cray's Cray-I Super Computer: Almost Five Times Faster Than a 7600," 21 *Datamation* 71 (July 1975).

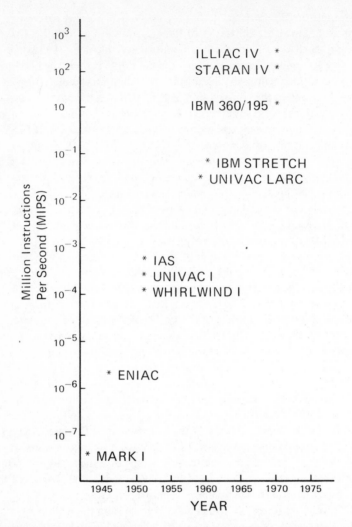

Sources Consulted: R. Turn, *Computers in the 1980's*, 95 (1974); Barr and Knight, "Technological Change and Learning in the Computer Industry," 14 *Management Science* 676 (July 1968).

Figure 1-5. Performance of Selected Computers.

United States and internationally. Commercial development has already begun that is applying the network technology previously developed under the ARPA contract.[107] In the case of computer networks, the development cycle was

---

[107] The Air Force is also planning to use the ARPA network technology in its future data communications. Electronics Systems Division Air Force Systems Command, *Support of Air Force Automatic Data Processing Requirements Through the 1980's* (1974) (Hanscom Field).

completed in four or five years from the original ARPA contract for data communication research to commercial use of the developed technology.

Time-Sharing. Early development on time-sharing began in the 1950s at MIT with the development of the Semi-Automatic Ground Environment (SAGE) system for the radar defense of North America. Later, Project MAC (Machine Aided Cognition and Multiple Access Computer) was funded by ARPA at MIT. Originally using an IBM 7094, the system then developed on a GE 645 computer.[108] In 1961 MIT completed the first general purpose time-sharing system known as the Compatible Time Sharing System. Of the twelve time-sharing advanced research projects funded during the early 1960s, ARPA sponsored six of them.[109] Since the early 1960s, further development on time-sharing has occurred. Today, time-sharing has entered the commercial stage of development with many firms producing time-sharing systems.[110] Thus as in the case of computer networks, the full cycle of events has occurred in the development of time-sharing technology.[111]

Minicomputers. Originally, minicomputers were really small-scale general purpose computers.[112] By the mid 1960s, however, there was a substantial reduction in the price-to-performance ratio.[113] Annual cost reductions of 70 or 80 percent were common during the late 1960s.[114] The cause of this large cost

---

[108] Strachey, "Time Sharing In Large Fast Computers," *First International Conference on Information Processing* 1 (June 1959) (Paris) (Early technical reference to time sharing as known today).

[109] Glauthier, "Computer Time-Sharing: Its Origin and Development," 16 *Computers and Automation* 23 (Oct. 1967) (Excellent review and bibliography of time sharing). *See also* R. Riley, *A Case Study of a Differentited Oligopoly: The Computer Time Sharing Industry* (1970) (Ph.D. Dissertation, University of Cincinnati).

[110] *See* Arden, "Interactive Computing," 63 *I.E.E.E. Proceedings* 836 (June 1975) (Excellent report on the current technical status of time sharing). Laven, "Time Sharing Grows Up," 22 *Infosystems* 32 (Feb. 1975) (Discussion of the present status and economic viability of time sharing).

[111] Commercial information retrieval systems such as Dialogue by Lockheed Corporation are recent developments made possible by advances in networking and time-sharing technologies. Dialogue was originally funded under a NASA contract to catalogue by computer the thousands of public documents made available through NASA contracts. Interview, Richard Caputo, Lockheed Information Systems, Washington, D.C., July 1975.

[112] For example, in 1956 Burroughs marketed the E-101, which sold for under 50,000 dollars. Koudela, "Past, Present, and Future of Minicomputers: A Scenario," 61 *I.E.E.E. Proceedings* 1526 (Nov. 1973).

[113] Gruenberger, "Are Small, Free Standing Computers Here to Stay," 13 *Datamation* 67 (April 1966).

[114] D. Kenney, *Minicomputers: Low-Cost Power For Management* 5 (1973).

reduction was the ability of minicomputer manufacturers to use integrated circuit technology.[115] This cost decrease combined with the fact that large general purpose computers are not well suited for many smaller applications, led to a rapid rise in minicomputer sales.[116] Presently, there are over forty manufacturers of minicomputers.[117] The major cost factor of a complete minicomputer system is the software. Kenny estimated that software costs will be as high as ten times greater than hardware costs.[118] Despite the high overall cost of a minicomputer system, there is a definite trend toward minicomputer systems composing an increasing percentage of all computer installations.[119] The trend is likely to continue due to the minicomputer advantages of organizational control by the physical on-site location of the minicomputer in the end user's establishment. The minicomputer cost-effective, on-line capability is an additional factor influencing this trend toward minicomputer installations composing an increasing percentage of all computer installations.

Change in Emphasis from Hardware to Software Development. There has been a long-term trend in change of emphasis from hardware to software. The origins of computer programming date back before the zero generation of computers. By the late 1930s the theoretical basis of programming was established in both the United States and in Britain.[120] In the zero and first system generations, little emphasis was placed on programming. In fact, the work of Hopper on the Harvard MARK I and Goldstine on ENIAC are the only high points of early software development.[121]

---

[115] Kaenel, "Mini Computers: A Profile of Tomorrow's Component," 18 *I.E.E.E. Transactions on Audio and Electroacoustics* 354 (Dec. 1970) (Comprehensive treatment of early minicomputer development).

[116] Bowers, "Predicting Future Computer Developments," 6 *Modern Data* 62 (May 1973).

[117] Hobbs and McLaughlin, "Minicomputer Survey," 20 *Datamation* 50 (July 1974); McCartney and Wilkinson, "The Year Mini Users Shed the Security Blanket," 21 *Infosystems* 26 (Jan. 1974). The leading minicomputer firm, Digital Equipment Corporation, was formed around an early Army contract to produce a programmed data processor (PDP-1). Interview, Earl Haight, Digital Equipment Corporation, Maynard, Massachusetts (July 1975). The first PDP-1 could perform .003 million instructions per second (MIPS). Barr and Knight, "Technological Change and Learning In the Computer Industry," 14 *Management Science* 676 (July 1968).

[118] D. Kenney, *Minicomputers: Low Cost Computer Power for Management* 168 (1973).

[119] McDermott, "Take-Your-Pick Software is Making the Mini Mighty, But Watch Out-It Costs," 22 *Electronic Design* 78 (April 1974). General purpose computers still lead in overall dollar costs. Minicomputer popularity is high, as seen in an entire issue of the IEEE being devoted to minis (Nov 1973).

[120] E. Post, *Finite Combinatory Process—Formulation I* (1936) (American); A. Turing, *On Computing Numbers* (1936) (British).

[121] C. Eames, *A Computer Perspective* (1973).

   The middle of the 1960s marked the point where software and hardware development and application costs became equal.[122] Wise reported that IBM spent upward of half a billion dollars on software development for the 360 series.[123] Figure 1-6 is an approximation of this long-term trend. In Figure 1-6, time is on the horizontal dimension, whereas the software as a percentage of total end user system cost is on the vertical axis. Thus over time, there has been a major shift in both development and implementation costs from hardware to

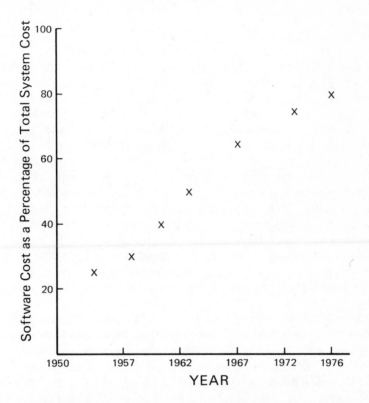

Source: Electronics Systems Division Air Force Systems Command, *Support of Air Force Automatic Data Processing Requirements Through the 1980's* 2-121 (1974) (Vol. 3-- Technology) (Hanscom Field) (*A.D. Little Report*).

Figure 1-6. Hardware and Software Costs.

---

[122] "The Growth of the Computer Industry," Computers in Higher Education, Report of the President's Science Advisory Commission to the U.S. Congress, *Data Processing Management in the Federal Government,* Hearings Before a Subcommittee of the Committee on Government Operations, House of Representatives, 90th Cong. 1st Sess, July 1967 (p. 318).

[123] Wise, "IBM's $5,000,000,000 Gamble," 74 *Fortune* 139 (Oct. 1966).

software.[124]   As systems become more complex, software development will play the major role in the future success of computer systems.[125]

Due to the development of large scale integration (LSI), computer design opportunities are available in which software is implemented in hardware. That is, through the use of programmable read-only memories (PROM's), repeatedly used standard software subroutines are implemented in hardware. This technique is used in the ILLIAC IV and STAR 100 computers.[126]

Conclusion

The economic development of the computer industry has been examined from the perspective of a repetitive development cycle. The beginning point of the cycle is a requisite demand for information processing by the government in both military and civilian areas, as well as scientific and commercial demand for computational power. Given this underlying demand for information processing, the Federal Government wisely funded numerous computer projects. Early federal funding was necessary due to the existing development positive externalities. Private firms were effectively deterred from investing in early computer development due to these huge positive externalities. In addition, these projects had specific goals. Although not always the case, the university environment acted as a bridge from the government-sponsored research and development to the business community. The free flow of information provided by the academic environment insured that all ideas would be available on an equal basis to all parties. Finally, private commercial development of the new technologies occurred to fulfill the large underlying demand by business and academic institutions.

Although the cycle was not always as clear as previously outlined, the general pattern did exist. Over time, various federal agencies have played key roles in funding. Originally, the Army and Navy were the large funding organizations, followed by the National Bureau of Standards. Next, the Atomic Energy Commission funded several projects in the 1950s, and finally, the Advanced Research Projects Agency of the Department of Defense has recently been a large provider of funds. In each case, however, the research funds were provided for specific projects.

The relation between the growth of the computer industry and the rate of

---

[124] See S. Wooldridge, *Software Selection* 13 (1973).

[125] M. Abrams and P. Stein, *Computer Hardware and Software: An Interdisciplinary Introduction* (1973) (Introduction to the technical aspects of hardware and software).

[126] L. Jones and R. Merwin, "Trends in Microprogramming: A Second Reading," 23 *I.E.E.E. Transactions on Computers* 755 (Aug. 1974).

technology can be seen in Figure 1-7. The horizontal axis represents time in
Figure 1-7. The horizontal axis represents time in Figure 1-7. The vertical axis
shows the relation between information-processing demand and technology.
Given the technology of the 1940s and early 1950s, the demand for computers
would have grown very slowly as denoted by line $D1$. As technology improved
the cost-to-performance ratio for information processing, the computer industry
stepped up to the second star and technology demand curve $D2$. This stepping
process repeated several times with each computer system generation, and thus
as long as technology continues to advance, the growth rate of the industry will
continue to rise along the path denoted by the stars and vertical bars. During
the present consolidation period of computer technology, the industry is at a

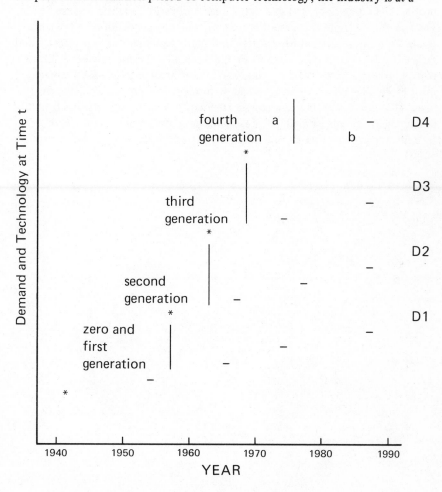

Figure 1-7. Demand and Technology.

critical point. If technology does not move forward, the industry will move
along line $D4$, as denoted by point b. On the other hand, if technology advances,
then the industry will shift to the higher demand-technology curve (upward
along point a) resulting in the continued rapid growth rate of the computer
industry.

Policy Recommendations

For computer technology to continue in the future, several policy proposals can
be extracted from the development cycle model. First, funding of development
projects should be early, and due to the huge positive externalities existing in the
projects, the Federal Government is probably the only source of development
funds when the goal is to prove the technological feasibility of the projects. Next,
during this research stage, all results should be freely communicated to interested
parties. It also appears that academic institutions provide an excellent environment in which this development can be performed. Within this academic environment, all interested parties can interact to obtain the maximum benefits from the
development funding. Finally, new technologies must rapidly diffuse through
the industry in order that all end users benefit from them.

2 The Legal Environment

In a recent study, Gilchrist and Wessel stated that "the computer industry is subject to a splintered, uncoordinated form of regulation."[1] Chapter 2 is divided into six parts. Each part examines one facet of the legal environment surrounding the computer industry. Antitrust regulation is first examined, followed by a discussion of the protection of proprietary property through patent, copyright, and trade secret protection. Major emphasis is placed on software protection in that cross-licensing agreements between computer firms combined with the rapid pace of computer technology have decreased the relative importance of hardware patent protection. Taxation and leasing are then discussed as well as federal communication regulations affecting the computer industry. International considerations with particular emphasis on computer export controls are examined next.[2] Finally, federal government procurement policies are reviewed. This examination of the legal environment of the computer industry serves as the foundation for the technological forecast in Chapter 3.

Antitrust

Overview. This section on antitrust first reviews the major antitrust statutes. Federal antitrust enforcement related to the computer industry is then examined, followed by a discussion of private antitrust actions. Barriers to entry are then discussed, and finally, several proposed restructuring plans are reviewed.

---

[1] B. Gilchrist and R. Wessel, *Government Regulation of the Computer Industry* 3 (1972). Time Incorporated, and the American Federation of Information Processing Societies, *A National Survey of the Public's Attitudes Towards Computers* 51 (1971) (Large majority surveyed believed the government should be concerned over the regulation of the computer industry). Much has been written concerning the governmental regulation of the computer industry. *See, e.g.*, R. Bernacchi and G. Larsen, *Data Processing Contracts and the Law* (1974) (Excellent up-to-date "gap-bridger" between the data processing profession and the legal profession); C.G. Gibson and Wilkinson, "Government and Industry: Should the Two Mix," 21 *Infosystems*, 28 (May 1974).

[2] Contract law relating to the purchase, maintenance, and leasing of computers will not be directly addressed. These issues, however, will be examined where relevant. Many articles have appeared on the general area of contract law related to computers. *See, e.g.*, Moorhead, "Limiting Liability in an Electronic Data Processing Service Contract," 4 *Rutgers J. Computers and Law* 141 (1974); Ridloff, "Procurement of Computers and Computer Services," 17 *Practical Lawyer* 73 (1971).

Antitrust considerations are of major importance in the computer industry.[3] The major antitrust statutory provisions affecting the computer industry can be categorized into three parts. Section 1 of the Sherman Act prohibits every "contract, combination . . . or conspiracy in restraint of trade of commerce among the several States."[4] The second statutory provision affecting the computer industry is found in Section 2 of the Sherman Act, which states that every person who shall

monopolize, or attempt to monopolize, or combine or conspire with any other person or persons, to monopolize any part of the trade or commerce among the several states, or with foreign nations, shall be deemed guilty of a misdemeanor . . .[5]

The regulation of mergers found in Section 7 of the Clayton Act is the third major statutory area affecting the computer industry. The main paragraph of Section 7 states that:

No corporation engaged in commerce shall acquire, directly or indirectly, the whole or any part of the stock or other share capital and no corporation subject to the jurisdiction of the Federal Trade Commission shall acquire the whole or any part of the assets of another corporation engaged also in commerce, where in any line of commerce in any section of the country, the effect of such acquisition may be substantially to lessen competition, or to tend to create a monopoly.[6]

Government Antitrust. The earliest significant antitrust litigation affecting the computer industry originated in the middle of the 1930s. In this suit against IBM and Remington Rand, the Justice Department charged that the requirement to use only punch cards produced by the respective manufacturers when leasing

---

[3] *See, e.g.*, W. Shepherd, *Market Power and Economic Welfare* 227 (1970); Jacobs, "Computer Technology (Hardware and Software): Some Legal Implications for Antitrust Copyrights, and Patents," 1 *Rutgers J. Computers and Law* 50 (1970).

[4] 15 *U.S.C.* sec. 1 (1973). *See generally* G. Holmes and C. Norville, *The Law of Computers (1971).* In United States v. Gerald Electronics, Corp., 365 U.S. 567 (1961), defendant was held not to have violated Section 1 of the Sherman Act by tying its several service contracts to the sale of CATV equipment because of the infancy of the industry. After thirty years, the computer industry is hardly an infant, and thus, the exception from illegal trying in all likelihood does not apply to the computer industry.

[5] 15 *U.S.C.* sec. 2 (1973). Several landmark antitrust cases have been brought under Section 2 of the Sherman Act. *See, e.g.,* United States v. United Shoe Machinery, Corp., 110 F. Supp. 295 (Mass. 1953), *aff'd per curian,* 347 U.S. 521 (1954); American Tobacco Co. v. United States, 328 U.S. 781 (1946); Standard Oil Co. v. United States, 221 U.S. 1 (1911).

[6] 15 *U.S.C.* sec. 18 (1973).

tabulating machines was an unlawful restraint of trade. IBM consented to stop agreeing with competitors on prices or conditions for leasing tabulating machines, and after a contest, IBM was also prohibited from requiring any purchaser or lessee of IBM tabulating machines to purchase IBM punch cards.[7]

The Federal Government filed a second suit against IBM in 1952.[8] The second suit was based on several IBM practices including restricted leasing agreements, refusals to deal, and price discrimination. The suit was settled by a consent decree in 1956. As part of the consent decree, IBM agreed to operate its software business (Service Bureau Corp.) as a separate subsidiary. The decree also required IBM to sell as well as lease equipment. The consent decree, however, did not specify the lease-purchase ratio, and thus, IBM has traditionally made it more attractive to lease rather than purchase its equipment. IBM was also required to train personnel from third party maintenance organizations to maintain purchased IBM equipment. Finally, the 1956 consent decree required IBM to reduce its share of the punch card market as well as to sell rotary presses for producing punch cards to independent card producers. The use of punch cards reached its peak in the early 1970s. IBM's share in the punch card market slowly declined, but in the long run, the effect of this part of the decree has not been great because computer technology shifted away from punch cards to time-sharing systems using interactive terminals.[9]

A third suit by the Federal Government against IBM is presently pending. Filed in 1969, the Justice Department charged IBM with four specific practices that allegedly contributed to IBM's monopolization of the computer industry. The complaint charged that IBM maintained a single price for hardware, software, and related support (i.e., bundled its prices for computer services), and thus forced customers to purchase all IBM equipment. Second, IBM used "its accumulated software and related support to preclude its competitors from effectively competing for various customer accounts." Third, IBM "restrained and attempted to restrain competitors from entering or remaining in the general purpose digital computer market by introducing selected computers, with unusually low profit expectations, in those segments of the market where the competitors had or appeared likely to have unusual competitive success, . . ." Fourth, IBM's educational discounts led to the IBM domination of the educational market.[10]

---

[7] United States v. International Business Machines Corp. 13 F. Supp. 11 (S.D.N.Y. 1935), *aff'd* 298 U.S. 131 (1936).

[8] United States v. IBM, 1956 CCH Trade Cas. par. 68, 245 (S.D.N.Y. 1956) *amended,* Civil No. 72-344 (S.D.N.Y. 1963 and 1970.

[9] *See generally* T. Billings and R. Hogam, *A Study of the Computer Manufacturing Industry in the U.S.* (1970) (Masters Thesis, Naval Post Graduate School, Monterey, California).

[10] United States v. International Business Machines, Corp., Divil Action No. 69-200 (S.D.N.Y. 1969).

IBM denied the four specific practices and requested dismissal of the complaint. The request was denied and a long discovery process began in 1969. By the spring of 1975, the discovery process was near completion and the trial began. At present, the suit continues and with appeals can be expected to last well into the early 1980s.

In responding to the first allegation of bundling, IBM announced a major change in its pricing policy. These changes were stated to have unbundled the purchase of software and hardware. Equipment prices were reduced by approximately three percent, and relatively high prices were set for consulting assistance and education. For most users, however, the "unbundling" announcement in 1969 merely represented a price increase.[11]

IBM also reduced its educational allowance from 30 percent to 10 percent. Although reduced to this official rate of 10 percent, IBM reported in internal documents obtained from the *Telex* v. *IBM* decision that the actual educational allowance was 27 percent when special programs and grants were counted. This 27 percent educational discount was allegedly sufficient to maintain IBM's educational goals.[12]

Private Antitrust Litigation. Major private antitrust litigation began in the late 1960s with the Control Data Corporation suit against IBM.[13] The Control Data

---

[11] *See* G. Brock, *The U.S. Computer Industry: A Study of Market Power* 157 (1975). Following the unbundling price change, IBM's system engineering force was reported to have dropped from 10,000 to 4,500. "Rumors and Raw Random Data," 16 *Datamation* 18 (Nov. 15, 1970).

[12] Telex Corp., v. IBM Corp., (Civil No. 72-C-89 (N.D. Okl.) (Minutes of the Management Review Committee, July 1, 1971, Plaintiff's Exhibit No. 391A-085). *See generally* G. Brock *The U.S. Computer Industry: A Study of Market Power* 158 (1975).

[13] In 1955, Sperry Rand filed an antitrust suit against IBM in an attempt to obtain access to IBM's patent portfolio. Shortly after the filing, the Justice Department and IBM agreed to a consent decree ending the 1952 government antitrust case against IBM. Under this 1956 consent decree, IBM was required to grant licenses on all tabulating equipment and computer patents applied for before 1961. IBM was allowed to charge a reasonable royalty on all patents except those applying to tabulating and manufacturing. During this same time period, the Sperry Rand ENIAC patent was still pending before the Patent Office.

Sperry Rand naturally wanted to limit any settlement to tabulating machine technology to protect its forthcoming ENIAC patent. IBM refused, and the parties finally agreed to a secret settlement in late 1956. Both parties agreed to cross license all patents applied for before October 1956 as well as to exchange technical information on all machines announced or in production by October 1956. Finally, IBM agreed to pay Sperry Rand $10 million. If the ENIAC patent was ever issued, IBM agreed to pay Sperry Rand a royalty of one percent of manufacturing costs for all infringing computers between 1956 and 1964. The $10 million was to be credited toward any royalty payments.

Therefore, although on its face the case was an antitrust suit, in actuality, it was a patent licensing dispute. *See generally* Honeywell v. Sperry Rand Corp., Civil No. 4-67-138 (D.Minn., 1973). (Findings of fact, Conclusions of law, and Order for judgment.) (Reprinted in *Hearings on S. 1167 Before the Subcommittee on Antitrust and Monopoly of the Senate Committee on the Judiciary,* 93rd Cong., 2d Sess., pt. 7, at 5794 (July 23-26, 1974) (The Industrial Reorganization Act–The Computer Industry)).

suit originated from IBM's marketing practices of its large-scale computer called the 7030 or STRETCH.[14] The IBM-STRETCH was discontinued because of its failure to meet design performance goals. Some deliveries, however, were made, but the price was cut from $13 million to $8 million to conform the price to performance capabilities.[15]

Control Data took the lead in large computers after the STRETCH was discontinued by IBM. In 1964, IBM announced the System/360. This announcement did not contain any large machines competitive with the CDC 6600. The large-scale scientific market was, therefore, left to Control Data. In 1963 IBM began informally discussing with potential customers of the CDC 6600 a large forthcoming IBM scientific computer. In August 1964, IBM announced its 360/91, which was competitive with the yet to be delivered CDC 6600. In September 1964, the first CDC 6600 was delivered. Supposedly due to difficulty in production, the IBM 360/91 was not delivered until early 1967. CDC alleged the IBM 360/91 announcement delayed orders for the CDC 6600.

After two and one-half years of discovery and several counter suits against each other, the trial was set for late 1973. In January of 1973, however, Control Data and IBM announced an out-of-court settlement.[16] As part of the settlement, IBM agreed to pay Control Data $101 million, and IBM sold its Service Bureau Corporation (SBC) to Control Data for its book value. Considering legal expenses and the actual value of SBC, the net transfer to Control Data was approximately $75 million.[17]

Many companies manufacture replacement products for IBM equipment. Typically, these products plug into the IBM main central processing unit (CPU). In the late 1960s and the early 1970s this business was quite profitable for these independent peripheral manufacturers. Timing is a critical factor in the introduction of peripheral products. If the products are introduced early during the cycle of the main IBM unit, then the independent firm can expect large profits. Knowledge of the IBM product is critical for the success of the independent manufacturer. As a result, many questionable practices have occurred whereby the independent peripheral manufacturers obtained specifications of IBM products

---

[14] Control Data Corp. v. International Business Machines Corp., Civil No. 3-68-312 (D. Minn. 1968). Many other firms also began filing antitrust suits against IBM after the Control Data Corporation suit. See e.g. Applied Data Research, Inc. v. IBM, Civil No. 69-1682 (S.D.N.Y. 1969). See, generally, B. Gilchrist and M. Wessel, Government Regulation of the Computer Industry 168 (1972).

[15] "The Shrinking of Stretch," 7 Datamation 17 (June 1961) (Thomas J. Watson, Jr., IBM Board Chairman at a press conference stated that every one of "the machines we sell will be a substantial loss to the IBM Company. We will make delivery of these machines because we do not want to break our promise to customers.")

[16] Lundell, "IBM/CDC Pact: 'No user distruption,'" 7 Computer World 1 (January 24, 1973). See also G. Brock, The U.S. Computer Industry: A Study of Market Power 170 (1975).

[17] "IBM-CDC Settlement," 19 Datamation 7 (March 1973) (As part of the settlement, the index prepared by Control Data as part of its trial preparation was destroyed by Control Data).

under development. From the perspective of IBM, these companies are stealing proprietary information. On the other hand, the independent peripheral manufacturers view IBM changing specifications as violations of antitrust laws through IBM's use of its market power to restrain competition. This intense competition spills over into numerous lawsuits.[18]

Many of these suits are brought and then settled out of court as both sides decide it is more economical to settle than to carry on a costly and lengthy suit.[19] Thus, the full explanation of the contents of the suit are never revealed to the public. A few suits and an occasional settlement of a suit are announced in trade journals. Memorex Corporation was sued by IBM for theft of trade secrets concerning the 3300 disk drive in 1970. Memorex filed a counter suit charging IBM with antitrust violations. IBM wanted the court to enjoin Memorex from marketing its compatible 3300 type disk drive until July 1973. The parties settled the suit and Memorex agreed not to market its product before July 1972. In economic terms, therefore, IBM won the case by slowing the delivery of competing disk drives.[20]

In another suit, Advanced Memory Systems (AMS) sold a memory adapter that could expand the memory capacity of the IBM/360 beyond the IBM set limits. This product threatened the entire IBM/360 marketing scheme, because end users could avoid the costly upgrade to a larger IBM system. As a result, IBM sent letters to customers using the AMS memory adapter stating that IBM would no longer provide maintenance on such equipment. In response, Advanced Memory Systems filed a private antitrust suit against IBM asking for a temporary restraining order against IBM to prohibit IBM from withdrawing its maintenance support. The temporary restraining order was granted.[21] AMS reasoned that IBM was required to provide maintenance for all equipment based on the 1956 IBM consent decree. On the other hand, IBM argued that maintenance of the altered memory was outside of the scope of the 1956 consent decree. The antitrust suit was settled with a compromise whereby AMS dropped its antitrust suit in return for IBM's agreement to provide best efforts, but not guaranteed maintenance, on extended memory machines.

---

[18] G. Brock, *The U.S. Computer Industry: A Study of Market Power* 173 (1975). *See* Automatic Radio Manufacturing v. Ford Motor Co., 242 F. Supp. 852 (D. Mass. 1965), in which Automatic Radio alleged that Ford redesigned its radio instrument panels to force Ford dealers to purchase factory-installed radios. *See also* Jordon, "Physical Tieins as Antitrust Violations," *Ill. L. Forum* 224 (1975).

[19] Several smaller suits are presently pending against IBM. *See, e.g.,* Forro Precision, Inc. v. IBM, 697 *B.N.A.-A.T.R.R.* A-10 (Jan. 21, 1975).

[20] "Memorex, IBM Ends Squabble Involving Trade Secret Suits," 6 *Computer World* 29 (Jan. 26, 1972).

[21] "IBM Discontinues Maintenance On CPU's Substantially Altered For Extended Memory: Court Order Status Quo For ITELANS Users Until March 2 Hearing," 7 *E.D.P. Industry Report* 2 (Feb. 22, 1972).

In a third suit between IBM and peripheral manufacturers, Telex Corporation charged IBM with attempting to monopolize and monopolizing the IBM plug-compatible peripheral market.[22] The amended complaint asked for $1.2 billion in damages (over $400 million trebled—based on the antitrust laws). After a short trial of twenty-nine days, Telex was found guilty of infringing IBM copy-righted manuals as well as illegally inducing former IBM employees to reveal trade secrets. IBM was found guilty of monopolizing and attempting to monopolize the market for peripheral equipment compatible with IBM's CPUs.

The original actual damages suffered by Telex were set at $117 million, which was then trebled to over $350 million plus costs and attorney fees. A series of restrictive measures were also placed on IBM, including a prohibition from collecting penalty payments for termination of IBM leases. These penalty payments had been invalidated as anticompetitive. IBM was also required to publicly disclose electronic interface standards at the time a product was announced or released for production. Third, IBM was prohibited from charging a single price for CPU and memory, and fourth, IBM was required to separately price the different parts such as tape drives and associated control units.[23] In November of 1973, the judgment was reconsidered, and the treble damage award was reduced to $259 million.[24]

IBM appealed to the Tenth Circuit Court of Appeals. In a three judge *per curiam* decision, the Tenth Circuit reversed, reasoning that the relevant market definition used by the trial court was incorrect. The trial court had limited the market to IBM plug-compatible equipment. The Court of Appeals reasoned that the relevant market was all peripheral equipment that was "reasonably inter-changeable," and relied on the *Cellophane* decision in which du Pont's Cellophane was ruled interchangeable with other types of wrapping material such as white paper and wax paper.[25] Based on this extended market definition, the Court of Appeals reasoned that the IBM practices were "ordinary market methods avail-able to all in the market." The Telex petition for an *en banc* rehearing was denied.[26] Apparently fearing the IBM $18 million counterclaim, Telex withdrew its petition for *certiorari* with no payments between the parties.[27] IBM, there-fore, could risk losing $300 million, but Telex could not risk an $18 million loss.

---

[22] *See generally* Wessel, "The Real Meaning of Telex," 21 *Datamation* 52 (July 1975).

[23] 367 F. Supp. 258 (N.D. Okla. 1973).

[24] *See* Note, "Telex v. IBM: Monopoly Pricing Under Section 2 of the Sherman Act," 84 *Yale Law J.* 558 (1975); Note, "Telex v. IBM: Implications for the Businessman and the Computer Manufacturer," 60 *Virg. L. Rev.* 884 (1974).

[25] United States v. duPont Nemours Co., 351 U.S. 337 (1956).

[26] 510 F.2 at 928 (10th Cir. 1975). *See* "Nanoseconds, Megabytes, Antitrust," 706 *B.N.A.-A.T.R.R.* B-1 (March 25, 1975).

[27] 55 *Wall Street J.* 8 (Oct. 6, 1975).

There are also many private suits between firms other than IBM.[28]   In *Honeywell, Inc.* v. *Sperry Rand Corporation et al.*[29]   Sperry demanded royalties for its ENIAC patent from all major firms in the computer industry at the rate of 1.5 percent of the net selling price of each computer system. After determining that Honeywell would owe over $200 million for the life of the ENIAC patent, Sperry Rand filed a patent infringement suit against Honeywell in 1967. Honeywell responded with an antitrust counterclaim charging that the Sperry Rand–IBM cross licensing agreement in 1956 was a conspiracy to monopolize the computer industry. The trial began in 1971, and in April 1973 the court ruled that Honeywell had infringed the ENIAC patent, but the patent was invalid due to its public use for over a year before the patent application was filed. The 1956 Sperry Rand–IBM agreement was ruled a "technological merger" and a conspiracy in restraint of trade violating Section 1 of the Sherman Act. The statute of limitations ran out in 1963, and consequently, Honeywell was not entitled to any relief because the suit was not filed until 1967.[30]

Some IBM critics complain whenever IBM lowers its prices to meet competition. The lowering of its prices by itself is a natural competitive response. Any sanctions against IBM for merely lowering its prices would in effect prevent IBM from competing.[31]   In the suits against IBM, however, plaintiffs generally charge IBM with the attempt or actual monopolization of various computer industry parts by a combination of lowering its prices and making computer design changes aimed at destroying IBM competitors.

If computer technology was not advancing as rapidly as it presently is, victories by IBM in private antitrust cases such as *Telex* would be very detrimental to the competitive structure of the computer industry. Computer technology is rapidly advancing, and thus, although private litigant victories in most cases against IBM would have aided the industry structure in becoming competitive, advancing computer technology will also cause the industry to become, at a greatly reduced pace, competitive. It should also be noted that the mere presence of antitrust regulations, both civil and criminal, prevents IBM from becoming even more dominant.

---

[28] *See, e.g.,* United Software, Corp. v. Sperry Rand Corp., Civil No. 74-1214 (E.D. Pa. 1974), 691 *B.N.A.-A.T.R.R.* A-20 (Dec. 3, 1974).

[29] Reprinted in *Hearings on S. 1167 Before the Subcommittee on Antitrust and Monopoly of the Senate Committee on the Judiciary,* 93rd Cong., 2d Sess., pt. 7, at 5794, (July 23-26, 1974) (The Industrial Reorganization Act–The Computer Industry). IBM was originally a defendant, but settled out of court with Honeywell.

[30] *See generally* "How the Judge Looked at the IBM-Sperry Rand ENIAC Part," 20 *Datamation* 78 (Jan. 1974).

[31] *See* Spiegal, *"Telex v. IBM:* Monopoly Pricing Under Section 2 of the Sherman Act," 84 *Yale L. J.* 558 (1975).

Barriers to Entry. Continued advancement of computer technology is critical to the future growth of the computer industry. Low barriers to entry will aid the advancement of computer technology, and thus, the future growth of the computer industry by enabling smaller firms with innovations to enter the industry. An understanding of the barriers to entry presently existing is needed before an adequate examination of restructuring proposals can be made. The major barrier existing in the computer industry is the need for massive "front end" capital required for the leasing of computer equipment.[32] Computer leases are generally for one to two years and contain a thirty- or ninety-day cancellation clause. Consequently, banks require large discounts in purchasing the leases due to the high risk of cancellation.

In the recent Industrial Reorganization Hearings, Collins testified that the first-year operation of a hypothetical firm selling its equipment would yield profits of $20 million. On the other hand, the leasing operations for the first year of that same hypothetical company would yield a net loss of $36 million.[33] Large banks such as the Continental Illinois National Bank and the Bank of America, backers of Telex and Memorex respectively, are extremely cautious of providing additional venture capital in light of the *Telex* and *Memorex* cases. The large paper losses the first few years after initial entry also naturally deter equity investors.

The problems with raising capital can also be seen in the present venture by Gene Amdahl. Domestic banks were apparently unwilling to fund Amdahl in his development of a central processing unit (CPU) competitive with the IBM 370 CPU. Thus, foreign capital was raised from Fujitsu and Nixdorf.[34] Therefore, the leasing capital barrier is very large, and effectively deters firms from entering the computer industry.[35]

One method to avoid the entire capital entry barrier is to enter the industry

---

[32] Interview, Daniel Slotnick, Professor, Department of Computer Science, University of Illinois (June 1975).

[33] *Hearings on S. 1167 Before the Subcommittee on Antitrust and Monopoly of the Senate Committee on the Judiciary,* 93rd Cong., 2nd Sess. pt. 7, at 5383 (July 23-26, 1974) (The Industrial Reorganization Act–The Computer Industry) (Statement by Eugene K. Collins, Director of Research, Evans and Co., N.Y., N.Y.).

[34] *Hearings on S. 1167 Before the Committee on Antitrust and Monopoly of the Senate Committee on the Judiciary,* 93rd Cong., 2nd. Sess., pt. 7, at 5417 (July 23-26, 1974) (The Reorganization Act–The Computer Industry) (Statement by Maryland Walter-Carlson, Vice President and Associate Director, Research Shareholders Management Co., Los Angeles, California).

[35] *See generally* J. Sood, *A Study of the International Computer Industry and A Projection of the Effect of the American Computer Industry of the United States Balance of Payments from 1969 to 1975* 57 (1971) (D.B.A. Dissertation, The George Washington University).

in one of the smaller subparts. A study by the Organisation for Economic Cooperation and Development concluded that partial entry into the hardware peripherals or software segments is a more effective way to enter the computer industry.[36] Partial entry makes the entering firm dependent on products compatible with the existing firm's CPU. Thus, the entering firm is in a very precarious position, because its market can be totally eliminated by the existing firm changing its product specifications.[37]

An additional barrier to entry is the large capital investment needed for research and development. As a firm captures more and more of the market, these research and development costs can be spread over more units produced.[38] As the cost of research and development rises, it becomes more natural for fewer firms to be in the industry on account of the huge research and development costs that are needed to develop computer products. It should be noted, however, that with the advancement in electronic component technology, the cost to develop and package computer products from electronic components is reduced. In the future, therefore, this barrier to entry should continue to decrease. Counterbalancing this high research and development cost is the fact that as a firm becomes more dominant, it is economically unwise for it to use all its newly developed research and development because of its existing revenue producing product base.[39] This bias against new product introductions is especially strong if existing products are under thirty-day cancellation leases, because end users will immediately demand the new product if it has a better cost-to-performance ratio than the old product.

There is also the entrenchment phenomenon. That is, once any computer firm is established with an end user, that company is very hard to dislodge.[40] It has been estimated that at least a 10 percent improvement in the price-to-

---

[36] Organisation for Economic Cooperation and Development, *Electronic Computers:* (Gaps in Technology) 23 (1969).

[37] *See, e.g.,* Telex Corp., IBM Corp., 367 F. Supp. 258 (N. D. Okla. 1973) (Plaintiff's exhibit 391A-0A8, p. 10 and 13, IBM Management Review Committee Minutes, July 15, 1971).

[38] Organisation for Economic Cooperation and Development, *Gaps in Technology—* (Electronic Computers) 22 (1969).

[39] *See* W. Banks, Jr., *An Inquiry Into the Growth Factors and Financial Policies of International Business Machines Corporation and into the Possibility and Probability of the Company's Continued Dominance of the Electronic Data Processing Industry* (1968) (Ph.D. Dissertation, University of Arkansas). *See generally* W. Nordhaus, *Invention, Growth and Welfare A Theoretical Treatment of Technical Change* (1969); F. Scherer, *Industrial Market Structure and Economic Performance* (1970).

[40] Organisation for Economic Cooperation and Development, *Gaps in Technology* (Electronic Computers) 113 (1969).

performance ratio is needed before an entrenched customer will even look at a competitor's computer.[41]

Most end users require extensive service support in the operation of their computers. *Datamation* conducted a survey of end users to determine the factors end users considered important in comparing manufacturing firms.[42] The survey ranked IBM first in after-sales service, product reliability, and support. IBM was last in the ranking of product performance per dollar. Other surveys have also shown the importance of vendor support in ranking computer manufacturers.[43] Therefore, with no independent third party maintenance subindustry, an entering firm must also immediately provide a large maintenance service for all the equipment it sells.

One final strategy used as a barrier to entry is the high cost of antitrust litigation. Existing firms know that any new firm entering the industry can sue them. This suit, however, does not prevent the existing firms from approaching and at times violating the antitrust laws because of the large capital requirement needed to maintain a full antitrust suit. For example, at present it costs over $2000 a year just to purchase a recording service that maintains records on all IBM litigations.[44]

Manufacturing economies are a natural barrier to entry. Unfortunately, few studies have been made to determine the existing manufacturing economies of scale.[45] In examining the IBM studies on peripheral production costs, Brock concluded that a company having 10 percent of IBM's share would incur about a 10 percent higher manufacturing unit cost. In approximate terms, a company with half of IBM's share would incur practically no cost disadvantage. Due to the fact that selling costs make up a large percentage of total cost, these approximate estimates indicate that the present size of IBM is not needed to achieve any natural economies of scale.[46]

---

[41] E. Shuster, *Selective Demand Determinants in the Computer Acquisition Process,* (1969) (Ph.D. Dissertation, American University).

[42] McLaughlin, "Monopoly is Not a Game," 19 *Datamation* 75 (Sept. 1973).

[43] *See, e.g.,* E. Shuster, *Selective Demand Determinants in the Computer Acquisition Process* 71 (1969) (Ph.D. Dissertation, The American University); *Hearings on S. 1167 Before the Subcommittee on Antitrust and Monopoly of the Senate Committe of the Judiciary,* 93rd Cong., 2nd Sess., pt. 7, at 5042 (July 23-26, 1974). (The Industrial Reorganization Act–The Computer Industry) (Statement submitted by the Auerbach Corp.).

[44] *See* 676 *B.N.A.-A.T.R.R.* A-26 (August 13, 1974) (IBM Litigation Reporting Service offered by International Data Corporation, Boston, Ma.).

[45] *See* G. Brock, *The U.S. Computer Industry: A Study of Market Power* 28 (1976).

[46] *See also Hearings on S. 1167 Before the Subcommittee on Antitrust and Monopoly*

Overall, Brock has estimated that the capital requirements to enter the integrated systems market are over $1 billion. For the mini market, the capital barrier was estimated at approximately $5 million and for peripheral manufacturers required to lease their equipment, the barrier entry is considerably higher than the $5 million figure for minicomputer manufacturers.[47]

In addition to considering the effect restructuring the industry will have on barriers to entry, one should consider the effect technology will have on the future structure of the industry. Based on the past IBM consent decrees, one is also reminded of the need to consider the interaction between the terms of a consent decree and advancing computer technology. In the 1936 consent decree, IBM was successful in using its patents on the card making machine to effectively bypass many of the intended purposes of the 1936 decree.[48] In the 1956 consent decree, IBM was required to lease and sell computers on equal terms. The lease-purchase ratio, however, was generally more favorable to leasing equipment. Once the equipment was leased, IBM was successful in multipricing its product through extra user charges for usage over a standard forty-hour work week.[49]

Although greatly slowed by IBM's present dominance of the industry, a projected long-term trend exists towards atomization of the industry. This long-term trend towards atomization is due in large part to the developments in semiconductor technology that are discussed in Chapter 3. Therefore, any proposed restructuring remedies need to consider computer technology trends.

Restructuring the Computer Industry.   The IBM—Justice Department antitrust

---

of the Senate Committee on the Judiciary 93rd Cong., 2d Sess., pt. 7, at 5626 (July 23-26, 1974) (The Industrial Reorganization Act—The Computer Industry) (Statement by Ralph E. Miller) (Discussion of external economies in having large numbers of identical machines. External economies include a larger resale market, more abundant and reliable software, and larger user organizations.)

[47] G. Brock, *The U.S. Computer Industry: A Study of Market Power* 56 (1975). IBM also has a long history of maintaining a large cash position. This large cash reserve is an additional deterent to potential entrants because in any price war, the firm with the largest cash position is in a stronger competitive position. W. Banks, Jr., *An Inquiry Into the Growth Factors and Financial Policies of International Business Machines Corporation and Into the Possibility and Probability of the Companies' Continued Dominance of the Electronic Data Processing Industry* (1968) (Ph.D. Dissertation, University of Arkansas). Finance text books suggest that the deductability of interest payments makes a huge liquid position too safe to maximize shareholder wealth. J. Horen, *Financial Management and Policy* (1971) (2nd ed.). A huge liquid position, however, effectively maximizes shareholder wealth when the asset to be protected is monopoly power, and large liquidity allows immediate retaliation to all potential entrants. *See* Bower, "Market Changes in the Computer Services Industry," 4 *Bell J. of Econ. and Management Science* 539 (Autumn 1973).

[48] W. Sharpe, *The Economics of Computers* 248 (1969).

[49] W. Sharpe, *The Economics of Computers* 259 (1969).

case is presently in trial.[50] Any discussion of the actual case would be mere speculation. Several proposals for restructuring the industry, however, will be examined at this point.

Many judicial and legislative proposals for an appropriate remedy for the present IBM dominance of the industry have been made.[51] The various reorganization proposals can be grouped into two categories. The first category includes those proposals that will primarily affect the conduct of the industry.[52] The second category includes those remedies primarily affecting the structure of the industry. An example of conduct changes can be found in the *Telex* decision and its proposed remedies for IBM: requiring disclosure of specifications and interfaces between equipment at time of product announcement or first sale, for example.[53]

Proposed structural remedies also vary greatly. Brock proposed that IBM be broken up along functional lines such that the central processing unit (CPU) division, electronic components division, the peripheral division, etc., be required to sell the various parts to all willing purchasers.[54] The Justice Department in its preliminary memorandum on relief requested that IBM be broken into "several discrete, separate, independent and competitively balanced entities capable of competing successfully in domestic and international markets with one another and with other domestic and foreign competitors."[55] In a related area, should the Industrial Reorganization Act pass, the industry would also be restructured.[56]

---

[50] *See* Bigelow, "United States v. IBM 1969-1974," 4 *Comp. L. Serv.* sec. 7-1, art. 6 (1975) (R. Bigelow, ed.); Keefe, "Not all Quiet on the IBM Antitrust Front, 60 *A.B.A.J.* 850 (July 1974).

[51] *See, e.g.,* J. Stood, *A Study of the International Computer Industry and a Projection of the Effect of the American Computer Industry on the United States Balance of Payments from 1969 to 1975* (1971) (D.B.A. Dissertation, George Washington University); *Hearings Before the Committee on Antitrust and Monopoly of the Senate Committee of the Judiciary,* 93rd Cong., 2nd sess., pt. 7 at 5464 (July 23-26, 1974) (The Industrial Reorganization Act–The Computer Industry) (Statement of Dan L. McGurk, Computer Industry Association, Encino, Calif.); G. Brock, *The U.S. Computer Industry: A Study of Market Power* (1975).

[52] *See* F. Scherer, "Industrial Market Structure and Economic Performance," 5 (1970) (Paradigm of market structure-conduct-performance).

[53] Telex, Corp. v. IBM Corp, 367 F. Supp. 258 (N.D. Okla., 1973). *See also* Rubin, "IBM and the Industry," 21 *Datamation* 99 (Sept. 1975).

[54] G. Brock, *The U.S. Computer Industry: A Study of Market Power* (1975).

[55] United States v. International Business Machines Corporation, civil no. 69-200 S.D.N.Y. 1969 (October 13, 1972). The basis of these separate but balanced entities could presently be formed from several of the IBM operating divisions.

[56] *See generally Hearings on S.1167 Before the Subcommittee on Antitrust and Monopoly of the Senate Committee on the Judiciary,* 93rd Cong., 2nd Sess., pt. 7 (July 23-26, 1974) (The Industrial Reorganization Act–The Computer Industry).

Related Antitrust Considerations. On the international scene, there has been continuous rumbling of possible antitrust action against U.S. firms, and in particular, against IBM. Thus far, however, no significant action has emerged.[57] A final antitrust consideration is the interaction between patenting software and antitrust. Should a patent of a strategic program become progressively more important, the patent holder would be subject to antitrust action unless the use of the patent was licensed to everyone at reasonable royalties.[58]

The present antitrust environment can be expected to continue. The mere presence of antitrust prohibitions undoubtedly restrains IBM from strengthening its existing dominance. If the IBM-Justice Department case is resolved in favor of IBM, then the very gradual pace toward structural atomization will continue. On the other hand, if the case is resolved in favor of the Justice Department, any restructuring of the industry will aid the already existing long-term technologically induced trend toward structural atomization.

Protection of Proprietary Property

The software part of the computer industry is one of the fastest growing segments of the entire computer industry. In Chapter 1 the trend toward software costs becoming a large percentage of total system costs was discussed, and consequently, the legal status of software is increasingly more important. The legal structure surrounding the software industry has not, however, kept pace with the technological changes occurring within the industry. Although there is voluminous material on the legal protection of software, no definitive legal principles have emerged concerning the procedures used to protect software.[59]

Rapid software development, however, is essential for the continued growth of the computer industry. Today, software packages are commonly sold for thousands of dollars.[60] In addition, there are now large numbers of identical

---

[57] *See, e.g.,* Gardner, "Common Market May Step Up Probe of IBM's Dominance," 20 *Datamation* 54 (August 1974).

[58] *See,* Baker, "Antitrust Aspect of the Software Issue," 4 *Comp. L. Ser.* sec. 7-1 art. 1 (1975) (R. Bigelow, ed.) (Paper delivered to the Conference on Protecting Proprietary Rights in Software, March 4, 1969).

[59] *See, e.g.,* George Washington University, Computers in Law Institute, *The Law of Software* (1968 and 1969). For an up-to-date bibliography on software protection see American Bar Association, Section of Patent, Trademark and Copyright Law, *1974 Committee Report.*

[60] *See, e.g.,* 20 *Datamation* 138 (August 1974) (Advertisements of software packages selling for $4,000 or leasing for $99 per month). For that expenditure level, the purchaser should receive an operational system, adequate documentation, and a reasonable amount of technical support. The purchase price typically represents one-fifth to one-tenth the total cost to develop an equivalent package. Head and Linilk, "Software Package Acquisition," 14 *Datamation* 24 (Oct. 1968).

computers available, on which these software packages can be used. Large social gains exist if these software packages can be used on all machines rather than having a similar software package independently developed for each computer.[61] Consequently, some type of legal mechanism is essential to provide software developers with a means to protect their intellectual products. Once appropriate legal protection is provided, the developers of software will be willing to sell their products, and thus, wasteful duplication of effort can be avoided. By providing a viable method to protect software, public policy will, therefore, foster the commercial development of software.

Overview. The remainder of this section on protection of proprietary property first examines the legal protection of software through the use of patent, copyright, and trade secret law. Each of these methods offers a viable alternative, but each suffers from major weaknesses.

Patent Protection. Hardware is clearly patentable under existing patent statutes.[62] Software, however, does not conveniently fall into any of the present statutory classifications of patentable material. Patent protection is commonly accepted as the strongest form of software protection. Consequently, proponents of software patent protection have attempted to secure software patents in several cases.

The status of the various patent law revisions before Congress is constantly changing.[63] Consequently, this area will not be examined due to the speculative nature of any inquiry. Instead, the present focus will be on the current legal interpretation of the existing patent law with regard to software patentability.

In several early cases, the Supreme Court held that a newly discovered scientific truth or mathematical expression could not be patented, but that "a novel and useful structure created with the aid of knowledge of scientific truth may be."[64] From this line of cases, and others related to the field of electronics, the Court developed the mental steps doctrine.[65] In brief, the mental steps

---

[61] It has been conservatively estimated that as much as 5 percent duplication of programming effort occurs annually. A. Pritchard, *A Guide to Computer Literature* 16 (1972) (2nd. ed.).

[62] 35 *U.S.C.* sec. 151 (1973). All statutory requirements must naturally be met to secure a hardware patent. In the case of the ENIAC patent, commercial use beyond the one year limit occurred before the patent was applied for, and thus, the patent was invalid. *See* "Eniac In Court: What Might Have Happened," 19 *Datamation* 119 (June 1973).

[63] There are currently four patent reform bills before the Senate (S. 23, McClellan bill; S. 214, Fong bill; S. 473, Hart bill; S. 1308 Scott bill). *See* 14 *Ill. Pat., Trademark, and Copyright Newsletter* 1 (June 1975).

[64] Mackay Co. v. Radio Corp., 306 U.S. 86 (1938).

[65] *See, e.g.,* Cochrane v. Diener, 94 U.S. 780 (1876); O'Reilly v. Morse, 15 How. (56 U.S.) 62 (1853). *See also,* Woodcock, "Mental Steps and Computer Programs," 52 *J. Pat. Off. Soc'y* 275 (1970).

doctrine means that if an idea can be totally carried out by the human mind
without the aid of a mechanical device, then the idea is unpatentable. Applied
to computer programs, the result is devastating because most software can at
least theoretically be performed by the human mind.

Through a series of cases, the Court of Customs and Patent Appeals (CCPA)
attempted to distinguish computer programs that provided some physical change
on materials from programs that did not physically affect materials.[66] Based on
this distinction, the CCPA separated computer programs performing some physical act on materials from the mental steps doctrine and upheld several patents
on computer programs. While the Patent Office and CCPA were distinguishing
types of computer programs, the President's Commission on the Patent System
concluded that the Patent Office lacked adequate methods and facilities for
classifying computer programs, and thus, recommended against a patent policy
that would allow the patentability of computer software.[67]

Gottschalk v. Benson. In 1972, the Supreme Court attempted to clarify this
confused situation by deciding *Gottschalk* v. *Benson.*[68] Writing for a unanimous
Court with three justices abstaining, Justice Douglas held that the program was
not patentable under the existing patent laws. Based on the settled principle that
ideas were not patentable, the Court reasoned that granting a patent for converting binary coded decimals (BCD) to binary numerals with the aid of a digital
computer would in effect be a patent on the algorithm embodied in the computer program, since the use of the algorithm on a digital computer would be the
only practical method of implementation. Justice Douglas, however, stressed
that the decision was only limited to invalidating the overly broad claim of

---

[66] *See* Note, 14 *Boston Coll. Ind. and Comm. L. R.* 1050 (1973); Note, 4 *Loyola Univ. of
Chicago, L. J.* 560 (1973).

[67] Commission on Patent System, *The 1966 Report of the President's Commission on the
Patent System* (reprinted in S. Doc. No. 5, 90th Cong., 1st Sess. at 21). *See also* Evans,
"Computer Program Classification: A Limitation on Program Patentability As a Process,"
53 *Or. L. R.* 501 (1974) (Proposal for a software selection scheme to decide which computer programs should be patented).

[68] 409 U.S. 63 (1972). Gary Benson and Arthur Talbot filed an application with the
Patent Office in 1963 seeking a patent on a method of converting binary coded decimal
(BCD) numerals into pure binary numerals through the use of a mathematical algorithm.
Although this process could be performed mentally with the aid of pen and pencil, the
algorithm enabled one to program a computer to do the same conversion with large
savings in manpower and time. The Patent Office refused to issue the patent on the
grounds that the subject matter of the invention was not within any of the statutory
classes of patentable inventions. Reasoning that the application was within the mental
steps doctrine, the Patent Office ruled that the claims were outside the statutory class
of patentable material. On appeal, the CCPA reversed the Patent Office decision and
held that the patent application claims were within the statutory classification of
patentable inventions. Application of Benson, 441 F.2d 582 (CCPA 1971).

patenting a mathematical algorithm, and not the invalidation of all computer programs.

One possible interpretation of *Gottschalk* is to read the opinion narrowly and conclude that mathematical algorithms are not constitutionally patentable. Thus, the patenting of software is still permitted. A broad reading of *Gottschalk*, however, indicates that all software is unpatentable.[69]

The CCPA is still validating patents for computer programs that adequately describe the program and that do not relate to a purely mathematical algorithm.[70] The legal support for issuance of these patents, however, is based on cases before *Gottschalk*, which distinguished computer programs from the mental steps doctrine.[71] The Supreme Court in *Dann* v. *Johnston*[72] again faced the issue of software patentability. In *Dann*, however, the Court avoided the direct issue of software patentability by ruling the Dann computer program obvious under 35 *U.S.C.* sec. 103, and thus not patentable.

On the practical side, a strong deterrent exists against the use of patents to protect software. The minimum cost of legal fees in obtaining a patent is approximately one thousand dollars with many patent applications costing considerably more. The average cost for software patent applications may be considerably higher due to their controversial nature. In addition, the gestation period for a patent application averages three years, and thus, if a patent is finally disapproved, the developer of a program will be left in the same position as before beginning the patent application procedure. A patent application remains confidential unless a patent is issued. Many patents are invalidated in infringement suits.[73] Patent disclosure standards are quite high.[74] Once a patent is declared invalid in an infringement suit, its contents are known. Thus, trade secret protection is

---

[69] Note, 4 *Loyola Univ. of Chicago L.R.* 560 (1973).

[70] *See, e.g.,* Application of Brandstadter, 484 F.2d 1395 (CCPA 1973); Application of Doyle, 482 F.2d 1385 (CCPA 1973).

[71] *See* Application of Musgrage, 431 F.2d 882 (CCPA 1970); Application of Mahony, 421 F.2d 742 (CCPA 1970); Application of Bernhart, 417 F.2d 1395 (CCPA 1969); Application of Prater, 415 F.2d 1393 (CCPA 1969).

[72] ____U.S. ____, 44 *U.S.L.W.* 4463 (1976).

[73] Approximately 100,000 patent applications are annually filed, of which two-thirds result in the issuance of patents. The overall validation level is approximately 60 to 70 percent. Great variation in patent validation percentages exists between the circuit courts of appeals. Interview, Stanley Schlosser, Office of Legislation and International Affairs, Patent Office, U.S. Department of Commerce, Washington, D.C. (July 1975).

[74] *See* Application of Doyle, 482 F.2d 1285 (C.C.P.A. 1973) (Mere disclosure of computer program flow chart ruled insufficient disclosure.)

is no longer available.[75]   The net result of these difficulties is that the choice of patent protection for software is not particularly inviting.[76]

Copyright Protection.   The difference between patent and copyright protection is that a patent holder acquires exclusive right to the invention even if another individual later, but independently, discovers the same idea.[77]   A copyright, however only protects one from the mere copying of the idea or work. For example, if a computer program were patented, no one could use the same program, even if they independently discovered the program. A copyright, on the other hand, would only prevent others from copying the exact program. Consequently, if an individual could prove that the program was independently developed, then the individual could freely use that program.[78]

There are two types of copyright protection. One is based on common law and the other is based on federal statutes.[79]   While an author is preparing a work and up to the time the work is published, the author is protected under state common law copyright. This means that the author is protected from unauthorized copying, publishing, vending, performing, and recording.[80]   Under present law, until the author permits publication, this common law protection exists forever.[81]

Once the author decides to publish the work, one of two alternatives will occur. First, the author can publish the work without any copyright notice on the work. If this happens, the work is considered to have been donated to the

---

[75] *See* Dobyns and Block "Adequate Disclosure of Computers and Programs in Patent Specifications," 56 *J. Pat. Office Society* 574 (1974).

[76] The Canadian Government recently issued a patent on a computer program. *See* 8 *Computerworld* 1 (August 7, 1974). *See generally* Falk and Popper, "Computer Programs and Nonstatutory Subject Matter in Canada," 4 *Comp. L. Serv.* sec. 9-4, art. 2 (1975) (R. Bigelow, ed.) If any foreign government upholds a patent on a computer program, the patent may be valid in the U.S. under the various patent treaties. S. Ladas, *Patents, Trademarks, and Related Rights: National and International Protection* (1975); American Bar Association, Section of Patent, Trademark, and Copyright Law, *1974 Committee Report.*

[77] Galbi, "Copyright and Unfair Competition Law As Applied to the Protection of Computer Programming," 3 *Comp. L. Serv.* sec. 4-3, art. 1 (1975) (R. Bigelow, ed.).

[78] For a concise legislative history of copyright law see footnote 17 in Goldstein v. California, 412 U.S. 546 (1973).

[79] *See generally* Nimmer, *Nimmer on Copyrights* (1974); Nicholson, *A Manual of Copyright Practice for Writers, Publishers, and Agents* (1970) (2nd ed.).

[80] Nimmer, *Nimmer on Copyrights* sec. 111 (1974).

[81] Limited publication is permitted under common law copyright law. A limited publication is defined as a publication that "communicates the contents of a manuscript to a definitely selected group and for a limited purpose, without the right of diffusion, reproduction, distribution or sale." White v. Kimmell, 193 F.2d 744 (9th. Cir. 1952).

public. On the other hand, if all copies of the work that are authorized by the author are properly designated as copyrighted material, then the author is protected under federal copyright statutes.[82] Under both common law copyright and statutory copyrights, authors can sue for damages for illegal copying of their work.[83] Damages are based on either actual damages that they have suffered or the profits that the copier received from the unauthorized copying.

In 1965, the Copyright Office issued Circular 31D, which outlined the three basic rules for current registration of computer programs.[84] The first rule is that the individual applying for the copyright must be the original author. Next, all copies of the program must be published with the normal copyright designation. Finally, copies of the program must be deposited with the Copyright Office, and if the program is in machine language, copies of the program both in machine language and in a high-level language must be deposited with the Copyright Office.[85]

Telex v. IBM. On the practical side, one method to prevent copyright infringement is to insert meaningless statements into the program.[86] If the alleged infringer literally copied the program, these meaningless statements will appear, and thus, sufficient evidence will be available to prove infringement. If the program is extremely long, the proof of availability of the program to the defendant and nearly complete identity will also be sufficient evidence to prove

---

[82] The duration of the federal copyright protection is fifty-six years if the copyright is properly renewed after twenty-eight years. In 1974, the Senate passed a revision to the copyright law (S. 1361, 93rd. Cong., 2nd Sess.) in which the duration of the copyright would have been fifty years after the author's death. This provision applied to both common law and statutory copyright. Congress is presently considering several copyright revision bills.

[83] Nimmer, *Nimmer on Copyrights* sec. 150 and 151 (1974).

[84] 2 *Comp. L. Serv.* p. 4-3a (1975) (Bigelow, ed.)

[85] Copyright registration of computer programs started slowly, jumped in the late 1960s, but has since leveled off. The number of software copyright registrations is quite low when the total number of programs annually written is considered. The figures as of February 1975 are as follows for each fiscal year:

1965 – 20	1971 – 41
1966 – 33	1972 – 247
1967 – 37	1973 – 280
1968 – 28	1974 – 265
1969 – 10	1975 – 155
1970 – 34	(through Feb. 1975)

Interview, Harriett Oler, U.S. Copyright Office, Office of the Registry, Washington, D.C. (July 1975).

[86] Galbi, "Copyright and Unfair Competition Law as Applied to the Protection of Computer Programming," 2 *Computer Law Service* sec. 4-3, art. 1, p. 17 (1975) (R. Bigelow, ed.).

copyright infringement. In *Telex v. IBM*[87] one of the counterclaims by IBM
against Telex was for copyright infringement of IBM's Fast Running Interpreter
Enabling Natural Diagnostics (FRIEND) program. Both the trial court and the
Cour of Appeals accepted as sufficient evidence that out of the entire program
only a few minor deviations existed between the IBM original and Telex version.
In addition, IBM was able to prove that Telex personnel had access to the IBM
program.[88]

In *Walt Disney v. Alaska Television Co.*,[89] The court held that copyright
infringement had occurred when the defendant copied a television show and
transported it to Alaska on magnetic tape. The mere copying onto magnetic
tape was considered the critical element, not the rebroadcast of the performance.
By analogy, one can reason that the copying of a computer program that is on
magnetic tape is also a copyright violation. Translations of copyrighted material
are also prohibited, and thus, the conversion of a copyright program from one
language to another through a compiler should also constitute copyright
infringement.[90]

Williams and Wilkins v. U.S.   The National Institute of Health established a
policy whereby on request, they would provide single copies of various obscure
medical journals. Over a million single copies were made before Williams and
Wilkins sued. With a strong dissent, the U.S. Court of Claims reversed the trial
court and held—four to three—that the photocopying of a copyrighted article,
one copy at a time, was not an infringement of the copyright. Rather, the copying
fell under the fair use doctrine, which allows the paraphrasing and excerpting of
copyrighted material to encourage the dissemination of ideas.[91]   Without an
opinion, the Supreme Court split four to four and thus, upheld the Court of

---

[87] 367 F. Supp. 258 (N.D. Okla. 1973), *rev g in part and modified on other grounds,* 510
F.2d 894 (1975) (Discussed in "Nanoseconds, Megabytes and Antitrust," 706 *B.N.A.-
A.T.R.R.* B-1 (March 25, 1975)).

[88] IBM has favored copyright protection, and Elmer Galbi, Senior Patent Attorney for
IBM, has proposed a revision to the Copyright Act which includes a provision allowing
the copyrighting of computer software. *See* Galbi, "Proposal for New Legislation to
Protect Computer Programming," 17 *Bull. Copyright Soc.* 280 (1970); Morris, "Protecting
Proprietary Rights of Computer Programs: The Need for New Legislative Protection," 21
Catholic Univ. L. R. 181 (1970). IBM may favor copyrighting over patenting computer pro-
grams because of the inherent antitrust dangers in patent protection for a dominant firm
such as IBM.

[89] 310 F. Supp. 1073 (W.D. Wash. 1969).

[90] *See also* Prasinos, "Worldwide Protection of Computer Programs by Copyright," 4
Rutgers J. Comp. and Law 42 (1974).

[91] Williams and Wilkins v. U.S., 487 F.2d 1345 (1974). *See* L. Bernacchi and G. Larsen,
Data Processing Contracts and the Law 698 (1974); Note, "Technological Piracy in
Reprographic Revolution," 36 *Univ. Pitt. L. Rev.* 153 (1974).

Claims decision.[92] Applied to software, one can reason that a single use of a copyrighted computer program (or at least the use of one part of the program) would not currently be a copyright violation.[93]

Trade Secret Protection. A viable third alternative for many firms in the use of trade secret law to protect software. Just as common law copyright law originates in the common law of each state, the origin of trade secret law can also be found in the common law of each state.[94]

Judicial recognition of trade secret law has a long history. In *Board of Trade of Chicago v. Christie Grain and Stock Co.*, Justice Holmes stated that "the plaintiff has the right to keep the work which it has done, or paid for doing, to itself. The fact that others might do similar work, if they might, does not authorize them to steal plaintiff's."[95] In a later case, however, Justice Holmes pointed out that it is not the subject matter *per se* that gains for itself the status of trade secret, but rather "the primary fact that the law makes some requirements of good faith . . . The property may be denied, but the confidence cannot be."[96]

State courts have held that a trade secret must meet four major tests: (1) appropriateness of subject matter, (2) secrecy, (3) novelty, and (4) economic value.[97] Appropriateness of subject matter has three broad subcategories of protectable information: (1) patentable and unpatentable inventions along with know-how associated with these inventions (*e.g.*, secret processes, patterns, compounds), (2) abstract ideas of a commercial or industrial nature *e.g.*, advertising plans, schemes for media presentation), and (3) other sorts of information that

---

[92] Williams and Wilkins v. United States, 420 U.S. 376 (1975).

[93] Justice Blackmun did not participate in Williams and Wilkins, but did conclude in Withtol v. Crow, 309 F.2d 777 (8th Cir. 1962), that making forty copies of a song constituted infringement and not fair use. *See* Nimmer, "Photocopying and Record Piracy: Of Dred Scott and Alice in Wonderland," 22 *U.C.L.A.L.R.* 1052 (1975).

[94] *The Restatement of Torts* defines a trade secret as:

any formula, device, or compilation of information which is used in one's business, and which gives him an opportunity to obtain an advantage over competitors who do not know or use it.

Restatement of Torts, sec. 757, comment (b) (1939). *See also* Bender, "Trade Secret Protection of Computer Software, 38 *Geo. Wash. L.R.* 909 (1970).

[95] 198 U.S. 236, 250 (1905). *See also* Ellis, *Trade Secrets* sec. 12, (1953).

[96] Dupont Power Co. v. Masland, 244 U.S. 100, 102 (1917).

[97] *See* Wessel, "Legal Protection of Computer Programs," 43 *Har. Bus. Rev.* 97 (March-April 1965). Several of these requirements are discussed in Kewanee Oil Co. v. Bicron Corp., 416 U.S. 470 (1974).

are not novel, but which are of value to the owner (*e.g.*, customer lists, discount codes, supply sources).[98]

The second requirement of secrecy is rather vague and has at least two interpretations: internal and external secrecy.[99] The distinction between internal and external secrecy is basically one between in-house secrecy (which involves the steps taken by the owner of the secret to prevent its disclosure by those in contractual relationships with him) and industrywide secrecy (which involves the knowledge of the subject matter among those outside of the owner's control). When the secrecy requirement is mentioned by courts, they typically are referring to internal secrecy. The secrecy requirement is not absolute. Some disclosures are permissible, but the disclosures are limited to persons who enter into confidential relationships with the owner of the trade secret.[100] As long as all parties maintain the secrecy, the independent discovery of the information by others does not destroy its protectable status. If the secret is revealed by dissemination of the product containing it, the trade secret is no longer protected.[101]

The third requirement of novelty is not as stringent as its counterpart under the patent statutes,[102] but the novelty in trade secret law is more discriminating than the originality concept under copyright laws.[103] The fourth requirement dealing with economic value focuses on such factors as the value of the information, the amount of effort expended in obtaining the trade secret, and the difficulty of acquiring or reacquiring the trade secret.[104]

---

[98] Turner, *The Law of Trade Secrets* 12 (1962).

[99] *See* B.F. Goodrich Co. v. Wohlgemuth, 117 Ohio App. 493 (ct. App. 1963); Kaumagraph Co. v. Stampagraph Co., 235 N.Y. 1 (1923); National Tube Co. v. Eastern Tube Co., 3 Ohio Ct. C. Rep. N.S. 459 (Cir. Ct. 1902), *aff'd*, 69 Ohio St. 560, 70 N.E. 1127 (1903).

[100] Morris, "Protecting Proprietary Rights of Computer Programs: The Need for New Legislative Protection," 21 *Catholic Univ. L.R.* 181 (1970). *See also* DuPont Powder Co. v. Masland, 244 U.S. 100 (1917); General Aniline and Film Corp. v. Frantz, 50 Misc. 2d 994, 274 N.Y.S. 2d 634, 151 U.S.P.Q. 136 (N.Y. Sup. Ct. 1966); Cincinnati Bell Foundry Co. v. Dodds, 10 Ohio Dec. Rep. 154 (Super. Ct. 1887).

[101] *See* Wesley-Jessen Inc. v. Reynolds, 182 *B.N.A. Pat., Trademark and Copyright J.*, A-2 (June 13, 1974) (Trade secret no longer a trade secret if embodied in a product which is then sold and examined with reverse engineering techniques). *See also* Oppenheim, *Cases on Unfair Trade Practices* 237 (2d ed. 1965).

[102] W. R. Grace & Co., v. Hargadine, 392 F. 2d 9 (6th Cir. 1968) (Comparison of patent and trade secret novelty requirement).

[103] Alfred Bell and Co. v. Catalda Fine Arts Inc., 191 F. 2d 99 (2d Cir. 1951) (Example of copyright novelty). The degree of novelty will also enter into the determination of damages awarded by the courts. Binder, "Trade Secret Protection of Computer Software," 38 *Geo. Wash. L. Rev.* 909 (1970).

[104] In a few instances, heavy reliance on this fourth requirement has resulted in lowering of the requisite secrecy and novelty standards. Ellis, *Trade Secrets* sec. 14 (1953).

Federal Preemption of State Trade Secret Law.   Although both the definitions and actual requirements of a trade secret vary between states, a well-developed body of trade secret law exists at the state level. This state trade secret law existed for many years, but was recently threatened by a series of Supreme Court cases beginning in the middle of the 1960s.

   Sears Roebuck and Co. v. Stiffel Co.[105] and a companion case,[106] were the first Supreme Court cases in this series that threatened the very existence of state trade secret law. In *Sears*, a pole-lamp sold by Stiffel Co., had previously been held unpatentable. Sears copies Stiffel's design and sold lamps identical to the Stiffel pole-lamp. Stiffel then sued Sears under the Illinois unfair competition law. The Court stated that, an "unpatentable article, like an article upon which a patent has expired, is in the public domain and may be made and sold by whoever chooses to do so."[107]   In broad language threatening the very existence of state trade secret law due to existing federal patent and copyright policy, the Court held that "a state may not, when the article is unpatented and uncopyrighted, prohibit the copying of the article itself or award damages for such copying."[108]

   Five years later in *Lear, Inc. v. Adkins*,[109] the Court held that a licensee could not be required to pay royalties under a contract that challenged the validity of a patent.[110]   Therefore, although *Lear* actually rested on a contractual issue of licensees paying under a contract while testing the validity of a patent, the Court again questioned the validity of state trade secret law based on federal preemption of this law by the federal patent policy.

   In *Goldstein v. California*,[111] the Court held that the federal constitutional provision authorizing Congress to grant copyrights for "limited times" was only a limit on Congress and not on the states. Thus, a California statute making it a criminal offense to pirate recordings produced by others was not void for lack of a durational limit, despite the Constitutional durational limitation on the Congressional power to grant copyrights. The key to *Goldstein* is the Court's

---

[105] 376 U.S. 225 (1964).

[106] Compco Corp. v. Day-Brite Lighting, Inc., 276 U.S. 234 (1964).

[107] 376 U.S. at 231.

[108] 376 U.S. at 232.

[109] 396 U.S. 653 (1969).

[110] The Court reasoned that requiring such payments would undermine the federal policy favoring full and free use of ideas in the public domain.

[111] 412 U.S. 546 (1973). Chief Justice Berger, writing for the majority, merely distinguished *Sears* and *Compco* from *Goldstein*. Dissents by Justice Douglas and Justice Marshall (each concurred in by Justice Brennan and Justice Blackmun, however, relied on *Sears* and *Compco*).

conclusion that by Congressional silence, Congress indicated that states could regulate copyright matters of a purely local nature. If Congress were to determine that a matter warranted national copyright attention and then preempt the field by concluding that no copyright protection was needed, any state action that attempted to protect what Congress had intended to be free from restraint, would be *ultra vires.*

As seen from *Sears, Adkins,* and *Goldstein,* the status of state trade secret law was very unclear. During this same time period, the Court decided *Gottschalk v. Benson,* which has been previously discussed in the patent protection section. *Gottschalk* invalidated a patent for a computer program converting binary coded decimals (BCD) to binary numerals through the use of a mathematical algorithm. Reading *Gottschalk* broadly, one could conclude that all computer programs are unpatentable.[112] If this extreme position were taken, the combination of *Gottschalk* with *Sears, Adkins,* and *Goldstein,* leads one to conclude that because computer programs were unpatentable, they were outside the area of trade secret protection. Therefore, computer programs were unprotectable by either federal or state law.

The threat of federal preemption over state trade secret law was eliminated in *Kewanee Oil Co. v. Bicron Corp.*[113] Kewanee developed a patentable process that could grow a seventeen inch crystal of a type useful in detection of ionizing radiation. After deciding to forego patent protection, Kewanee relied on trade secret law for the protection of this process. Several Kewanee employees signed agreements not to disclose trade secrets obtained while employed for Kewanee. These employees left Kewanee and formed Bicron Corp., which competed with Kewanee in producing the seventeen inch crystals. Based on Ohio trade secret law, the District Court granted a permanent injunction against Bicron producing the seventeen inch crystals. The Court of Appeals, however, reversed on the ground that Ohio's trade secret law was preempted by the federal patent laws.[114]

The Supreme Court reinstated the District Court's opinion by holding that the Ohio trade secret law was not preempted by the federal patent laws. The Court distinguished three types of trade secrets: (1) The trade secret believed by its owner to be patentable; (2) the trade secret whose patentability is considered dubious; (3) the trade secret known by its owner to be unpatentable. The Court then upheld enforcement of trade secrecy rights under each of these

---

[112] Kaul, "And Now State Protection of Intellectual Property?" 60 *A.B.A.J.* 198 (Feb. 1974).

[113] 416 U.S. 470 (1974). *See* Stern, "A Reexamination of Preemption of State Trade Secret Law After Kewanee," 42 *Geo. Wash. L.R.* 927 (1974); Note, "Accommodation of Federal Patents and the State Interest in Trade Secrets," 16 *Will. and Mary L. Rev.* 171 (1974).

[114] 478 F. 2d 1074 (6th Cir. 1973).

categories. Unless Congress takes affirmative action, state trade secret law is not preempted by federal patent policy.

Software and Trade Secrets. With the very existence of state trade secret law settled in light of *Kewanee*, it is appropriate to return to the four requirements of trade secrets — (1) appropriateness of the subject matter, (2) secrecy, (3) novelty, and (4) economic value — to determine their applicability to the special case of software. Computer programs clearly fall within the first requirement of appropriateness of subject matter. Those programs that are in the developmental stage are not as safe as completed programs, but "as the idea becomes more detailed and moved toward implementation, it is more likely to be regarded as qualified for trade secret protection."[115] Mere documentation and data in the form of programs will probably fall in the least protectable class.

In order to insure fulfillment of the secrecy requirement, special care must be taken by the owner both in the case of maintaining in-house secrecy and in the case of selective proliferation of the program. The owner should ensure limited access to the program and all relevant documents should be stamped as secret or confidential. In the case of a sale or rental of a program package, the owner should contract with the vendee to insure that disclosures are limited and closely controlled to protect the trade secret status of the program package.[116]

Very little has been written on the novelty requirement of computer programs for trade secret protection due to the limited case law dealing specifically with trade secret protection of computer software. It would appear, however, that if a program involves many complicated subroutines, the novelty requirement would be satisfied.

For the fourth requirement, the greater the value of the program, the wider the scope of protection afforded by the law of trade secrets.[117] Consequently, the owner should establish a detailed log for each use of the program to provide tangible evidence of its value. Establishing the actual development costs of the program is also an important element in insuring common law protection.

Scope of Protection. The *Restatement of Torts* outlines the protection given by trade secret law. Generally a person is liable for the use or disclosure of another's trade secret when he or she either discovers the secret by improper means, or

---

[115] Irizarry y. Puente v. Harvard College, 248 F. 2d 799, (1st Cir.) *cert. denied*, 356 U.S. 947 (1957); Hamilton National Bank v. Belt, 210 F. 2d 706 (D.C. Cir. 1953).

[116] Various methods are available to facilitate maintaining this secrecy including (1) only allowing the transfer of object code, (2) limiting the amount of documentation transferred with the package, (3) establishing a licensing system on an individual installation basis, and (4) contractural provisions to limit the grantee or licensee in proliferation of the program from the installation site.

[117] Ellis, *Trade Secrets* sec. 14 (1953).

breaks a confidence with others. Further, an individual is liable, if with full knowledge of the facts he or she learns the secret from a third party. Finally, if disclosure is accidentially made to an individual, the individual is not liable for use of the secret until informed of the mistaken disclosure. Thereafter, the individual is liable if he or she uses the trade secret.[118]

A common method to protect computer software is the use of restrictive contractual agreements between the owner of the trade secret and all others with whom the owner deals.[119]   The two distinct categories of such contractual agreements are employee and nonemployee contracts. Clauses in employee contracts requiring nondisclosure both during employment and after employment are commonly used. Another device commonly used in employee contracts is the noncompetition clause.[120]

Nonemployee contracts are more difficult to deal with. If owners choose to lease their programs on a nonexclusive basis, the lessees will only acquire the right to use the programs while titles remain with the lessors. On the other hand, if the developer chooses to sell the software, full title and exclusive rights will be transferred to the vendee. A transaction similar to outright sale of software is a contract for development of a program. In this relationship, title may reside in either party to the contract, and therefore, the division of rights should be clarified before execution of the contract.

Criminal and Noncriminal Remedies Under Trade Secret Law. On the civil side, the owner of a trade secret may obtain injunctive relief to prevent an appropriator from either using the secret or disclosing the secret to a third party.[121]   If the secret has already been disclosed to a third party or used by the appropriator, the owner may seek damages resulting from the disclosure or from the profits accrued by the use of the trade secret.[122]

---

[118] *See Restatement of Torts*, sec.757 (1939).

[119] *See* Doerfer, "The Limits on Trade Secret Law Imposed by Federal Patent and Antitrust Supremacy," 80 *Harv. L. Rev.* 1432 (1967).

[120] These clauses simply limit an employee from competing with the employer for a definite time period and within a specified geographic area once the employee terminates the relationship with the employer. Courts have applied a rule of reason to both time and geographic limitations. The reasonableness of the time period in restrictive agreements will vary between jurisdictions, and may vary depending on the type of position held by the employee. *See* Klein, "The Technical Trade Secret Quadrangle: A Survey, 55 *Nw. U.L. Rev.* 437 (1960). Traditionally, geographic limitations have been viewed as the competitive region of the employer, but the software industry is national in scope, and thus, national territorial limitations should be valid. 10 Cavitch, *Business Organizations* sec. 234.02 (1974).

[121] *See* Kewanee Oil Company v. Bicron Corporation, 416 U.S. 470 (1974); Schulenburg v. Signatrol, Inc., 33 Ill. 2d 379 (1965), *cert. denied*, 383 U.S. 959 (1966) (Although an injunction is a drastic remedy, it may be granted in appropriate instances). *See also* "Software, Statutes, and Stare Decisis," 13 *How. L. J.* 420 (1967).

[122] Morris, "Protecting Proprietary Rights of Computer Programs: The Need for New Legislative Protection," 21 *Catholic Univ. L.R.* 181 (1970).

The use of state criminal sanctions is a relatively new aspect of trade secret protection.[123] Two methods of providing such sanctions presently exist: criminal prosecution for software theft if the stolen information is in such a form as to fit the relevant language of the existing statute, and specific criminal sanctions for misappropriation of trade secrets.[124]

At the federal level, no express trade secret statutes exist. There are, however, statutes that prohibit the transportation and sale or receipt of stolen goods, wares, merchandise, securities, or money.[125] It is still not settled whether the theft of computer programs falls under the federal statutes.[126] Further, no protection exists under these statutes against appropriation by memory.[127]

Overall, trade secret protection of software is a viable alternative for private industry. In a recent case, theft of trade secret protected software (and hardware) was ruled a violation of Oklahoma trade secret law.[128] Although trade secret protection has serious limitations, it currently appears to be the best alternative for private firms.[129]

---

[123] Trade secret theft continues in the computer industry. *See, e.g.*, Curtis, "Theft of Secrets Continue," 48 *Electronics* 63 (May 15, 1975); Hammer, "IBM–Tighter Reins on Trade Secrets; Pledges Fight on Lawsuits," *New York Times* 57 (April 30, 1974).

[124] The first category of general statutory sanctions may be further divided into those jurisdictions that define the subject matter of theft in terms of property, those jurisdictions that qualify or extend (in the form of lists) the property concept in the relevant statutes, and those jurisdictions that provide statutory protection for things of value.

Three complications arise when these statutes are used to protect trade secrets. First, many of the statutes do not carry significant penalties (if at all) for theft involving an "intent to return." Thus, the damage would have been done, but the appropriator would be immune from criminal prosecution under the general statutes. For a recent case in which the defendant was convicted under a felony theft statute rather than a specific trade secret theft statute, see Hancock v. Texas, 402 S.W. 2d 906 (Texas Crim. App. 1966), 379 F. 2d 552 (5th Cir. 1967). Second, if the relevant statutory wording only includes the article in which the secret is embodied (*i.e.*, magnetic tapes or sheets of paper), the protection is worthless. Third, the trade secret must qualify for protection, or the statute will be impotent against appropriation by memory rather than copying of the information.

[125] 18 *U.S.C.* sec. 2314 and 2315 (1973).

[126] In several cases the courts have held that the act of transporting photostatic copies of the stolen information (not computer programs) violated the federal statutes. *See, e.g.*, United States v. Greenwald, 479 F. 2d 320 (6th Cir.), *cert. denied*, 414 U.S. 854 (1973); United States v. Bottone, 365 F. 2d 389 (2d Cir. 1966), *cert. denied*, 385 U.S. 974 (1966); United States v. Lester, 282 F. 2d 750 (3rd Cir. 1960), *cert. denied*, 364 U.S. 937 (1961).

[127] *See* United States v. Bottone, 365 F. 2d 389 (2d Cir. 1966) (Court commented that 15 *U.S.C.* 2314 would not apply to the theft of trade secrets by memory).

[128] Telex, Corp. v. IBM Corp. 367 F. Supp. 258 (Okla. 1973); *rev'd on other grounds*, 510 F. 2d 894 (10th Cir. 1975).

[129] Telex Corp. v. IBM Corp. 367 F. Supp. 258 (Okla. 1973); *counterclaim aff'g with modification*, 510 F. 2d 894 (*10th Cir. 1975*).

Taxation and Leasing

Overview.   Leasing of computer equipment has been a major factor in the computer industry.   Leasing and taxation considerations are closely interwoven: a change in tax policy can dramatically affect the lease-purchase decision.   This section of Chapter 2 first examines the lease-purchase environment.   The development of third-party leasing firms is then discussed as well as the tax implications of third party leasing.   Finally, state software taxation is considered.

Purchase-Lease.   A major factor in the decision to lease or purchase is the difference between technological and economic obsolescence.[130]   Technological obsolescence occurs when new hardware or software performs faster or more efficiently than older hardware or software.   Economic obsolescence focuses on both performance factors as well as cost.   Therefore, when the combination of performance factors and costs of a newer price of equipment outweighs those of an older piece of equipment, the older piece of equipment is economically obsolete.   Taylor found that if economic obsolescence is expected within three years, then leasing is more economical.   In the three- to five-year range, the optimal mix between leasing and purchasing is unclear, and finally beyond five years it is generally more economical to purchase than to buy.   The purchase-to-monthly-lease ratio has traditionally been between 40 and 50 to 1.   Therefore, the item is paid for within forth to fifty months.[131]   Other factors in the lease-purchase decision include considerations such as the cost of available financing, required capacity, and finally, tax considerations.[132]

This purchase-lease ratio varies by type of equipment.   Generally equipment that is primarily composed of electrical components will have a lower lease-purchase ratio.   The reason for the lower ratio is that the computer related electrical technology has advanced very rapidly, resulting in predominantly electrical equipment (memory, CPU, etc.) being made obsolete very quickly.   On the other hand, mechanical equipment has generally had higher purchase-lease ratios because mechanical technology (printers, card readers, *etc.*) has not advanced as rapidly as electrical component technology.[133]

---

[130] D. Taylor, *Capital Budgeting Theory as Applied to the Leasing or Purchasing of Capital Assets—With Emphasis on Computer Equipment* 14 (1967) (Ph.D. Dissertation, Louisiana State University and Agriculture and Mechanical College).

[131] W. Sharpe, *The Economics of Computers* (1969).

[132] Gustafson, "Computers—Lease or Buy?" 41 *Financial Executive* 64 (July 1973). *See generally* McGugan and Caves, "Integration and Competition in the Equipment Leasing Industry," 47 *J. Bus.* 382 (July 1974) (Recent survey of the entire leasing industry); Pantages, "An Introduction to Leasing," 14 *Datamation* 26 (August 1968).

[133] *See generally* W. Armstrong, *Computer Leasing: Evaluating Criteria for Decision-Making* (1968) (American Management Association—Finance Division) (Early work on economic analysis of leasing problems).

IBM has traditionally favored leasing its equipment. Part of this reason may be the historical carry-over of leasing its tabulating equipment in the 1930s, 1940s and 1950s. Officially, IBM stated that its leasing policy was based on its emphasis of selling a service, resulting in the need for full control over its equipment to provide quality service.[134] Groppelli has estimated that the IBM profit rate is 50 percent more on rentals than in outright sales.[135]

At first glance, a high unit sale price policy would appear to maximize profits rather than a leasing policy. For short run maximization, a high unit price does profit maximize. In long-run profit maximization, however, a high unit price is not optimal. A high unit pricing policy would have several detrimental effects on IBM's long-run profits. High sale prices would first attract entrants into the industry. Once in the industry, firms are less likely to leave even if they experience lower than expected profits. A high sale price policy would also lower the capital barrier to entry as compared to thirty- to ninety-day cancellable leases. In outright sales, a firm naturally obtains the sale proceeds immediately. Under thirty- to ninety-day cancellable leases, however, banks may insist on some type of collateral, and will generally require large discounts when purchasing the leases due to the high risk caused by the lease cancellation clauses. Finally, an industry leasing policy causes new entrants to operate at a loss the first few years after entry. When operating at a loss, new entrants are less attractive to equity and debt investors.

In the 1950s and in the early 1960s, most equipment was on lease. Therefore, no secondary used-market existed. By the middle of the 1960s, however, a large enough supply of used computers existed for a used market to function.[136] The risk of economic obsolescence is resolved between mainframe manufacturers and end users by the use of short-term rentals (risk is on the lessor) and long-term leases (risk is on the lessee). Naturally, the purchaser of computer software and hardware always has the risk of economic obsolescence.[137] By the middle of the 1970s, however, purchasing has become relatively less attractive. The reason for this is that IBM is rumored to be readying a new future system. Therefore, third party leasing companies can currently only lease economically their presently owned older equipment. In addition, third party leasing firms who purchased IBM 370 systems have experienced less profits than were expected due to later

[134] T. Belden and M. Belden, *The Lengthening Shadow: The Life of Thomas J. Watson* 308 (1962). *See also* J. Phillips, *Patterns of Price in Competition in the Computer Industry* 45 (1971) (Ph.D. Dissertation, University of Illinois at Urbana-Champaign).

[135] A. Gropelli, *The Growth Process in the Computer Industry* 143 (1970) (Ph.D. Dissertation, New York University).

[136] Fueche, "Second-Generation Computers Live Again—In the Resale Market," 16 *Computers and Automation* 24 (Sept. 1967).

[137] W. Sharpe, *The Economics of Computers* 215 (1969). *See generally* Heiborn, "The Art of Leasing Computers," 16 *Computers and Automation* 42 (Jan. 1967).

announced, but more powerful, 370 computers.[138]   In theory, short-term leasing leaves the risk of economic obsolescence on the lessor. Due to its dominance, IBM controls the rate of technological change. Consequently, IBM does not bear the risk of economic obsolescence, even though a large lease base would generally place the risk of technological obsolence on the lessor.

Hardware and Software Tax Considerations.   The sale of hardware generally falls under the investment tax provisions, and thus, the purchaser will obtain an investment tax credit when purchasing hardware. In addition, purchased hardware is depreciable over the life of the equipment.

Software taxation is not as clear. If software and hardware are jointly purchased (*i.e.*, bundled), then the full price of the purchase will be eligible for the investment tax credit.[139]   Therefore, from the purchaser's tax perspective, it is better to purchase bundled software and hardware or contract for software development. Software development costs can generally be treated as an ordinary business expense.[140]   The ordinary business expense status must be applied to all software development costs and must be regularly used each year.

State Taxation.   State taxation of software and hardware is a final area of concern. Hardware is generally treated as tangible property, and thus no dispute on its taxation exists at the state level. Software, however, is a more difficult matter to tax. States have reasoned that software is tangible personal property, and thus, subject to state property tax provisions. Software owners have argued that software is personal intangible property, which under the laws of most states is not subject to property taxation.[141]   This issue is unresolved, and many cases still arise over the classification of software as tangible or intangible personal property and the resulting tax consequences.[142]

---

[138] Gardner, "Leasing: A Phenomenon that Drains the Balance Sheets of All But IBM," 21 *Datamation* 78 (July 1975). *See also* "Computer Leasing Today—Interview With J. N. Randolph, 42 *Financial Executive* 50 (May 1974).

[139] *Rev. Rul.* 71-177 (Investment Credit On Software).

[140] *Rev. Pro.* 69-21 (Software development costs can be expensed under Section 171 of the 1954 Internal Revenue Code, as a research and development expenditure). *See also* Computer Services Corp. v. Commission, 63 T.C. No. 30 (Dec. 1974), 1 *Computer Law and Tax Rep.* 2 (Feb. 1975) (Software development expenses granted ordinary expense status).

[141] *See* Bryant and Mather, "Property Taxation of Computer Software," 18 *N.Y.L. Forum* 59 (1972); Myers, "Software and Taxes: A Basic Question," 14 *Datamation* 34 (July 1972). *See also* Aronson, "Intangible Taxes: A Wisely Neglected Revenue Source for States," 19 *Nat'l Tax J.* 184 (1966); Blackburn, "Intangible Taxes: A Neglected Revenue Source for States, 18 *Nat'l Tax J.* 214 (1965).

[142] *See, e.g.*, MAI Equipment Corp. v. Courterfield, 3 *C.C. H. State Tax Rep.*, par. 200-433, at 10, (Ohio 1971). *See generally* Bigelow, "State and Local Taxation," 1 *Comp. L. Ser.* sec 2-3.2, art. 2 (1975) (R. Bigelow, ed.).

Debate over proper state taxation of computer software will continue. The battle will constantly shift between state courts and legislatures. Software, however, will eventually be taxed simply because its aggregate value is steadily increasing, and thus, it is a large potential source of state revenue. Although the investment tax credit provisions generally favor purchase of computer equipment, IBM's present dominance and policy favoring leasing will probably cause firms to continue leasing computer equipment. The other tax provisions effecting hardware and software can be expected to remain relatively constant.

Communications — FCC

Computer linked data communications began in the early 1940s.[143] Over time, the interaction of computers and communications has steadily grown. With the advent of time-sharing in the 1960s, use of computers from distant points through remote terminals has become a reality.[144] With the development of networking, computers are becoming increasingly more dependent on communications, and simultaneously, communication technology is becoming ever more dependent on computers in delivering faster and more efficient communication services.[145]

Overview. The remainder of this section on communication policy first examines the early Federal Communication Commission decisions on the interrelationship of computers and communications. The FCC Computer Inquiry is then examined followed by a discussion of the cases resulting from it. The long-run effect of the FCC Computer Inquiry is considered as well as the latest developments in packet switching and value added communication services

Early Federal Communications Decisions. The Federal Communications Act of 1934 created the Federal Communications Commission, which was charged with "regulating interstate and foreign commerce in communications by wire and

---

[143] *See* Stibitz, "The Relay Computers at Bell Labs," 35 *Datamation* 44 (April 1967) (Data communications between Hanover and New York City as part of a demonstration in 1940 to the American Mathematical Society meeting at Dartmouth College).

[144] *See generally* L. Loevinger, "Communications Regulations, *The Law of Computers* (1971) (G. Holmes and C. Noville, eds.); Bigelow, "Some Legal and Regulatory Problems of Computers with Communication Capabilities," 4 *Comp. L. Ser.* sec. 6-1, art. 1 (1974) (R. Bigelow, ed.).

[145] *See generally* S. Mathison and P. Walker, *Computers and Telecommunications: Issues in Public Policy* (1970); A. Zellwager, "Five-Year Computer Technology Forecast," (1972) (U.S. Department of Transportation Rep. #DOT-TSC-DST-72-23); Irwin, "Computer Utility: Competition or Regulation," 76 *Yale L. J.* 1299 (1967).

radio . . ."[146] The Commission has broad powers to regulate the communications industry through both legislative rule making and judicial procedures.[147]

An early case affecting the interaction of computers in communications was *Hush-a-Phone Corp. v. United States*,[148] which tested the legality of the tariff prohibiting all foreign attachments. Hush-a-Phone manufactured and sold a device that coupled over the speaker of a telephone in such a manner that speech into the phone could not be overheard by third parties near the speaker. After the sale of numerous devices, the telephone companies threatened to suspend or terminate service of subscribers who continued to use Hush-a-Phones based on the foreign attachment tariff. The FCC concluded that the use of devices such as Hush-a-Phones were "deleterious to the telephone system" and would result in a general degration of quality service.[149] On appeal, the decision was reversed and remanded to the Commission. The circuit court stated that the tariff was an "unwarranted interference with the telephone subscriber's right reasonably to use his telephone in ways which are privately beneficial without being publicly detrimental."[150] On remand, the Commission invalidated the tariff prohibiting foreign attachments as they related to Hush-a-Phones.

After World War II, microwave communications grew slowly and the FCC generally only assigned frequencies to common carriers and government agencies. By the 1950s, numerous corporations also applied for licenses to operate their own microwave systems. The Commission consolidated all the applications, and over the objections of common carriers, changed its no entry policy to allow private firms entry into the microwave field.[151] Each applicant was assigned a portion of the radio spectrum above 890 millicycles. The private applicants, however, were not allowed to share construction or use of the microwave system among themselves. The carriers reacted to the *Above 890* decision with drastic reduction in long distance rates such as the Bell System Wide Area Telephone Service (WATS).[152]

In 1964, Microwave Communications, Inc. (MCI) applied to the Commission

---

[146] 47 *U.S.C.* sec. 151 (1973).

[147] *See, e.g.,* United States v. The Southwestern Cable Co., 392 U.S. 157 (1968).

[148] 238 F. 2d 266 (D.C. Cir. 1956).

[149] Hush-a-Phone, Corp. v. American Tel. and Tel. Co., 20 F.C.C. 391, 420 (1955).

[150] 238 F. 2d at 269 (1956).

[151] In re Allocation of Frequencies In the Banks Above 890 Mc., *petition for reconsideration denied*, 29 F.C.C. 825 (1960).

[152] *See In re, American Tel. and Tel. Co.*, 38 F.C.C. 370 (1964) (List of Telpak price reductions, the largest price reduction amounting to 85 percent). *See generally* "Regulation of Computer Communication," 7 *Harv. J. Leg.* 208 (1970).

for a permit to provide low cost voice and data communication links between urban centers. Substantial price reductions were offered compared to the existing common carrier rates. Consumers were also granted complete flexibility in the use of the terminal equipment in an unqualified sharing of lines. The Hearing Examiner approved a limited MCI application connecting Chicago and St. Louis.[153] In affirming the Hearing Examiner, the Commission stated that the MCI proposed service would meet a significant unfulfilled communication need.[154]

After the initial MCI application was granted, numerous other applicants petitioned the Commission for construction of commercial microwave systems. After realizing it faced a general licensing question, the Commission grouped several of the applications together.[155] Again, over the objection of the common carriers, the Commission established a policy of granting individual petitions.[156] Subsequently, the FCC granted numerous applications for the establishment of commercial microwave services.[157] The existing common carriers responded with announcements of plans to construct nationwide digital data networks.

While *MCI* was in progress, a dispute between Bunker-Ramo Corporation and the common carriers developed. Bunker-Ramo had previously provided a national stock quotation service on leased common carrier lines, but in 1965 included a buy-sell provision in its service such that brokers using the stock quotation service could also transact business. The common carriers responded that the additional service proposed by Bunker-Ramo was within the traditional communications monopoly, and thus, denied Bunker-Ramo access to the necessary communications lines. Bunker-Ramo finally withdrew its FCC message offering petition. Western Union then filed a tariff in 1967, which provided the same service that Bunker-Ramo had applied for. The Western Union tariff was approved over the objection of Bunker-Ramo.[158]

In early cases, therefore, the Commission allowed Hush-a-Phone to enter the limited mechanical phone attachments market and allowed MCI to establish

---

[153] *In re Application of Microwave Communication Inc. for Construction Permits to Establish New Facilities in the Domestic Public Point-to-Point Microwave Radio Service,* 18 F.C.C.2d 979 (1967).

[154] 18 F.C.C.2d 953 (1969).

[155] *In re Establishment of Policies and Procedures for Consideration of Application to Provide Specialized Common Carrier Service in the Domestic Public Point-to-Point Microwave Radio Service and Proposed Amendments to Parts 21, 43 and 61 of the Commission's Rules,* 24 F.C.C.2d 318 (1970).

[156] 29 F.C.C.2d 910 (1970).

[157] Taub, "Federal Communications Commission Regulation of Domestic Computer Communications: A Competitive Reformation," 22 *Buffalo L. Rev.* 947 (1973).

[158] *In re Western Union Tel. Co.,* 11 F.C.C.2d 1 (1967).

voice and digital communication service between major cities. But the Commission did not permit Bunker-Ramo to establish a message switching service in addition to its stock quotation service.[159]

Carterphone. Carterphone Corporation produced a radio transmitter that automatically switched on when the telephone caller was speaking and then returned the radio to receiving status when the speaker was finished. The device was connected to the phone system enabling a user to call anywhere on the phone system from a remote radio connection. After the sale of several thousand devices, the common carriers announced that the use of Carterphones on the telephone network was prohibited under the tariff prohibiting foreign attachments. Carterphone Corporation filed a private antitrust suit against the telephone companies to invalidate the tariff on antitrust grounds.[160] The court ruled that the FCC had primary jurisdiction, and thus, referred the case to the Commission. The Hearing Examiner approved the Carterphone radio transmitter for use on the telephone network, and ordered the carriers to change their tariffs to allow the use of the Carterphone device.[161]

On appeal, the Commission without a hearing affirmed the Trial Examiner and broadened the Trial Examiner's decision to include all harmless attachments provided by customers.[162] The Bell and General Systems appealed the decision, but the appeal was later withdrawn when the parties settled out of court.[163]

The FCC Inquiry. Against this backdrop of FCC rulings and policies, the Commission determined that a full examination of the computer and the communication regulatory interface was needed. In 1966, the Commission initiated a public inquiry designed to answer the following two questions:

1.   Under what circumstances should data processing, computer information, and message switching, or any particular combination thereof be deemed subject to regulation pursuant to the provisions of the Communications Act?

2.   Whether the policies and objectives of the Communications Act will be served better by such regulations or by such services evolving in a free,

---

[159] *See generally* Comment, "Computer Services in the Federal Regulation of Communications," 116 *U. Pa. L. Rev.* 328 (1967).

[160] Carter v. American Tel. and Tel. Co., 250 F. Supp. 188 (N.D. Tex), *aff'd*, 65 F.2d 456 (5th Cir. 1966).

[161] *In re American Tel. and Tel. Co.*, 13 F.C.C.2d 430 (1967).

[162] Carter v. American Tel. and Tel. Co., *13 F.C.C.2d 420 (1968).*

[163] *See generally* Walker, Mathison, and Jones, "Data Transmission and the Foreign Attachment Rule," 16 *Datamation* 60 (Feb. 1969).

competitive market, and if the latter, whether changes in an existing provisions of the law or regulations are needed.[164]

The Commission received over 3,000 pages of correspondence and submitted these responses to the Stanford Research Institute (SRI) for analysis.[165] In its final decision, the Commission made three major rulings. It retained broad jurisdiction over those aspects of the computer industry that in any way related to communications. Common carriers could not favor their own affiliates if they chose to enter the data processing industry. Third, the principle of maximum separation was established in which the data processing affiliates were to be totally separate from their parent common carriers.[166]

By deciding not to regulate the data processing industry, the Commission faced the issue of defining the difference between data processing and message switching. Data processing is:

the use of a computer for the processing of information as distinguished from circuit or message-switching. "Processing" involves the use of the computer for operations which include, *inter alia*, the functions of storing, retrieving, sorting, merging or calculating data, according to programmed instructions.[167]

On the other hand, message switching is:

the computer-controlled transmission of messages between two or more points, via communications facilities, wherein the content of the message remains unaltered.[168]

The Commission further refined the difference between message switching and data processing by defining hybrid data processing and hybrid communication. These two categories were defined as follows:

---

[164] *In re Regulatory and Policy Problems Presented by the Interdependence of Computer and Communication Services and Facilities*, 7 F.C.C.2d 11, 17-18 (1967) (An additional issue relating to privacy was originally raised, but was later dismissed as being beyond the jurisdiction of the Commission).

[165] Dunn, "Policy Issues Presented by the Interdependence of Computer and Communications Services," 34 *Law and Contemp. Prob.* 369 (1969).

[166] 28 F.C.C.2d 265 (1971). *See generally* B. Gilchrist and M. Wessel, *Government Regulation of the Computer Industry* 70 (1972); Note, "The FCC Computer Inquiry: Interfaces of Competition and Regulated Markets," 71 *Mich. L. Rev.* 172 (1972).

[167] Final Decision and Order, 28 F.C.C.2d at 287 (1971) Codified at 47 *C.F.R.* sec. 64.702 (a) (1) (1972).

[168] Final Decision and Order, 28 F.C.C.2d at 287 (1971) (Codified at 47 *C.F.R.* sec. 64.702 (a) (2) (1973)).

(i)   Hybrid Data Processing Service is a hybrid service offering wherein the
        message switching capability is incidental to the data processing function
        or purpose.
(ii)   Hybrid Communication Service is a hybrid service offering wherein the
        data processing capability is incidental to the message switching function
        or purpose.[169]

The overall effect of the data processing definition is that firms whose "primary
thrust" is data processing will not be regulated. The FCC assumed that communications carriers would police the line between hybrid data processing and
hybrid communication.[170]

        After exhausting administrative procedures, the common carriers appealed
the FCC decision in the *Computer Inquiry*. *GTE Service Corp. v. FCC* affirmed
the Commission's right to regulate common carriers who entered the data
processing field, but held that the FCC could not regulate data processors using
communications networks.[171] In addition, the FCC could not require common
carriers to use a separate name for their data processing entities. But the FCC
could require the common carriers to establish a totally separate corporate subsidiary for data processing. The carriers were also allowed to purchase data
processing services from their separate corporate subsidies.[172] The decision
basically supported the FCC in its *Computer Inquiry*. Common carriers are
allowed to enter the data processing industry, but they may do so only through
separate entities. The possibilities of cross subsidization, therefore, are greatly
reduced.

        The overriding silent fact in the entire *Computer Inquiry* is that the Bell
System companies are precluded from entering the data processing field by a
1956 antitrust consent decree between Western Electric Company and the
Justice Department.[173] The interesting point is that as the FCC defines the difference between hybrid data processing and hybrid communications, the limits
of the 1956 Western Electric consent decree are defined. Therefore, by

---

[169] Final Decision and Order, 28 F.C.C.2d at 287 (1971) (Codified at 47 *C.F.R.* sec. 64.702
(a) (5) (1972)).

[170] Final Decision and Order, 28 F.C.C.2d at 279 (1971), *reconsideration denied*, 34
F.C.C.2d 557 (1972). *See Berman, "Computer or Communications? Allocation of* Functions and the Role of the Federal Communications Commission," 27 *Fed. Comm. Bar. J.*
161 (1974).

[171] 474 F.2d 724 (2d Cir. 1973).

[172] Note, "Federal Communications Commission—Review of Regulations Relating to Provisions of Data Processing Services by Communications Common Carriers," 15 *Bost. Coll.
Ind and Comm. L. Rev.* 162 (1973).

[173] United States v. Western Elec. Co., 1956 *C.C.H.—Trade Cas.* par. 71, 134 (D.N.J. 1956).

indirect means, the FCC defines the boundaries for the Bell System to operate in the data processing industry.

State Regulatory Policy.   Entry by firms other than common carriers into interstate communications is now permitted under the various FCC rulings. At the state level, a great diversity of regulatory policies exists. In a recent dispute between state utility commissions and the FCC, plaintiffs argued that the FCC could not grant specialized communication tariffs to noncarrier firms in the microwave transmission area.[174] The court held that the FCC did have the right to authorize new carriers into the specialized communication field of microwave transmission. Therefore, although these firms were directly affecting intrastate communications, the FCC could authorize licenses to those firms that were competing with intrastate common carriers. Many states do not allow interconnection between noncarriers and carriers in intrastate networks.[175]   State regulatory policy, therefore, can have a major impact on the communication-computer interface.

Value-Added Networking—Packet Switching.   The FCC has authorized packet-switching communication services.[176] Packet switching has been classified as hybrid data communications, and is thus within the FCC regulatory sphere. Numerous applications have been granted, and several networks are emerging. The major problem in developing the networks, however, is the shortage of requisite capital.[177] As in the case of MCI application, the Bell System is also responding with its data phone digital service (DDS).[178]

The FCC has begun an inquiry into the interconnection issue between common carriers and noncarriers.[179] The Commission role in the interface between the

---

[174] National Association of Regulatory Utility Commissioners and the Washington Utilities and Transportation Commission v. Federal Communications Commission, 513 F.2d 1142 (9th Cir. 1975), 43 *U.S.L.W.* 2341 (1975).

[175] *See, e.g.,* Phonetele, Inc. v. General Tel. of Calif., 3 *Comp. L. Rep.* 1192 (1972).

[176] Application of Packet Communications Inc., 43 F.C.C.2d 922 (1973), FCC File No. P-C-8533) (Memorandum Opinion, Order and Certificate). *See generally* Berman, "Computer or Communications? Allocation of Functions and the Role of the Federal Communications Commission," 27 *Fed. Com. Bar J.* 161 (1974).

[177] Himsworth, "Funding Cash for Communications," 21 *Datamation* 49 (March 1975).

[178] Frank, "DDS Users in 19 Cities to Pay More," 8 *Computerworld* 1 (Dec. 25, 1974/ Jan. 1, 1975); Frank, "Firm Testing Datran's Digital Dial-up Service," 8 *Computerworld* 15 (Dec. 25, 1974/Jan. 1, 1975). The issue of electronic funds transfer (EFT) is also looming in the future. Congress has recently created an EFT Commission. P.L. 93-495, Title 2. *See also* Address by Donald I. Baker, Deputy Assistant Attorney General, 704 *B.N.A.-A.T.R.R.* A-9 (March 11, 1975).

[179] In the Matter of Economic Implications and Interrelations Arising From Policies and Practices Relating to Customer Interconnection, Jurisdiction or Separations and Rate Structures, FCC 74-344, Dk. #20003 (April 10, 1974).

computer and communications industry will continue to evolve as computer and communications technology converge.[180]

The Federal Government has broad authority to set computer standards, which includes computer-communication specifications. In areas where firms do not agree on communication standards, the Federal Government, through the Brooks Law, does have authority to establish such standards.[181]

In some areas, the Bell System charges for local calls on a time basis. As this practice widens, the cost of dial-up terminals used in time sharing systems will increase. Bell is also developing a new short hold tariff in which a terminal is on-line for long periods of time but is only charged for the actual communication time to the central computer. Therefore, although local calls will be billed on a time basis, the charge will be computed on the net quantity of communication rather than the gross connect time.[182]

Satellite Communication Regulation. Satellites provide the opportunity for major cost reductions. Significant cost reductions provide dramatic opportunities for computer design innovations.[183] The Communications Satellite Act of 1962 established the Communications Satellite Corporation (COMSAT), which is owned half by the general public and half by overseas carriers.[184] The Office of Telecommunications Policy of the President has recommended that an open entry policy for satellite communication be established.[185] The Bell System is

---

[180] Williams, "FCC Defines Its Impact Into Interconnect Impact," 20 *Electronic News* 38 (Jan. 22, 1975). It was recently reported that A.T.T. could lose as much as one-third of a $1 billion in the New York market to interconnect firms based on the present high A.T.T. tariff structure. *See* "AT&T Seen Losing 37 Percent of $1 Billion N.Y. Market to Interconnect Firms," 20 *Electronic News* 1 (April 14, 1975).

[181] Brooks, "A Federal Government and Computer Compatibility," 13 *Datamation* 24 (Feb. 1969).

[182] Interview, Peter Alsberg, Associate Director, Center for Advanced Computation, University of Illinois, Urbana-Champaign (July 1975).

[183] *See generally* Gottlieb, Dalfen and Katz, "Transborder Transfer of Information by Communications and Computer Systems: Issues and Approaches to Guiding Principles," 68 *Am. J. International Law* 227 (April 1974); Evans, "Satellite Communications – The Legal Gap," 11 *Jurimetrics* J. 92 (Dec. 1972); Powell, "Satellites, Sovereignity and Speculation," 22 *Fed. Comm. Bar J.* 218 (1968).

[184] 47 *U.S.C.* sec. 701 (a) (1973). Taub, "Federal Communications Commission Regulation of Domestic Computer Communications: A Competitive Reformation," 22 *Buffalo L. Rev.* 947 (1973).

[185] Office of Telecommunications Policy, Executive Office of the President, Recommendations on Domestic Satellites (Oct. 28, 1971). (Reprinted in 4 *Comp. L. Ser.* app. 6-7A (1974) (R. Bigelow, ed.))

jointly developing a satellite system with GTE-Sylvania after a lengthly battle over permission to enter satellite communications.[186]

IBM is also interested in participating in satellite communication technology. Initially, IBM requested FCC permission to purchase 55 percent of CML Satellite Corporation. CML is made up of COMSAT, General Corporation, MCI Communications Inc., and Lockheed Aircraft Corp.[187] IBM proposed to buy out MCI and Lockheed. The Federal Trade Commission (FTC) objected to the FCC reasoning that the IBM proposal would be a violation of Section 7 of the Clayton Act.[188] As a result of the FTC objection, IBM has now been ordered to participate in the domestic satellite corporation in a fashion such that IBM and COMSAT do not individually own less than 10 percent of the domestic satellite corporation, nor more than 45 percent of the corporation. Therefore, IBM and COMSAT will need a third party to purchase the remaining interest to the domestic satellite corporation.[189]

Computer-related satellite communication policy remains in a state of flux. The cost of establishing the satellite communication networks are exceedingly high, and therefore, establishment of a satellite network will not occur in the immediate future.

This section on communication regulations has examined various communication policies related to computers. Based on the *Computer Inquiry*, the FCC will undoubtedly play an active role in regulating the computer-communication interface. Through its ability to define hybrid data processing and hybrid communication, the FCC will greatly influence the role played by the Bell System in the data processing industry. The trend toward open entry in data communications will likely aid the continued decrease in communication costs.

---

[186] Domestic Communications—Satellite Facilities, 38 F.C.C.2d 665 (1972), 38 Fed. Reg. 1180 (1972). *See also* Bigelow, "Some Legal and Regulatory Problems of Computers with Communications Capabilities," 4 *Comp. L. Serv.* sec. 6-1, art. 1 (1974) (R. Bigelow, ed.).

[187] 673 *B.N.A.-A.T.R.R.* A-30 (July 23, 1974).

[188] 62 *B.N.A.-A.T.R.R.* A-21 (Nov. 1, 1974).

[189] Frank, "FCC Restricts IBM's Satellite," 9 *Computerworld* 1 (Feb. 5, 1975) (In addition, IBM is prohibited from directly promoting or selling services from the satellite corporation, but rather must establish a separate corporate entity. Concern exists in the computer industry over IBM's potential ability to control the satellite-computer communications by the establishment of IBM-type standards. *See, e.g., Hearings on S. 1167 Before the Subcommittee on Antitrust and Monopoly of the Committee of the Senate Judiciary*, 93rd. Cong., 2d Sess., pt 7 at 5463 (July 23-26, 1974) (The Industrial Reorganization Act—The Computer Industry) (Statement by Royden C. Sanders, Jr.)

Export and Import Regulations—The International Setting

Overview. Estimates of the world computer market—excluding the United States—range from $18 billion in 1977 to as much as $40 billion by 1980.[190] Various studies have examined technology transfers as well as the international computer industry.[191] This section, dealing with export and import regulation policy, first examines export regulations. Particular emphasis will be addressed toward governmental policies encouraging computer exports, followed by a discussion of the regulations prohibiting the export of computers and computer technology. The existing foreign economic-legal import environments of Western Europe, Japan, developing countries, and the communist countries are briefly examined.

Promotion of Exports. The Department of Commerce periodically publishes marketing guides to major countries and also helps organize exhibitions in various foreign countries.[192] The export-import bank also aids in the export of computers.[193] The bank has two methods for encouraging the expansion of foreign trade. The first is through direct credits to private companies in which the export-import bank guarantees the second half of the foreign payment. The second is through guaranteeing loans made by U.S. banks to exporters. In addition, the President has established an Export Council.[194] The Council is made up of industry members and is to advise the President on export policy.[195]

The General Agreement on Tariffs and Trade (GATT) prohibits governmental favoritism toward exporters. There are, however, numerous exceptions to GATT.[196] One exception to GATT is the Domestic International Sales

---

[190] *See, e.g.*, U.S. Department of Commerce—Domestic and International Business Administration, *Global Market Survey—Computer Equipment* (1973); Gross, "World Computer Market, 9 *Columbia J. World Bus.* 13 (March 1974); McGovern, "World Computer Market, 6 *I.E.E.E. Intercon Technical Paper* 2511 (March 26-30, 1973); Statement by Loren A. Schultz, Decision Data Computer Corporation, *Wall Street Transcript* 39567 (Feb. 17, 1975).

[191] *See, e.g.*, W. Lee, *The International Computer Industry* (1971); Lesher and Howick, *Assessing Technology Transfer* (1966) (Published by the National Aeronautical and Space Administration, Rep. #SP-5076); Houser and Frahn, "Technology, Trade and the Law: A Preliminary Exploration," 6 *Law and Policy in Int. Bus.* 85 (1974).

[192] *See generally* Department of Commerce, *Electronic Data Processing Equipment, Peripherals Services and Software* (1970).

[193] 12 *U.S.C.* sec. 635 (1973).

[194] Executive Order No. 11753, 38 *Fed. Reg.* 34983 (December 20, 1973).

[195] *See generally* Staff of Subcommittee on Europe of the House Committee of Foreign Affairs, 90th Cong. 2d Sess., *Basic Documents on East-West Trade* (Aug. 1968) (Committee Print); Y. Hu, *The Impact of U.S. Investment in Europe: A Case Study of the Automotive and Computer Industries* (1973).

[196] W. Gifford, *Exporting: Government Assistance in Regulations* (1975) (Practicing Law Institute, Course Handbook Series #128 on Commercial Law and Practice).

Corporation (DISC). Many technical rules must be followed for a company to gain the benefits from a DISC organization.[197] One major requirement of DISC regulations is that the receipts from the sale of the exports must return to the United States for a net tax benefit to accrue to the exporter.[198] There are also numerous ways to transfer software abroad, which have major tax implications. For example, if software is expensed as a research and development (R & D) expense, there is a low or even zero basis for the transfer. The transfer, however, may be nontaxable by the nonrecognition procedures of Section 351 of the Internal Revenue Act of 1954.[199]

Export Controls. The Department of Commerce has supervisory power over the exports of all computers. The present export control regulations divide export licenses into two broad categories: (1) General licenses that authorize export without special license documents for each shipment; (2) Validated licenses that are subject to specific limitations.[200] A commodity control list is maintained stating which commodities can be exported to individual countries by type of license. Presently, there is a lengthy procedure to obtain permission to export under either a general license or a specifically validated license based on the commodity control list.[201]

The export regulations were recently amended in the Export Administration Act of 1974.[202] Under the 1974 amendments, the export license must either be granted, denied, or a reason given for the delay within ninety days. Congress is also to be given a report in one year on the present status of the Export Administration Act Amendments.[203] Under the new procedures, the Department of

---

[197] *See* National Export Expansion Council, *A Report of the Industry Advisory Committee on Office Machines and Computers* (1972) (Department of Commerce No. C-1.42/3:IN 2/4) (Discussion of the technical aspects of DISC arrangements).

[198] *See generally* J. Sood, *A Study of the International Computer Industry and a Projection of the Effect of the American Computer Industry on the United States Balance of Payments from 1969 to 1975* (1971) (D.B.A. Dissertation, The George Washington University): Guttentage, "Prospects for New Tax Legislation Affecting Exports," *Exporting Governmental Assistance and Regulation* (1975) (Randall, Chairman, Practicing Law Institute, Commercial Law and Practice Handbook Series, No. 128).

[199] Flyer and Buell, "Tax Free Transfers of Computer Software to Foreign Corps: An Up-to-date Analysis," 41 *J. Tax.* 26 (July 1974).

[200] Department of Commerce, *A Summary of U.S. Export Control Regulations* (Feb. 1971).

[201] *See generally* Davison, "Export Controls on Computers," 4 *Comp. L. Serv.* sec. 9-3, art. 2 (1974) (R. Bigelow, ed.). Part 376, Special Commodity Policies and Provisions, requires detailed technical specifications on all exports of computers. 15 *C.F.R.* sec. *376.10.*

[202] 58 app. *U.S.C.* sec. 2402 (1974).

[203] Conference Report No. 93-1412 (Joint Explanatory Statement on the Committee of Conference) 3 *U.S. Code–Cong. and Adm. News* 6245 (1974) 93rd Cong., 2nd Sess., (1974). *See generally* Robertson, "New Export Law Stakes Out DOD Role," 19 *Electronics News* 1 (Nov. 18, 1974).

Defense (DOD) may object within thirty days to the issuance of a license. If the President overrides the DOD objection, Congress has thirty days of continuous session to disapprove the President's override of the DOD objection to the export license. This Congressional override is by majority vote.

There are naturally some difficulties in enforcing the computer export regulations. In *Lorenz EDV-Unternehmensberatung*,[204] the Director of the Office of Export Control issued an order temporarily denying the export privileges to the plaintiff because the parties first exported a computer to Germany and then re-exported the computer to Russia.[205]

The commodity control list maintained by the Department of Commerce, is identical to the Coordinating Committee list (COCOM). The membership of COCOM is made up of NATO members, except Iceland, but including Japan. COCOM maintains a list of commodities that can be exported to Communist   . countries. The Department of State represents the United States in COCOM, but is advised by the Economic Defense Advisory Committee.[206] The Economic Defense Advisory Committee is composed of representatives from the Department of State, Department of Commerce, Department of Defense, Central Intelligence Agency, and where appropriate, the Atomic Energy Commission and the National Aeronautics and Space Administration. All COCOM members must agree to remove an item from the control list. During each of the COCOM meetings, intense bargaining occurs to determine the prohibited export items.[207]

The International Computer Market.   Authorities agree that a computer technological gap exists between the United States and the rest of the world. This technological gap can be divided into three parts.[208] Invention rate is the first criterion used to measure the technological gap. The second measure is the development and innovation of various countries. Development and innovation include the combination of a high technology as well as marketing skill in molding the technology into economically viable products. The third criterion is the utilization of computers in each country. Utilization is estimated from the number of computers per billion of gross national product and the number of computers per million of working population. Based on 1965 data, the United States was a major step above in both computer utilization measures.[209]

---

[204] 37 *Fed. Reg.* 12980 (June 23, 1972), 3 *Comp. L. Ser. Rep.* 235 (1972).

[205] The order later was extended indefinitely. 37 *Fed. Reg.* 21545 (1972).

[206] B. Gilchrist and M. Wessel, *Government Regulation of the Computer Industry* 63 (1972).

[207] National Export Expansion Council, *A Report of the Industry Advisory Committee on Office Machines and Computers* (1972) (Department of Commerce, No. C 1.42/3:IN 2/4).

[208] Organization for Economic Cooperation and Development, *Electronic Computers* (Gaps in Technology) 9 (1969).

[209] Organization for Economic Cooperation and Development, *Electronic Computers* (Gaps in Technology) 11 (1969).

Compared to the nearest country, the United States has twice the number of computers per billion dollars of gross national product, and twice the number of computers per million of working population.[210]

A brief overview of the present economic-legal export environment of Western Europe, Japan, the developing countries, and the communist countries, follows. Emphasis is on the qualitative aspects of the present computer technology status of these major areas of the world.

Western Europe. The Europeans have generally lagged behind the United States in computer development.[211] In response to its lagging computer technology, the Europeans merged various smaller companies to form larger companies, which theoretically were better able to compete against IBM and other U.S. companies.[212] According to Hayes, 1965 was the watershed year for the computer technology race between the United States and Western Europe.[213] After the middle of the 1960s, the United States effectively took the lead in world computer technology.[214] The Western European computer market will undoubtedly remain competitive, especially in the data services and software development areas. These areas have lower barriers to entry than the traditional hardware mainframe systems market.[215] In Figure 1-6, the trend toward increasing software costs was discussed. With software development and applications becoming the major cost of computer installations, a large potential software market exists. Due to the lower barriers to entry in software, this market will remain competitive.[216] As

---

[210] *See generally* Phillip, "Economic Development in the Use of Computers," 2 *Management Informatics* 265 (1973) (Phillips found a high correlation between economic development and computer usage); Atlantic Institute, *The Technology Gap—U.S. and Europe* (1970).

[211] *See generally* J. Sood, *A Study of the International Computer Industry and a Projection of the Effect of the American Computer Industry on the United States Balance of Payments from 1969 to 1975* (1971) (D.B.A. Dissertation, George Washington University).

[212] Council of Ministers of European Communities Resolution Re Common Industrial Policy, "A Community Policy on Data Processing," (July 5, 1974) (Reprinted in *Hearings on S. 1167 Before the Subcommittee on Antitrust and Monopoly of the Senate Committee on the Judiciary* 93rd Cong., 2d Sess., pt. 7 at 5333 (July 23-26, 1974) (The Industrial Reorganization Act—The Computer Industry).

[213] Hayes, "Western Europe: Problems of Computer Industry Government Subsidizations," 9 *Columbia J. of World Bus.* 113 (Summer 1974). *See generally* B. Murphy, "The Computer Industry Itself, *Computers and the Year 2000* 181 (1972) (Avebury, *et al.*, eds.)

[214] *See generally* Lord Avebury, "The Economic Role of Government in Computing and Computer Development," 12 *Computing Economics* 353 (1973) (Infotech Information, Ltd.); Smith, "Unidata Starts Long Climb Upward," 47 *Electronics* 1 (March 7, 1974).

[215] *See generally* C. Freeman, "Research and Development in Electronic Capital Goods," 34 *National Institute—Economic Review* 40 (Nov. 1965); Hayes, "Western Europe: Problems of Computer Industry Government Subsidizations Examined," 9 *Columbia J. of World Bus.* 113 (Summer 1974).

[216] Shortland, "Developments in European Mini-Computer Technology," 86 *Bulletin Scientifique del'Association des Ingenieurs Electriciens Sortis de l'Institut Electrotechnique Montefiore* 27 (Jan. 1973) (*Bull. Sci. A.I.M.*).

long as the United States, however, maintains its technological leadership in the computer industry, exports to the Western European countries can be expected to continue.[217]

Japanese Market. The Japanese market is much harder to penetrate that Western Europe. Although always remaining within GATT requirements, the Japanese make it as difficult as possible for foreign imports to enter Japan.[218] The Japanese have established the Japan Electronic Company (JECC), which purchases a large majority of all computers in Japan and then leases them to end users. Domestically produced Japanese computers are favored by JECC.[219]

The Japanese have used licensing agreements from U.S. computer firms to accelerate their computer technology. Japan has also initiated an eight-year project to develop pattern information processing systems. The funding of this project, however, has been drastically curtailed in the last few years.[220] Based on the large expenditures for research and development, which the Japanese financed in the 1960s, Japan will probably only narrow the gap between U.S. and Japanese computer technology.[221] Therefore, as in the case of Western Europe, Japan is generally behind the United States in computer technology. As compared to Western Europe, however, the barriers to entry from U.S. exports into Japan are considerably greater due to the Japanese internal control over most leasing.

The Developing Countries. The developing countries are obviously far behind the United States in computer development. Traditionally, developing countries have lagged an entire system generation in computer usage. The major issue for developing countries, however, is the types of computers that they can best utilize.[222] With the growth of minicomputers, developing countries will be able to more rapidly assimilate both hardware and software technology into their economies.[223]

---

[217] Forest, "How to Build a Computer Industry: Is the Issue as Critical as Oil?" 21 *Datamation* 98 (1975).

[218] See W. Lee, ed., *The International Computer Industry* (1971).

[219] Szuprowicz, "Informationalization of Japan," 15 *Angewandie Informatik–Applied Informatics* 317 (Aug. 1973).

[220] Yaskai, "Japanese Slash AC Project Funds," 20 *Datamation* 111 (Aug. 1974).

[221] Organization for Economic Cooperation and Development, *Gaps in Technology* (Electronic Computers) 58 (1969).

[222] United Nations Department of Economic and Social Affairs, *The Application of Computer Technology for Development* (1973). *See generally* F. Rodriquez, *The Role of the Private Sector in Applying Computer Technology to the Development of Latin American Countries* (1969) (United Nations No. ED-055-601, Vol 72 #07 5B).

[223] *See generally* W. Sharpe, *The Economics of Computers* 264 (1969).

Eastern Europe and Russian Computer Markets. Although data are difficult to obtain on the present status of the Soviet bloc computer technology, a qualitative perspective can be obtained.[224] In the 1940s and 1950s, the Soviets placed little emphasis on computer development.[225] As a result, Russia has historically lagged the United States in computer technology.[226] This gap today between the U.S. and the Soviet bloc appears to be remaining relatively constant.[227] The communist nations, therefore, are generally believed to be eight to ten years behind the United States in computer technology.[228] In addition, with their scarcity of trained computer manpower, Russia and Eastern European countries can only annually absorb a limited amount of additional computational capacity. Therefore, a large commercial market exists in Russia and Eastern Europe for the sale of slightly dated computers. The major legal regulatory block in the sale of commercial computers is the present COCOM agreement, which limits the sale of computers to the communist bloc nations.

Imports. There has been little governmental concern for the import of computers, primarily because imports have been negligible to date. With the rise of the Japanese computer industry, this situation may change. Again, based on the

---

[224] *See, e.g.*, R. DiPaloa, *A Survey of Soviet Work in the Theory of Computer Programming* (1967) (Rand Corp. #RM 5424PR) (Study of Russian Software Development); B. Doncov, *Soviet Cybernetics Technology: Time-Sharing in the Soviet Union* (1971) (Rand Corp. #R-522PR) (Soviet communication network far behind United States, and thus, networking lagging United States by many years. In addition, time sharing is far behind the United States.); Maltson, "Soviet Integrated Circuit Technology," 6 *I.E.E.E. Intercon Technical Papers 30/5* (March 26-30, 1973) (New York, New York Meeting) (Soviet Union well behind U.S. in integrated circuit technology).

[225] *See generally* Miliner, "Lessons from U.S. Electronic Boom," 2 *Soviet Cybernetics Review* 7 (Sept. 1972) (Rand Corp. #R-960/5-PA).

[226] P. Armer, *The Systems Gap* (1967) (Rand Corp. #PR 3641) (Comparison of U.S. and USSR computer technology in 1959 and 1967 with no change in U.S. lead noted.) U.S. Central Intelligence Agency, *Intelligence Report: U.S. Computers in Soviet Management* (1967) (U.S. five years ahead of Russia in computers.); "Soviet Union: The Computer Gap," 39 *Electronics* 187 (Jan. 24, 1966).

[227] *See, e.g.*, French, "Should DP Firms Trade with the East?" 8 *Computerworld* 1 (May 8, 1975) (Statement by William C. Norse, Chairman of Control Data Corporation, that the Russians were three to four years behind the U.S. in computer technology); Szuprowica, "Soviet Bloc's RIAD Computer System," 19 *Datamation* 80 (Sep. 1973) (Discussion of Russian 1973 Exhibit of Computers in Moscow).

[228] *See generally* Holland, "Ryad Details Begin to Emerge," 2 *Soviet Cybernetics Review* 18 (March 1972) (Rand Corp. #R-960/2-PR) (Ryad computer developed in early 1970s in the 360/20 to 360/65 class); Machan, "Vacillation in Czech Computer Policy," 2 *Soviet Cybernetics Review* 37 (May 1972) (Rand Rep. #R-960/3-PR); Psurtsev, "Solving the Data Transmission Problem," 2 *Soviet Cybernetics Review* 46 (July 1972) (Discussion of a 200 baud network planned for the 1973-75 time frame. The ARPA Network operates on 50K baud lines.). Ershov, "A History of Computing in the U.S.S.R.," 21 *Datamation* 80 (Sept. 1975).

discussion of Figure 1-7 dealing with the continuing advancement of U.S. computer technology, imports of computers into the United States will not pose a major problem as long as our computer technology continues to advance. The computer products that are most likely to enter the United States market are those that are based on the more stable electromechanical technology. Those products that are based on purely electronic computer technology will probably not pose a threat to the U.S. computer industry. Should any products enter on bids to the Federal Government, it appears that the Buy American Act would effectively prevent the Federal Government from purchasing any large amounts of foreign computers.[229] Therefore, computer imports will not be a major factor in the domestic U.S. computer industry for the foreseeable future.

Federal Procurement Policies

Overview. The Federal Government is the largest single purchaser of computers. By purchasing well over 10 percent of the industry output, federal procurement policies greatly affect present as well as future computer industry developments.[230] The Government even has difficulty determining the annual total amount of money spent on computers.[231] This section, dealing with federal procurement policies, first examines the federal computer acquisition process. Federal standardization policy is then considered. Finally, several future standardization trends are discussed.

Federal Acquisition Policies. Until the middle of the 1960s, government agencies purchased computers without governmentwide coordination. In 1965, Congress enacted the Brooks Law.[232] Under the Brooks Law, the General Services Administration (GSA) is mandated to coordinate all government purchases of electronic data processing equipment. In addition, GSA may transfer equipment between agencies, as well as establish a revolving fund for the purchase of computers without fiscal year limitations. The Department of Commerce is authorized to research and to make recommendations to the President for establishment of

---

[229] 41 *U.S.C.* sec. 10 (a) (1973).

[230] Univac Division—Sperry Rand Corporation, *Technology and Changes in the 1970's: A Basis for Perspective and a Better Understanding of Some of the Forces Which Influence Industrial, Economic, and Social Change in the Years Ahead* (1970) (Statement by Herbert Grosch).

[231] *See Hearings on Economy and Management—Procurement Data Processing Equipment, Joint Economic Committee, Subcommittee on Economy in Government*, 91st Cong., 2d Sess. (July 1, 1970).

[232] 40 *U.S.C.* sec. 759 (1973) (Congressman Brooks sponsored PL 89-306).

federal automatic data processing standards. The Office of Management and Budget (OMB) has overall policy control over governmentwide computer procurement.[233]

Under GSA policy there are three computer procurement procedures:

1. General purpose computers costing under $50,000 may be purchased directly by each agency. Each agency, however, is still required to follow GSA procurement regulations;
2. Purchases may be made through the Federal Supply Contracts Schedule. Contracts are negotiated individually with each supplier on a noncompetitive basis. Under these contracts, the supplier agrees to provide the stated items at the agreed price.
3. Separate competitive contracting is the third method by which computers are purchased. Under this procedure, the contract awards are determined by a competitive bidding process.[234]

The competitive bidding process incurs a large cost to determine appropriate standards. The standards, called benchmarks, state that each bidder must provide a computer that can perform the benchmarks. The benchmark procedure is very expensive for each bidder to follow, thereby limiting the use of benchmark bidding to large procurements.[235] Benchmarking procedures allow no deviations, and thus, even though a bidder might be able to provide computers that could do more than the required standards, the bidder will not be given any credit for performance above the benchmark. Instead, bidders are encouraged to lower their price, because once the benchmarks are achieved, competition is based solely on price. If the benchmarks do not fully take advantage of the latest available technology, the Government will purchase lower quality computers.[236]

Federal procurement policy has shifted from leasing to purchasing computer equipment.[237] For equipment having an economic obsolescence of five or more years, the Federal Government saves money in purchasing the computer

---

[233] *See generally* Federal Management Circular 74-5, "Management, Acquisition and Utilization of Automatic Data Processing (ADP)," 34 *C.F.R.* 282 (July 30, 1974).

[234] *See* B. Gilchrist and M. Wessel, *Government Regulation of the Computer Industry* 16 (1972).

[235] *See* G. Brock, *The U.S. Computer Industry: A Study of Market Power* 45 (1975).

[236] Interview, William Bittner, Captain, Judge Advocate General, Systems Command, U.S. Air Force, Hanscom Field, Bedford, Massachusetts (July 1975).

[237] *See* D. Taylor, *Capital Budgeting Theory as Applied to the Leasing or Purchasing of Capital Assets—With Emphasis on Computer Equipment* (1967) (Ph.D. Dissertation, Louisiana State University and Agriculture and Mechanical College).

equipment [238] This shift in purchasing policy also enables smaller firms lacking the huge leasing capital resources to enter the industry. Therefore, federal procurement policies can have a powerful effect on the computer industry.

Changes in federal procurement policies have resulted in savings on numerous occasions. In the late 1960s, IBM plug compatible manufacturers (PCM) offered substantial price reductions over IBM tape drives and disk drives. GSA requested that all agencies switch to save money in renting tape and disk drives.[239] In another area, once an initial computer was purchased on competitive bidding, the upgrading of the system was not done by competitive bidding but rather was sole sourced from the original manufacturer. Consequently, small systems grew into large systems without competitive bidding. In 1971, the Department of Defense changed its policy to eliminate this procedure of noncompetitive bidding in the upgrading of large systems. Thereafter, all government agencies were also required by OMB to have competitive bidding in upgrading systems.[240]

Third party suppliers who cannot provide an entire system have also effectively been excluded from the General Services Administration (GSA) automatic data processing (ADP) schedule of contracts awarded by the GSA.[241] In effect, this policy means that the Federal Government does not want to act as a general contractor and assemble mixed systems for governmental use.[242]

---

[238] When the Government leases computer equipment, it is effectively borrowing money at commercial computer rates in the 8-12 percent range. Considering that the Federal Government can borrow at treasury rates in the 5-8 percent range, leasing computer equipment is additionally unwise. If the risk of economic obsolescence is high, buy-back provisions can be included in the purchase contract to place the risk of economic obsolescence back onto the computer vendor.

[239] See G. Brock, U.S. Computer Industry: A Study of Market Power 112 (1975).

[240] See Memorandum, Assistant Secretary of Defense, "Replacement of Installed Leased Computers with Compatible High Performance and/or Lower Cost Units Without Competition" (March 4, 1971); Director, Office of Management and Budget, Transmittal Memorandum No. 3 Amending Circular No. A-54 to the Heads of Executive Department and Establishments (Aug. 26, 1971).

[241] See In re Tom Disco (No. B-181956, Feb. 13, 1975), 570 B.N.A.—Fed. Cont. Rep. A-17 (March 3, 1975).

[242] See generally Scaletta and Walsh, "Comparison of Provisions in Government Computer Purchase Contracts and the Standard Commercial Purchase Contracts, 10 Data Management 14 (Dec. 1972). In the early 1960s, many universities received funds for partial payment of computer facilities based on federal research contracts. Under the provisions of these contracts, the Federal Government paid for its share of computer usage. At the same time, computer utilization was not at full capacity. As the university itself began to utilize more of the computer during third shifts, the percentage of federal government utilization declined. Therefore, many universities were required to pay additional funds for the rental or purchase of computers, and the Federal Government paid less for its same usage, but smaller relative percentage usage. The Government used the full cost pricing rule, which was calculated by taking the total annual cost of the computer and dividing it by the total hours of utilization. Hirschel, Arnold, Neil, "The Allocation of

There are numerous instances where federal procurement policies have been modified to cope with changing computer technology. Federal procurement policies will continue to evolve as computer technology advances. Overall, the Brooks Law has been effective in helping to reduce computer procurement costs, especially on the hardware side. The Brooks Law has also focused attention on the federal computer procurement process.[243]

Third Party Maintenance. The barriers to entry into the computer industry were discussed in the antitrust section of this chapter. One barrier to entry is the computer maintenance function. For a firm to succeed in the computer industry, historical experience has shown the need for a massive maintenance organization. Under the Brooks Law, the Federal Government, where feasible, may contract with third party firms to provide maintenance to government computers. Federal procurement policy can greatly aid the third party independent maintenance submarket by contracting with third party firms to perform maintenance on government purchased computers. The third party maintenance submarket however, has grown very slowly.[244]

Independent organizations providing maintenance service to computer installations need trained manpower.[245] As the third party maintenance submarket develops, the maintenance barrier to entry will decline. Smaller firms that only sell part of a total computer system will be able to exist in the computer industry when reliable nationwide service of mixed computer systems is available.[246]

Government Procurement of Software. Software costs are a large part of total system costs, and thus, software procurement is an important part of federal procurement policies. Software is often not directly purchasable, but rather

---

Computer Time by University Computer Centers," 41 *J. Bus.* 383 (July 1968). The problem of average costing has not been resolved, and is generally settled on an *ad hoc* basis because there are simply no "correct" answers which are consistent with federal procurement policy and still equitably charge users in multiprogram, multiprocessor, and multiuser machines. W. Sharpe, *The Economics of Computers* 448 (1969).

[243] *See generally* B. Gilchrist and M. Wessel, *Government Regulation of the Computer Industry* 17 (1972) (GSA and OMB have informed Congress that the Brooks bill has been very effective, but GAO has been critical of the Brooks Law's effectiveness).

[244] *See generally* Comptroller General of the United States, *Report to Congress on Maintenance of Automatic Data Processing Equipment in the Federal Government* (April 3, 1966) (No. BB-197 941, Vol. 71 #09-9b); Russell and Howe, "Building a Hardware Team," 18 *Datamation* 92 (Nov. 1972); Wessel, "Third Party Maintenance for Those Above and Beyond Unbundling," 16 *Datamation* 177 (June 1970).

[245] Interview, Edward Cohler, Computer Signal Processors, Inc., Burlington, Massachusetts (July 1975).

[246] *See generally* 2 *Comp. L. Serv.* sec. 3.1 app. (1974) (R. Bigelow, ed.) (Copies of maintenance contracts presently used by third party maintenance firms).

must be developed. In-house development is difficult because salaries of trained software computer personnel frequently range in the $20,000-$35,000 region. This range is difficult to accommodate under the present civil service salary system, and thus, software development is contracted to private firms.[247]

Although direct sale of patented or copyrighted software would be the best legal method for the Government to procure software, such situations are atypical.[248] Consequently, the Government must normally contract for the development of software. There are three methods to contract for software development.[249] First, a firm may contract to supply trained personnel on a daily basis to develop software for the Government. If this procedure is followed, it is clear that the Government is entitled to exclusive rights to all software developed. Another method is to bid for a contract, but to include a cost plus clause in which the Government agrees to absorb any additional costs above a specified amount under various cost overrun conditions. The Government again pays for all software development, and thus, is entitled to exclusive rights to the software.

The third approach is to contract for software development, but the cost is a fixed item in the contract. Again, if the Government supplies all the resources to develop this software, then the Government has exclusive rights to the software. The difficulty arises, however, when the software developer supplies some of the resources in the software development. In this situation, the software developer and the contracting agency must determine the appropriate rights that the Government will obtain to the software.

In governmental supply as well as research and development contracts, two provisions are generally used to define the intellectual property rights.[250] These two provisions are the patent and data clauses. Although software is generally unpatentable as previously discussed in the proprietary section of this chapter, the patent rights clause requires that the contractor supply the Government written disclosure of each invention conceived under the contract or the first reduction to actual practice. Although most rights that the Government has under the patent clause are specifically spelled out, the list of specific rights does not cover software. NASA adopted a broader patent provision referred to as the new technology clause, which replaces the traditional patent rights clause.[251]

---

[247] 2 *Comp. L. Serv.* sec. 3, art. 3 (1974) (R. Bigelow, ed.).

[248] *See* Saragovitcz, "Patents-Trade Secrets—Technical Data Use and Misuse by the U.S. Government," 15 *Vill L. Rev.* 331 (1970).

[249] Wofsey, "Contracting for Software," 2 *Comp. L. Serv.* sec. 3-3, art. 2 (1975) (R. Bigelow, ed.).

[250] *See* Levy, "Computer Programs in Government Procurement," 10 *Will. and Mary L.R.* 658 (1969). *See also C.C.H.-Gov't. Cont. Rep.* par. 14,110; 14,200; 14,205; 14,220.

[251] *N.A.S.A.* par. 9.101-4.

The NASA new technology clause requires reporting of all inventions, and in addition, the reporting of all innovations, and thus, would include the development of software.

The second major provision in government contracts is the rights in data clause, which is used by most government agencies when contracting for the delivery of specified data. This clause does not specifically call for acquisition of data, but rather defines the rights that the Government has in the specified data. The rights which the Government has under the rights and data clause are either limited to various specific uses or unlimited.[252]

Recently, a new clause has been introduced into the Armed Services Procurement Regulation (ASPR) entitled restricted rights. The restricted rights clause must be negotiated on a case-by-case basis. Under the restricted rights, the Government still has the right to use the software-developed product, but depending on the contract terms, it is not allowed to distribute it to other governmental agencies or to individuals outside the Government.[253] Assuming the contractor chose trade secret protection as the means to protect its software, the contractor must attach restricted legends listing the software as proprietary to any proposals and correspondence with the contracting federal agency.[254]

Originally, the exclusive remedy for federal breach of contract providing for limited use of proprietary data was a damage action in the Court of Claims pursuant to the Tucker Act.[255] In *International Engineering Co. v. Richardson*,[256] plaintiff obtained an injunction against governmental misuse of proprietary information. Other remedies include requests to the General Accounting Office to have the Comptroller General order cancellation of bids if proprietary data is disclosed by the Government. The Boards of Contracts Appeals is another alternative to prevent the governmental misuse of proprietary data.[257] The Boards, however, only have jurisdiction over current contracts. Finally, a suit for unauthorized use of proprietary information

---

[252] Under *A.S.P.R.* sec. 9-201, unlimited rights in data means that the Federal Government has the right to use, duplicate, or disclose technical data in any manner and for any purpose.

[253] *A.S.P.R.* sec. 7-104.9 ("Rights in Data and Computer Software"). *See generally* 209 *B.N.A.-Pat., Trademark, Copyright, J.* A-3 (Jan. 2, 1975).

[254] *A.S.P.R.* 3-507.1(8), 32 *C.F.R.* sec. 3.507-1(A). *See also* Quest Electronics Corp., Comp. Gen. B-163200 (March 12, 1968).

[255] 28 *U.S.C.* sec. 1494 (1973). *See generally* Hinricks, "Proprietary Data and Trade Secrets Under Department of Defense Contracts," 36 *Mil. L. Rev.* 61 (1967).

[256] 490 *B.N.A.-Fed. Contract Rep.* D-1 (July 23, 1973).

[257] *See* "Unauthorized Use of Proprietary Information by the Government: A Mixed Bag of Remedies," 512 *B.N.A.-Fed. Contract Rep.* K-1 (July 1, 1974).

could be brought in the Court of Claims.[258]   In extreme cases where a U.S. employee discloses trade secrets, criminal penalties of $1,000 in fines and one year in prison are applicable.[259]   These provisions, however, have not been used.

If a recalcitrant trade secret or patent owner refuses to sell a product, the Government can reverse engineer to obtain the trade secret,[260] and by its power of eminent domain use the patent.[261]   The patent owner may sue in the Court of Claims for reasonable compensation.[262]   Although it is not the policy of the Federal Government to use copyrighted material without the author's permission, if unauthorized use occurs, the copyright owner may recover damages in the Court of Claims.[263]

Therefore, the Government possesses several methods to procure both software and hardware. Under the Brooks Law, the General Services Administration (GSA) coordinates the purchase of all computer related equipment. On the hardware side, the procurement regulations are reasonably straightforward. The outright purchase of hardware is favored. On the software side, however, numerous problems occur in software procurement. The major problem is that most software is contracted for development rather than as an off-the-shelf purchase. In software development contracts, procurement regulations have evolved to allow a variety of options—ranging from total purchase of the developed product (leaving the Government with unlimited rights) to the contractor maintaining possession of its trade secret protected software (leaving the Government limited rights to the use of the developed software).

Federal Standardization.   Attempts to standardize hardware and software have a long history.[264]   Computer industry standards would lower the barriers to entry because smaller firms would be able to provide a subpart of a total system, and therefore, breach the systems barrier to entry. Standards would also enable users to more easily switch between computer manufacturers. Currently, the cost of conversion from one manufacturing system to another is several times higher than the cost savings realized from buying another computer system. The

---

[258] *See* Kostos, "Unauthorized Use of Technical Data in Government Contracts: Remedies of the Data Owner," 6 *Boston Coll. Ind. and Com. L.R.* 753 (1965).

[259] 18 *U.S.C.* sec. 1905 (1973).

[260] *See A.S.P.R.* 1-304.2B(4), 32 *C.F.R.* sec. 1.304-2(4) (1968), as amended (Supp. 1969).

[261] Crozier v. Crupp, 224 U.S. 290 (1912).

[262] 28 *U.S.C.* sec. 1498 (1973).

[263] 28 *U.S.C.* sec. 1498 (1973). *See* M. Nimmer, 2 *Nimmer on Copyright* sec. 131.4 (1974).

[264] *See* Steel, "Standards for Computers and Information Processing," 8 *Advances In Computers* 103 (1967).

major cost of conversion is the lock-in effect of software.[265] As the trend toward electronic miniaturization continues with the advent of large-scale integration (LSI), additional pressure to standardize electronic components will occur due to the large economies of scale obtainable through mass production of LSI electronic components.[266] The Europeans are also attempting to standardize their hardware and software.[267]

Chapter 1 discussed the early software standardization efforts in the late 1950s. Realizing that a standardized language was needed to avoid massive duplication in software procurement, the Department of Defense (DOD) established a committee to create a common business language. In a few months the Common Business Oriented Language (COBOL) was developed.[268] After the establishment of COBOL, DOD required that all computers purchased for business applications have a COBOL compiler.[269] By 1964, DOD stated that COBOL compiler efficiency would be a consideration in competitive bid evaluation.[270] COBOL has continuously been developed and is now a major recognized language.[271] The effect of the government backing of COBOL was great. In the middle of the 1950s, 90 percent of all medium-sized computer installations used software written directly in assembly language. By the middle of the 1960s, only one-third of the medium-sized computer installations still used software directly written in assembly language. Instead, they were using higher level languages due to the availability of efficient compilers for these higher level languages.[272]

The Brooks Law. Except in the case of COBOL, the development of federal software and hardware standards has been slow. Under the Brooks Law, the Department of Commerce now has responsibility to establish governmental standards for computer procurement.[273] Within the Department of Commerce,

---

[265] Interview, John Bracket, SOFTECH, Inc., Waltham, Massachusetts (July 1975).

[266] *See generally* N. Foy, *Computer Management: A Common Sense Approach* (1972).

[267] *See* Y. Hu, *The Impact of U.S. Investment in Europe: A Case Study of the Automotive and Computer Industries* 276 (1973).

[268] *See* S. Rosen, "Programming Systems and Languages, a Historical View," *Program Systems and Languages* 13 (1967) (S. Rosen, ed.).

[269] "Policy on Selection of Computers," DOD Directive #41055.55 (August 15, 1961).

[270] *See generally* M. Rose, *Computers, Managers and Society* 63 (1969).

[271] J. Maginnis, *Fundamental ANSI COBOL Programming* (1975).

[272] Cunningham, "The Need for ADP Standards in the Federal Community," 15 *Datamation* 28 (Feb. 1969). With an efficient compiler, there is no gain in using assembly languages over easier-to-program higher level languages.

[273] 40 *U.S.C.* sec. 759 (1973).

the National Bureau of Standards has been delegated the responsibility to establish computer procurement standards.[274]   Based on the Brooks Law, the Center for Computer Sciences and Technology of the National Bureau of Standards was created in 1965 to advise executive agencies on computers, to conduct research on computers for government use, to support development of computer standards, and to improve compatibility among government computers by recommending uniform federal standards.[275]   Final approval of all computer standards rests with the Office of Management and Budget (OMB).[276]   All standards accepted by OMB must be published in the Federal Information Processing Standards Registry.[277]

A natural hesitancy exists within the federal bureaucracy to establish any standards. Grace Hopper, in the Navy, is currently pushing for complete standardization of COBOL as well as FORTRAN. Standardization at the federal level takes as long as ten years to complete. Consequently, visibility is low for anyone working in standards. Therefore, standardization efforts must be led by well-known individuals who can maintain the requisite momentum. Adequate qualified supporting staff must also be committed to any standardization project.[278]

There are, however, forces pushing the computer industry away from standardization. First, it is difficult to break the inertia once a computer installation and its supporting manpower has been trained in one specialized language. In addition, it is exceedingly difficult to require programmers to ignore the special features of a machine and to write programs in only standard languages, thereby writing inefficient (as far as computer utilization is concerned) software.[279]

---

[274] *See* Brooks, "The Federal Government and Computer Compatibility," 15 *Datamation* 24 (Feb. 1969).

[275] 30 *Fed. Reg.* 12549, 4 *Comp. L. Serv.* app. 7-2A (1974) (R. Bigelow, ed.).

[276] Presidential Memorandum, "Automatic Data Processing Standards for Use by Federal Agencies," 36 *Fed. Reg.* 8721 (April 30, 1971). Based on the Brooks Law, the President has delegated the responsibility of establishing computer standards to the Director of the Office of Management and Budget.

[277] The Federal Information Processing Standards Registry is reprinted in 4 *Comp. L. Serv.* app. 7-2A (1974) (R. Bigelow, ed.). *See* Cook, *et al.,* "An Overview of the 1974 COBOL Standard," 44 *A.F.I.P.S. Proceedings* 301 (1975) (The Federal COBOL Compiler Testing Service (FCCTS) is now operated by the Navy).

[278] Interview, John Bracket, SOFTECH Incorporated, Waltham, Massachusetts (July 1975). *See* "NBS Plans to Clarify a Rule on ASCII Use," 20 *Electronic News* 31 (Jan. 20, 1975) (Ruth L. Davis, Director of NBS, Institute for Computer Science, requested that her staff clarify the Federal Information Processing Standards to be more specific on ASCII.); Address by Jacques S. Gansler, Deputy Assistant Defense Secretary for Installations and Logistics (Material Acquisition to the American Institute of Aeronautics and Astronautics, Portions reprinted in 57 *B.N.A.-Fed. Contract Rep.* A-3 (March 3, 1975).

[279] Edwin McCauley, Assistant Research Professor, Center for Advanced Computation, University of Illinois, Urbana-Champaign (June 1975).

The American National Standards Institute (ANSI) acts as a clearinghouse and coordinating agency for voluntary standardization.[280] Although the use of uniform standards as a price fixing device is illegal,[281] due to the advancing rate of computer technology, the price fixing aspects of computer standardization are not relevant.[282] A unanimous decision is needed before ANSI can promulgate a new standard. Consequently, progress is relatively slow.

In the 1950s, most computers used a binary coded decimal procedure for communications within the computer. This binary coded decimal system (BCD) was found to be insufficient for computers being developed in the early 1960s. Therefore, the ANSI began development of the American Standard Code for Information Interchange (ASCII). IBM developed the Extended Binary-Coded Decimal Interchange Code (EBCDIC). Consequently, by the mid 1960s, two industry standards were in effect. These two standards existed even though ANSI only endorsed ASCII.[283]

An improved ASCII is being developed by ANSI called the Advanced Data Communications Procedure (ADCP). IBM is also developing an alternative called the Synchronous Data Link Control (SDLC), which will be an alternative to the ADCLP. Therefore, the industry may again be faced with two standards in which the majority of the nongovernment computer centers use the IBM standard (which can be modified by IBM), whereas many other commercial computer centers and some federal agencies will undoubtedly adopt the standard eventually developed by the ANSI.[284] Beyond COBOL, data base standardization is needed to allow portable data files. The Data Base Task Group (DBTG) is beginning work to develop a standardized Information Management System (IMS).[285]

Various user groups have formed around each major computer manufacturer. These user groups generally attempt to exchange programs and, in effect, standardize programs around particular computer systems.[286] There are also many private disputes over standardization.[287]

---

[280] See Grove, "Information Processing Standardization: An Evaluation," 29 Datamation (Feb. 1969).

[281] United States v. American Radiator and Standard Sanitary Corp. 433 F.2d 174 (3d Cir. 1970).

[282] See generally B. Slome, Computer Technology and Standardization in U.S. Trade and Production Abroad: A Case Study of the Vernon Product Cycle Model (1972) (Ph.D. Dissertation, City University of New York).

[283] "IBM Votes No on Seven Bit Code," 7 Datamation 17 (March 1962).

[284] See Hirsch, "Does SDLS Stack the Deck for IBM," 20 Datamation 121 (March 1974).

[285] Bachman, "Trends in Data Base Management—1975," 44 A.F.I.P.S. Proceedings 569 (1975).

[286] See, e.g., White, "Software Standards," Digital Equipment Computer Users Society (DECUS) 338 (Nov. 28-30, 1973).

[287] See Hearings on S.1167 Before the Subcommittee on Antitrust and Monopoly of the Senate Committee on the Judiciary, 93rd Cong., 2d Sess., pt. 7 at 5445 (July 23-27,

Existing federal procurement and standardization policies will continue. The emphasis on purchasing rather than leasing will aid in lowering the capital barriers to entry. Federal procurement policy should continue to favor third party maintenance firms where feasible. In the standardization area, constant pressure must be applied to insure that uniform standards will emerge in the computer industry. If additional standards emerge, smaller firms will be able to supply subparts of total systems.[288]

The Legal Environment — Final Remarks

Chapter 2 outlined the legal environment existing in the computer industry. Computer technology has advanced very rapidly, and in many instances, outpaced the development of supporting legal regulations and policies. In many instances *ad hoc* regulation has occurred, while in other areas, no regulation was the stated policy. This legal environment will now be used as the backdrop for the technological forecast in Chapter 3. Various assumptions will be made concerning the legal environment for the technological forecast in Chapter 3.

In antitrust, the pending *United States v. IBM* case presents an element of uncertainty. As will be seen in Chapter 3, computer technology is predicted to gradually edge the industry towards a more atomized structure. Should the Government win the suit, the industry structure will more quickly atomize. With a more atomized structure, computer technology will not be hindered by the dominance of IBM. If IBM wins, its dominance will continue, and computer technology will continue to evolve at a greatly reduced rate.

The legal proprietary environment will be assumed to remain approximately the same. Both patent and copyright revision appear far off. In the immediate future, therefore, trade secret protection will be the primary software protection method. Should either patent or copyright software protection emerge as a viable alternative to trade secret software protection, costly duplication of effort will be reduced. Consequently, software development may increase slightly. Due to the rapid hardware development, hardware patents will not hinder computer development.

Within the taxation and leasing areas, no change is expected. The Federal Communications Commission will continue to regulate data transmission. The present FCC regulatory policy of limited entry, will allow the noncommon carrier firms to compete with common carriers, and therefore, aid the declining

---

1974) (The Computer Industry—Industrial Reorganization Act) (Statement of Royden C. Sanders, Jr.); 1 *Comp. L. and Tax Rep.* 5 (March 1975) (Discussion of the Sanders Associates suit against IBM over compatibility of software in the IBM Operating System (OS)).

[288] *See* Hopper, "Standardization and the Future of Computers," 8 *Data Management* 32 (April 1970).

communications cost trend. Within the export area, some movement toward faster export procedures can be expected. Finally, federal procurement policies will continue to evolve to keep pace with advancing computer technology. The Federal Government will support third party maintenance firms and their development as a viable subindustry. A purchase policy rather than a leasing policy will aid in lowering the barriers to entry to the systems market. The standardization battle will continue with slow progress as long as computer technology advances.

shift" in which individuals are unwilling to change their positions until there is a low risk that their shift will result in a poor choice of alternatives.[8] Consequently, emerging trends may be overlooked due to the natural conservative basis of most individuals who wish to stay with the consensus. Third, the written questionnaire used in the Delphi method is inflexible, whereas personal contact permits greater flexibility as well as clarification of questions in ambiguous areas.

Information for the scenario forecast was obtained from several sources. Library research served as the primary source of information. Field interviews supplemented this primary source of information. For the field interviews, a structured interview technique following standard guidelines established by the University of Michigan Survey Research Center was followed.[9] Because of the rapid technological change involved, however, the interviews were open-ended to insure full development of all interviewee ideas.

The form followed in the structured interview was developed at the University of Illinois on individuals in computer science, in electrical engineering, and on staff at the Center for Advanced Computation. Once this questionnaire was developed, it was interactively developed by a type of snowballing. This snowballing effect was simply that as each interview was completed, additional information was acquired as to future technological developments in the industry. The questionnaire is reproduced in Appendix A, and the list of interviewees is in Appendix B.

Several other information-gathering techniques were examined, but each was inadequate based on the type of information needed. A series of mailed questionnaires was considered, but there are several objections to mailed questionnaires.[10] First, questionnaires are impersonal, and thus, tend to discourage interview cooperation and creativity. Next, the personal contact permits new ideas to be developed in interviews. Mailed questionnaires lack this flexibility to develop new ideas. Third, the field interview permits clarification of questions wherever ambiguities arise.

Underlying Assumptions. Chapter 2 examined the legal environment surrounding the computer industry. Antitrust considerations will predominate within the computer industry. The pending Justice Department-IBM case with all appeals will last for several years. Therefore, it is assumed that the status quo will remain; and thus, IBM will continue to dominate the industry. Should the Justice

---

[8] L. Hoffman, "Group Problem Solving," *Advances in Experimental Social Psychology* (1965) (L. Berkowitz, ed.).

[9] University of Michigan, Survey Research Center, Institute for Social Research, *Interviewer's Manual* (1969). *See also* G. Shouksmith, *Assessment Through Interviewing* (1968); J. Smith, *Interviewing in Market and Social Research* (1972).

[10] *See* C. Cannell and R. Kahn, "Interviewing," *The Handbook of Social Psychology* (1968) (2d ed. L. Lindzey and E. Aronson, eds.).

Department win, no effect on the industry structure would occur for at least four to seven years due to the necessary appeals and implementation period of any competitive restructuring plan.

In the software area, the present use of the trade secret protection will continue. Any new software protection statutes are five to seven years away from enactment and well over ten years away from having a major effect on the industry. The status of taxation is assumed to remain constant; however, most states will eventually tax software as personal property. The FCC policy of open entry into data communications is assumed to remain. This open entry policy effectively eliminates the regulatory data communications barrier. In the international area, export regulations are assumed to continue, but the controls over exports of commercial computers to the communist nations will gradually be relaxed. Federal computer procurement policy is assumed to continue with continued emphasis on buying rather than leasing, as well as continued standardization efforts.

In the scientific area, a technologically surprise-free forecast is assumed. The surprise-free assumption means that no technologies that are not currently being actively researched in laboratories will occur in the forecast period.[11] Under the surprise-free assumption, any bias in the forecast will be on the conservative side. For example, it is assumed that no technological breakthroughs like biological memories or new energy sources will be discovered and become commercially available during the forecast period.

Computers are based on electrical as well as mechanical technologies. Mechanical technologies in card readers, printers, and keyboards, are not expected to advance rapidly in the fifteen-year time period.[12] On the electrical side, as theoretical limitations of size, switching speed, reliability, and power dissipation are approached, technological advancement will become less rapid.[13] Large scale integration (LSI) is assumed to be the dominant electrical building block during the forecast period.[14]

A final delimiting assumption concerns the concept of artificial intelligence.

---

[11] R. Turn, *Computers in the 1980's* (1974).

[12] *See generally* Hoagland, "Mass Storage—Past, Present, and Future," 41 *A.F.I.P.S. Proceedings* 985 (1972) (Pt. 2) (Fall Joint Computer Conference). Nonmechanical keyboards with no moving parts are presently available, but a feedback mechanism is needed for touch typing. Keyboards with no mechanical-circuit parts are also technologically feasible. For touch typing, however, these keyboards would still require some moving parts for a feedback mechanism.

[13] Bowers, "Predicting Future Computer Developments," 6 *Modern Data* 62 (1973).

[14] *See generally* A. Zellweger, "Five-Year Computer Technology Forecast," (1972) (U.S. Department of Transportation Rept. No. DOT-TSC-OST-72-23); Rudenberg, "Large Scale Integration: Promises versus Accomplishments, A Dilemma of Our Industry," 35 *A.F.I.P.S. Proceedings* 359 (1969) (Fall Joint Computer Conference).

Numerous articles have been written on artificial intelligence.[15] Under the classic definition of artificial intelligence devised by Turing, a human in a room is allowed to communicate through a terminal into a second room to a machine and another human. If the first human cannot tell the difference between the communications with the second human and the machine, then the machine is defined as possessing artificial intelligence.[16] Other definitions of artificial intelligence simply state that when a machine is able to do things which require intelligence, then the machine is said to possess intelligence.[17]

The definition of artificial intelligence is in a constant state of flux. Generally, once a concept is understood, it no longer is classified in the artificial intelligence framework.[18] For example, speech output and visual input systems were originally part of artificial intelligence.[19] The development of artificial intelligence, therefore, is an evolutionary process. All interviewees agreed that artificial intelligence based on the Turing definitions would not occur within the fifteen-year forecast frame. Therefore, it is assumed that artificial intelligence will not emerge during the forecast period.

Stage I – Technological Forecast: Scientific Considerations

The scientific section of the technological forecast first examines electrical component developments. Input and output (I/O) devices are then reviewed followed by a discussion of system developments. Communications and network technology are then reviewed as well as software developments. Finally, emerging computational patterns are examined. Emphasis is placed on nonnumeric computation, Computer Aided Instruction (CAI) developments, and computer graphics.

Electrical Components

Overview. This section dealing with electrical component technology examines

---

[15] *See, e.g.,* M. Minsky, ed., *Semantic Information Processing* (1968). *See also* D. Michael, *Cybernation: The Silent Conquest* (1962).

[16] Turing, *Intelligent Machinery* (1947) (Reprinted in B. Meltzar and D. Michie, eds., *Machine Intelligence* 3 (1970). *See also* Stell, "Artificial Intelligence Research–Retrospect and Prospects," 16 *Computers and Automation* 22 (Jan. 1967).

[17] P. Jackson, Jr., *Introduction to Artificial Intelligence* (1974).

[18] Interview, Wesley Snyder, Assistant Research Professor, Coordinated Science Laboratory, University of Illinois, Urbana-Champaign (June 1975).

[19] Minsky, 49 *I.E.E.E. Proceedings* 8 (Jan. 1961). *See generally* Tatham, "The Use of Computers for Profit," 141 (1969) (Artificial intelligence now beyond numerical control).

the development of integrated circuits, followed by a discussion of components used in processors. In the discussion of processors, particular emphasis is placed on semiconductor technology. Component technologies such as super conductivity, magnetic film, charged coupled devices (CCD), acoustic wave, and electrical optical technologies are also briefly examined. Finally, the electrical component technology relating to memories is examined. Memory technology is divided between those electrical component technologies affecting random access memories (RAMs) and those related to bulk memory.

Integrated Circuit Technology. Electrical components are the fundamental building blocks of the electronic digital computer. The early electrical component development was discussed in Chapter 1, which examined the original vacuum tube technology through the discovery of the transistor effect and the development of integrated circuits.[20] Integrated circuit development has evolved to large scale integration (LSI) in which thousands of electrical units are placed on a single silicon chip.[21] At present, as well as during the fifteen-year forecast period, integrated circuit technology will be the foundation of all computer development.

The trend within integrated circuit technology is to place more functions on a single chip. This trend toward placing more functions on a single chip is in response to the interconnection problem at the macro level. Macro level interconnections (*i.e.*, between silicon chips) pose problems of reliability in that they have a relatively low mean time between failures (MTBF's). Interconnections between functions in a silicon chip (*i.e.*, micro level) have higher MTFB's. Macro level connections are also more expensive than micro level connectors. Therefore, as more of these functions are placed on a single chip, the reliability of the overall system is increased because fewer macro interconnections exist between chips.[22] Electronic signals travel the speed of light. Consequently, there is a finite time period for an electronic signal to travel between two points. As computer speeds increase, distances between electrical components begin to limit overall computer speed. Placing more functions on a chip reduces distances between functions, and thus, minimizes the speed of light-distance problem. Counterbalancing this gain in system reliability due to additional functions being placed on a single chip is the problem of chip manufacturing whereby lower yields are obtained as additional functions are placed on a chip.

---

[20] *See generally* D. Kleiman, *The Integrated Circuit: A Case Study of Product Innovation in the Electronics Industry* (1966) (D.D.A. Dissertation, George Washington University).

[21] *See* A. Khambaga, *Introduction to Large Scale Integration* (1969) (Technical discussion of LSI).

[22] Interview, George Anner, Professor, Department of Electrical Engineering, University of Illinois, Urbana-Champaign (June 1975).

As manufacturing techniques gradually improve, the cost to produce more complex chips will decline.

Integrated circuit manufacturing techniques are presently based on photolithographic pattern-generation technologies. This photolithographic technology makes use of photographic masks that must be produced with great precision. Conventional optical processing techniques currently used to manufacture these masks are hard pressed to meet the continually decreasing tolerances caused by the increase in the number of functions per chip. Consequently, electron-beam masking techniques are beginning to emerge commercially.[23] Present electron beam techniques, however, cause radiation damage to the chip, which results in chip failures.

Once the more precise masks are produced, there is the additional problem of using the masks in the production of integrated circuits. Presently used contact printing operations often damage the mask during manufacture of the first chip. This results in an entire defective batch of chips. Projection printing techniques now being used on an experimental basis will eventually solve the damaged mask problem.[24] Therefore, integrated circuit manufacturing techniques in both mask production and the actual process of placing the chemical substances onto the integrated circuit chip will continuously improve during the fifteen-year forecast period.

Processors. Processors contain the arithmetic and control unit of a computer.[25] The major part of modern processors are composed of semiconductor devices. Basic to all semiconductor technology is the fundamental tradeoff between speed and power consumption. Speed is generally measured as the switching time for a semiconductor device. As speed increases, the amount of power needed to produce this speed also increases. Heat is a byproduct of this power consumption. Driven to its limit, the semiconductor device will overheat and no longer function properly. The fundamental limits of switching speed and the resulting power dissipation have not been reached. As these fundamental limits are approached, however, switching speed increases will gradually decline.[26]

Several different types of semiconductor technology are presently used in processors. Emitter-coupled logic (ECL) is currently the fastest semiconductor

[23] *See Brewer*, "The Application of Electron-Ion Beam Technology to Micro Circuits," 10 *I.E.E.E. Spectrum* 30 (May 1971).

[24] Allen, "Circuit/System Building Blocks," 12 *I.E.E.E. Spectrum* 49 (Jan. 1975). *See generally* R. Turn, "Computers in the 1980's: Trends in Hardware Technology," (1974) (Rand Corp. Rep. No. P-5189).

[25] A. Zellweger, "Five-Year Computer Technology Forecast," (1972) (Department of Transportation Rep. No. DOT-TSC-OST72-23).

[26] W. Ware, *On Limits In Computing Power* (1969) (Rand Corp. Rep. No. P-4208) (Fundamental switching speed estimated at 10 to the –13th second).

technology. ECL speed, however, is gained at a cost of high power consumption and resulting high heat dissipation within the integrated circuit.[27] Bipolar semiconductors are the second type of technology presently available. The bipolar manufacturing process is well established and bipolar speed is also relatively fast, but again power consumption is also relatively high.[28] Metal oxide semiconductors (MOS) are a third type of semiconductor technology presently used. Although relatively slow in switching time, power consumption is also low. P and N channel are two types of MOS technology.[29] MOS technology has gradually improved in speed while maintaining low power consumption.[30]

A fourth semiconductor known as complementary metal oxide silicon (CMOS) combines N and P channel MOS on the same chip. Charged coupled devices (CCDs) are a fifth type of semiconductor technology presently under development. The CCDs, however, are still in the early commercial production stage.[31] A final type of semiconductor technology presently under development is the integrated injection logic (IIL—also commonly known as I squared L). IIL has the speed of bipolar technology but the power consumption level of MOS.[32] The semiconductor technologies that are used in processors are also used in random access memories.[33]

Several other types of component technologies are currently under laboratory investigation. Superconductive cryogenic devices have been extensively investigated. At very low temperatures (from 2 degrees K to 7 degrees K), the resistivity of certain materials is essentially zero, and thus, circulating currents can be maintained almost indefinitely without additional power. One popular type of superconductive cryogenic device is the Josephson junction.[34] IBM is supporting a large effort in Josephson junction research. Josephson devices, however, are still in laboratory development, and commercial development is expected far in the future. One of the problems with the use of Josephson devices is the thermal shocking encountered when the device is removed and then

---

[27] See "A TYRO Challenges IBM in Big Computers," *Business Week* 65 (May 12, 1975) (Gene Amdahl using emitter-coupled logic (ECL) in his central processor).

[28] See generally Turn, *Computers in the 1980's* 159 (1974).

[29] See generally B. Streetman, *Solid State Electronic Devices* 294 (1972).

[30] See generally M. Rock, *A Survey of MOS Devices and Processing* (1974) (Masters Thesis, University of Illinois) (Excellent technical review of MOS technology).

[31] B. Streetman, *Solid State Electronic Devices* 48 (1972).

[32] Allan, "Circuit/System Building Blocks," 12 *I.E.E.E. Spectrum* 49 (Jan. 1975).

[33] Turn estimated that by 1990, MOS and bipolar semiconductor gates would cost approximately 1.0 to 0.2 cents. R. Turn, *Computers in the 1980's* 159 (1974).

[34] Keyes, "Physical Limits in Digital Electronics," 63 *I.E.E.E. Proceedings* 740 (May 1975).

returned to the very low temperature range.[35] Consequently, commercial use of superconductive cryogenic devices is not expected within the fifteen-year forecast time frame.[36]

Magnetic film, domain-wall motion devices are under investigation for use as processor components. Charged coupled devices (CCDs) are also under extensive development and may be used in processors. Other long-range technologies include acoustic surface wave technology, as well as electrical-optical logic elements.[37] Although several substitutes for semiconductor technology are currently being studied, semiconductor technology will dominate in processor design during the next fifteen years.[38] Improvement in semiconductor performance (increased speed while decreasing power consumption and resulting heat dissipation), however, will be gradual, but steady.[39] Parallelism in chip design whereby a repeatedly used function is reproduced several times on the same chip will also increase semiconductor performance.

Memories. Memory technology is divisible into two broad categories. Random access memories (RAMs) allow the processor to directly address individual words. Due to their high cost, RAM usage is limited, and thus, mass memory is the second broad category of memory technology. Mass memories are slower because they are not directly accessible by the processor, but have a lower cost per bit. Therefore, mass memories are capable of storing large amounts of information at a low cost. A basic objective in memory design has been to provide the end user with large amounts of memory, which are accessible at speeds comparable to processor speeds. As a result, a hierarchy of memories has evolved whereby RAMs are used closest to the processor and mass memories are indirectly connected to the processor through the RAMs. In the following discussion, RAM technology will first be examined, followed by a review of mass memory technology.

RAMs. Magnetic core memory has dominated RAM usage since its original development in the early 1950s at M.I.T. Core memory uses the magnetic

---

[35] Allan, "Technology Forecasting V–Components," 12 *I.E.E.E. Spectrum* 9 (April 1975).

[36] Interview, Wesley Snyder, Assistant Research Professor, Coordinated Science Laboratory, University of Illinois, Urbana-Champaign (June 1975).

[37] *See generally* R. Turn, *Computers in the 1980's* 173 (1974).

[38] Interview, Daniel Slotnick, Professor, Department of Computer Science, University of Illinois, Urbana-Champaign (June 1975); John Stiffel, Senior Research Engineer, Computer-Based Educational Research Laboratory (PLATO), University of Illinois, Urbana-Champaign (June 1975).

[39] Interview, George Anner, Professor, Department of Electrical Engineering, University of Illinois, Urbana-Champaign (June 1975).

properties of small donut-shaped ferrite substances to provide fast access time. RAM magnetic core technology is now threatened by semiconductor technology. One advantage of magnetic core memory is its nonvolatile storage capability when power is suddenly lost.[40] Semiconductor RAMs are volatile, and thus, lose any information stored in them when power is lost. The nonvolatile characteristic of high speed memory is very important in some real time applications such as monitoring manufacturing processes. Therefore, if the information stored in RAMs is valuable, either core RAMs must be used, or the additional expense of backup battery power supplies must be incurred to use semiconductor RAMs.

Semiconductor RAMs are based on the same electronic component technology which was previously discussed in the processor section.[41] Bipolar, MOS, and CMOS RAMs are currently used. The other semiconductor technologies of emitter-coupled logic (ECL), charged coupled devices (CCD), and integrated injection logic (IIL or I squared L) are in early commercial development.[42]

Figure 3-1 highlights the predicted cost performance of semiconductor RAMs. In Figure 3-1, the 1970 semiconductor RAM cost was approximately 1 to 10 cents per bit. This price range made semiconductor RAMs barely competitive with core storage. Core reliability was also better than semiconductor RAM reliability. Since the early 1970s, semiconductor RAM prices have decreased, while reliability has increased. In addition, the required wire linkages between each miniature core limit core density. Semiconductor RAMs are now replacing core memory. By the late 1970s, the semiconductor price per bit will approach one-hundredth of a cent.[43] Therefore, no matter which RAM technology emerges by the 1980s, the RAM price per bit will be in the .01 cent range.

Several other types of RAM technology are commercially available or under development. Plated wire memories consist of a series of very small diameter plated wires each containing a thin, magnetic film. The magnetization direction of the cylindrical film is the storage mechanism. A single wire can store several hundred bits. The Univac 1100 Computer System contained 3.5 million bits of

---

[40] Interview, Thomas Miller, Digital Equipment Corporation, Maynard, Massachusetts (July 1975).

[41] In addition to semiconductor RAMs, there are also read-only memories (ROMs), as well as permanent read-only memories (EPROMs). *See generally* W. Riley, ed., *Electronic Computer Memory Technology* (1971).

[42] Allan, "Technological Forecasting V—Components," 12 *I.E.E.E. Spectrum* 58 (April 1975); Electronics Newsletter, *Electronics* 25 (June 26, 1975) (Discussion of IIL 4 K by 1 K bit memory in early commercial usage).

[43] "IC-Memory Reliability Called Superior to Core," 46 *Electronic Engineering Times* 7 (Feb. 24, 1975).

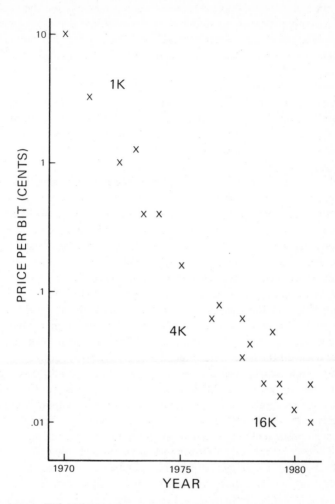

Sources: Altman, "The 16-K RAM is Coming," 48 *Electronics* 80 (June 12, 1975). Copyright © McGraw-Hill, Inc., 1975. *See also Hearings on S. 1167 Before the Subcommittee on Antitrust and Monopoly of the Senate Committee on the Judiciary,* 93rd Cong., 2d Sess., pt. 7, at 5434 (July 23-26), 1974) (The Industrial Reorganization Act—The Computer Industry) (Statement by Marilyn Water-Carlson).

Figure 3-1. Predicted Semiconductor Random Access Memory (RAM) Performance.

plated wire storage. Further developments will increase speeds as well as packing densities of plated wire memory.[44]

Bubble memories currently under development will bridge the gap between

---

[44] *See generally* R. Turn, *Computers in the 1980's* 183 (1974).

high cost but high speed of core and semiconductor memory, and the slower speed but lower cost of mass memories such as magnetic tape. Bubble memory technology is based on thin magnetic garnet films, which support small magnetic domains (bubbles). These magnetic domains move through the material based on external magnetic forces. Bits are either turned on or turned off by the presence or absence of the domain.[45]

Bell Labs recently delivered a prototype bubble memory to Western Electric for product development. Rockwell International also developed a bubble memory chip for use by NASA.[46] Commercial use of bubble memories will occur between the late 1970s and early 1980s.

Mass Memories. Large storage capacities, low cost per bit, and slow access times generally characterize mass memories. Four major types of mass memories are currently either in commercial use or in the research and development stage. Magnetic tape storage is currently used when mass storage is required but slow access times are acceptable. Disk storage is used when lesser amounts of data need to be stored and shorter access times are desired. Bubble, electronic beam, and holographic laser beam memory technologies are all currently under development. Each of these technologies are categorized in Figure 3-2. In Figure 3-2, the present and predicted 1980 access times and cost per bit characteristics of magnetic tape, disk, bubble, electron beam, and holographic laser beam memory technologies are outlined. These rough approximations indicate the orders of magnitude differences between the mass storage technologies. Presently, both magnetic tape and disk are commercially available with the tradeoff between the disk higher access times but higher costs and the magnetic tape lower cost but slower access times. By the early 1980s, bubble, electron beam, and holographic laser beam technologies will dramatically decrease access times and reduce mass memory storage cost. Consequently, huge quantum jumps in performance and decreases in costs will occur by the early 1980s in mass memory technology.[47]

Electron beam technology is the stronger candidate for future mass memories because electrons are easier to manipulate by either magnetic or electrical

[45] A. Zellweger, "Five-Year Computer Technology Forecast," 60 (1972) (Department of Transportation Rep. No. DOT-TSC-OST-72-23).

[46] Allan, "Circuit/System Building Blocks," 12 *I.E.E.E. Spectrum* 51 (Jan. 1975); Interview, Wolfgang Poppelbaum, Professor, Department of Computer Science, University of Illinois, Urbana-Champaign (June 1975) (Bubble memory will not surpass semiconductor for at least ten years); Falk, "Technological Forecasting II—Computers," 12 *I.E.E.E. Spectrum* 48 (April 1975) (Skepticism about the practical ability of magnetic bubble technology to compete with charged coupled devices (CCD's); Interview, Saburo Muroga, Professor, Department of Computer Science, University of Illinois, Urbana-Champaign (June 1975) (Expects bubble memory to emerge commercially within two to four years).

[47] Interview, Edward Cohler, Computer Signal Processors, Inc., Burlington, Massachusetts (July 1975).

TYPE	YEAR	ACCESS TIME (in seconds)	COST/BIT (in cents)
MAGNETIC TAPE	1975	$10-100$	$10^{-4}-10^{-6}$
	1980	$10-100$	$10^{-5}-10^{-7}$
DISK	1975	$10^{-1}-10^{-2}$	10^{-4}
	1980	$10^{-2}-10^{-3}$	10^{-5}
BUBBLE	1975	*	*
	1980	10^{-4}	10^{-3}
ELECTRON BEAM	1975	*	*
	1980	$10^{-4}-10^{-5}$	$10^{-2}-10^{-3}$
HOLOGRAPHIC LASER-BEAM	1975	*	*
	1980	$10^{-3}-10^{-5}$	$10^{-5}-10^{-6}$

Note: *Not Commercially Available at Present

Sources Consulted: R. Turn, *Computers In The 1980's* (1974); Electronics Systems Division Air Force Systems Command, *Support of Air Force Automatic Data Processing Requirements Through the 1980's* (1974) (Vol. 3–Technology) (Hanscom Field) (*A.D. Little Report*): Hughes *et. al.,* "BEAMOS–A New Electronic Digital Memory," 45 *A.F.I.P.S. Proceedings* 541 (1975); Speliotis, "Bridging the Memory Access Gap," 45 *A.F.I.P.S. Proceedings* 507 (1975); Ypma, "Bubble Domain Memory Systems," 45 *A.F.I.P.S. Proceedings* 523 (1975); "Electronic Beam Auxiliary Memory Offers Potential for Mass Storage Uses," 14 *Computer Design* 30 (1975).

Figure 3-2. Selective Commercial Mass Memory Characteristics

control.[48] Holographic and laser beam technology is a dark horse in the future mass memory market. The major problem in optical techniques is the limited substances capable of manipulating the photons in holographic and laser beam mass memories.[49]

Component technological developments are the fundamental building blocks

---

[48] Interview, Henry Krone, Assistant Director, Senior Research Engineer, Coordinated Science Laboratory, University of Illinois, Urbana-Champaign (July 1975).

[49] Interview, Donald Bitzer, Director, Computer-Based Education Research Laboratory (PLATO) University of Illinois, Urbana-Champaign, (June 1975); Interview, Michael Faiman, Associate Professor, Department of Computer Science, University of Illinois, Urbana-Champaign (July 1975). *See also* Gillies, Hoffman, and Nelson, "Holographic Memories–Fantasy or Reality," 44 *A.F.I.P.S. Proceedings* 529 (1975) (Holographic memories expected to be commercially available in late 1970s or early 1980s); Landauer, "Optical Logic and Optically Accessed Digital Storage," (Undated) (IBM Thomas J. Watson Research Center, Yorktown Heights, New York).

to all computer design. In the processor area, semiconductor technology will dominate processor design through the 1980s. For any additional processor technologies to emerge, they will have to be cost effective with semiconductor technology. Therefore, processor costs can be expected to decline as indicated by Figure 3-1. Semiconductor technology will also play a major role in RAM technology.[50] Finally, within the mass memory area, major developments can be expected in which large capacity mass memories with fast access times, but low cost per bit, will emerge commercially.[51]

Once low-cost, but high-performance, mass memory is available, large resource sharing data bases will become economically viable. In the technological forecast time frame, hierarchical memory systems will remain with fast memory used to match its speed with processor speeds, while mass memories will serve the large storage function.[52] In addition, low cost RAMs will provide computer system designers the opportunity of placing large amounts of memory in pheripheral units such as line printers and terminals.[53]

Input and Output (I-O) Devices

Overview. Combined with processors and memories, input and output devices are the third major part of modern computer systems. In this section on input and output devices, the advent of microprocessors and microcomputers is first examined, followed by a discussion of intelligent terminal development. Charged coupled devices (CCDs) as a direct input device are considered as well as current developments in output devices, such as light emitting diodes (LEDs) and liquid crystal displays (LCDs). Finally, speech understanding systems are reviewed.

Microprocessors and Microcomputers. A microcomputer is an LSI chip (or a group of chips) containing an entire data processing system including the processor, memory, and input and output components. A microprocessor contains only the processor or the processor and either memory or input and output components, but not all three of them.[54] Microprocessors are beginning to be

---

[50] *See generally* Greenblott and Hsiao, "Where is Technology Taking Us in Data Processing Systems," 44 *A.F.I.P.S. Proceedings* 523 (1975).

[51] Interview, Franklin Probst, Associate Director of Planning, Computer-Based Education Research Laboratory (PLATO), University of Illinois, Urbana-Champaign (July 1975).

[52] Electronics System Division Air Force Systems Command, *Support of Air Force Automatic Data Processing Requirements Through the 1980s* 2-2 (1974) (Vol. 3–Technology) (Hanscom Field) (*A.D. Little Report*).

[53] A. Zellweger, "Five-Year Computer Technology Forecast," 54 (1972) (Department of Transportation Rep. No. DOT-TSC-OST-72-23).

[54] Laliotis, "Microprocessors Present and Future," 7 *Computer* 20 (July 1974); Threewitt, "The Microprocessor Rationale," 44 *A.F.I.P.S. Proceedings* 20 (1975).

integrated into computer systems. The full integration of microprocessors into computer systems will have dramatic effects on computer design due to the ability of microprocessors to perform many simple processing functions traditionally performed by the central processing unit (CPU).[55] Numerous individuals interviewed stated that the integration of microprocessors into computer design would be the most dramatic development in computer technology in the next fifteen years.[56]

As of late 1974, over twenty microprocessors were commercially available.[57] Microprocessors are being used in numerous input and output devices such as control over printers and telecommunication interfaces.[58] With the continued decline in microprocessor costs, a major microprocessor application will be in control units of consumer goods such as automobiles and watches.[59]

Microprogramming replaces the hardwired logic control unit inside a CPU with a miniature high speed computer that performs the control function in the CPU.[60] Original theoretical work on microprogramming was completed in the early 1950s by Wilkes.[61] The design of microprograms becomes more difficult as microprograms are required to perform more complex tasks. Once a microprogram is developed and implemented, it is inexpensive to reproduce. Consequently, microprograms are very attractive to substitute in place of repeatedly

---

[55] Interview, Thomas Maggiacomo, Electrical Systems Group, Communications Division, GTE Sylvania, Needham, Massachusetts (July 1975). *See also* Laliotis, "Microprocessors Present and Future," 7 *Computer* 20 (July 1974) (Prediction that microprocessors will serve as the foundation for the fifth computer system generation).

[56] Interviews, *e.g.*, Edward Cohler, Computer Signal Processors, Inc., Burlington, Massachusetts (July 1975); Gilbert Falk, Bolt, Beranek, and Newman, Inc., Cambridge, Massachusetts (July 1975).

[57] Falk, "Computer Systems: Hardware/Software," 12 *I.E.E.E. Spectrum* 38 (Jan. 1975).

[58] Allan, "Circuit/System Building Blocks," 12 *I.E.E.E. Spectrum* 49 (Jan. 1975); Moore and Eidson, "Printer Control: A Minor Task for a Microprocessors," 22 *Electronic Design* 74 (Dec. 6, 1974).

[59] Interview, John Stifle, Senior Research Engineer, Computer-Based Education Research Laboratory (PLATO), University of Illinois, Urbana-Champaign (June 1975).

[60] *See generally* S. Husson, *Microprogramming: Principles and Practices* (1970); Jones and Merwin, "Trends in Microprogramming: A Second Reading," C-23 *I.E.E.E. Transactions on Computers* 754 (Aug. 1974).

[61] Wilkes, "The Best Way to Design an Automatic Calculating Machine," *Manchester University Computer Inaugural Conference* 16 (1951). *See generally* Agrawala and Rauscher, "Microprogramming: Perspective and Status, C-23 *I.E.E.E. Transactions on Computers* 32 (Aug. 1974); Opler, "Fourth Generation Software," 13 *Datamation* 22 (Jan. 1967) (First use of the term firm wiring); Stringer, "Microprogramming and the Choice of Order Code," *Automatic Digital Computation Proceedings of a Symposium held at the National Physical Laboratory* 71 (March 25-28, 1953) (No. 10) (Early discussion of the theoretical basis of microprogramming).

used software operations.[62] Within the forecast time frame, microprogramming will evolve from logic implementation within computer design to use as operating systems and higher level language compilers.[63]

In the broad spectrum of computational resources, microcomputers are one step above microprocessors. Microcomputers are currently being used as dedicated computers in many industrial control applications. As the processing power of microcomputers grows, they will be able to perform many functions traditionally in the minicomputer sphere. Therefore, microcomputers will be the smallest complete computer available for end users desiring a total (but very low capacity) computer system.[64]

Intelligent Terminals. With the advent of time sharing discussed in Chapter 1, the use of remote terminals has steadily increased. Interactive terminal usage is expected to increase during the forecast period, while the use of punch card equipment and card readers will steadily decline.[65] Numerous interactive terminals connected to a large computer through a time sharing operating system require a large amount of input and output (I/O) processing for control of these terminals. Large computers are very efficient in processing information; however, large computers are relatively inefficient in I/O functions. Therefore, as microprocessors and microcomputers are incorporated into terminals, these terminals will be able to perform many of the I/O functions traditionally performed by the central processing unit (CPU).

By the 1980s, terminals will possess large amounts of computational power. The exact tradeoff between local computation performed by an intelligent terminal and remote computation performed by the CPU is very hard to determine at this time.[66] This configuration of processing resources is one of the phenomena called distributed computation.[67]

As a rough approximation, an intelligent terminal in the early 1980s may

---

[62] *See generally* Ramamoorthy and Shankar, "Automatic Testing for the Correctness and Equivalence of Loop Free Microprograms," C-23 *I.E.E.E. Transactions on Computers* 37 (Aug. 1974).

[63] Broadbent, "Microprogramming and System Architecture," 17 *Computer J.* 2 (Feb. 1974).

[64] Vacroux, "Microcomputers," 232 *Scientific American* 32 (May 1975).

[65] P. Alsberg, *Research in Network Data Management and Resource Sharing* 13 (1975) (CAC Doc. 164 and JTSA Doc. 5510).

[66] Interview, Franklin Propst, Associate Director of Planning, Computer-Based Education Research Laboratory (PLATO), University of Illinois, Urbana-Champaign (July 1975).

[67] A. Zellweger, *Five-Year Computer Technology Forecast* 8 (1972) (Department of Transportation Rep. No. DOT-TSC-OST-72-23). *See generally* Irwin and Kosman, "Compact Computing Power for Terminals," 3 *Telesis* 239 (July–Aug. 1974); "Intelligent Terminals," 20 *Electronic News* 1 (March 3, 1975).

contain at least 64K of main memory plus secondary storage. In addition, the intelligent terminal will have keyboard input and visual output display capability as well as network communication interfaces.[68]

Although nonimpact keyboards are already economically feasible, the human element and psychological preference for key depressant devices will insure the continued use of mechanical keyboards.[69] In general terminal development, electromechanical technology will not dramatically improve during the forecast time frame as compared to electrically based terminal technology.[70]

Charge coupled devices (CCDs) are under development as input devices. CCD technology would be used as the basis of a visual image input processing system.[71] A visual output system similar to cathode ray tube (CRT) devices using CCD technology is also being developed. CRT technology is currently the most widely used visual soft copy output technology. In addition to CCD and plasma technology, CRT devices are also being threatened by newer developments in solid state electronics such as liquid crystal displays (LCDs) and light-emitting diodes (LEDs).[72]

Advances in hard copy output will be slower due to the underlying electromechanical technology of hard copy output. Electrostatic nonimpact printers are currently available, but their cost effectiveness is limited due to their special paper requirements. Thus, in the fifteen-year forecast framework, the major progress in output technology will be in visual soft copy output. The primary importance of these developments in output technology is that the visual output costs of intelligent terminals will continue to decrease during the fifteen-year forecast period.

Speech Understanding Input Systems. Research is continuing on speech

---

[68] *See generally* P. Alsberg, *Research and Network Data Management and Resource Sharing* 18 (1975) (CAC Doc. 164 and JTSA Doc. 5510). *See generally* "The H.P. Model 2640A," 26 *Hewlett-Packard J.* (June 1975) (H.P. Model 2640A presently selling for a base price of $3000).

[69] Electronic Systems Division Air Force Systems Command, *Support of Air Force Automatic Data Processing Requirements Through the 1980's* 2-41 (1974) (Vol. 3–Technology) (Hanscom Field) (*A.D. Little Report*). *See generally* Auerbach Info., Inc., *Auerbach Terminal Equipment Digest* (1970) (Early complete list of terminal equipment).

[70] Electronics Systems Division Air Force Systems Command, *Support of Air Force Automatic Data Processing Requirements Through the 1980's* 2-44 (1974) (Vol. 3–Technology) (Hanscom Field) (*A.D. Little Report*).

[71] *See generally* Chien and Snyder, "Hardware for Visual Image Processing," CAS-22 *I.E.E.E. Transactions on Circuits and Systems* 22 (June 1975).

[72] *See* Bursky, "Incandescents Fight for Life as LED's Improve," 52 *Electronic Engineering Times* 1 (May 19, 1975). *See generally* R. Turn, *Computers in the 1980's* 108 (1974); (Exhaustive survey of display technologies); Allen, "Circuit/System Building Blocks," 12 *I.E.E.E. Spectrum* 53 (Jan. 1975).

understanding systems.[73] Further development of speech understanding systems faces two closely related problems. The electronic problem of capturing the spoken word into machine-readable form is the first problem. Once obtained in machine-readable form, the second problem is the computer determination of the word meanings.[74]

This second problem—of determining the meaning of the word—approaches the artificial intelligence sphere. Development of artificial intelligence, however, is not expected until beyond the fifteen-year forecast time period. Consequently, this second problem of meaning interpretation is outside the time frame of the present technological forecast. Advances in basic linguistic theory must occur before the first problem of transforming spoken words into machine-readable form is resolved.[75] Within the underlying linguistics theory, the major difficulty is the disaggregation of continuous speech into discrete words.[76]

Speech understanding systems capable of one-hundred words are presently available. Larger vocabularies of one- to three-hundred words are also available through the use of a hierarchy system of key words.[77] Gradual enlargement of vocabularies and decreasing costs are expected. Researchers at Bolt, Beranek and Newman, Inc., hope to develop a one-thousand word vocabulary model by the early 1980s. Commercial voice recognition systems capable of several thousand words are not expected until the middle to latter 1980s.[78]

For the forecast period, therefore, speech understanding systems will not greatly affect the computer industry due to their commercial availability in the latter 1980s. Once speech understanding systems are commercially available (at cost effective prices compared to conventional key to machine-readable input techniques), a major input bottleneck will be eliminated.[79]

Voice response systems are currently available.[80] Banks are using voice

---

[73] A. Newell, *et al.*, *Speech-Understanding Systems* (1971) (Carnegie-Mellon University, Pittsburgh, Pennsylvania).

[74] Interview, David McKeown, Department of Clinical Engineering, George Washington University, Medical Center, Washington, D.C. (July 1975).

[75] Interview, John Stifle, Senior Research Engineer, Computer-Based Education Research Laboratory (PLATO), University of Illinois, Urbana-Champaign (June 1975).

[76] *See* Bolt, Beranek and Newman, Inc., *Natural Communications With Computers* (1974) (Report No. 2976 Vol. 1).

[77] Interview, Wesley Snyder, Research Assistant Professor, Coordinated Science Laboratory, University of Illinois, Urbana-Champaign (June 1975). *See generally* C. Weitzman, *Minicomputer Systems: Structured, Implementation and Application* 338 (1974).

[78] Interview, Bertram Bruce, Bolt, Beranek and Newman, Inc., Cambridge, Massachusetts (July 1975).

[79] *See generally* R. Turn, *The Use of Speech For Man-Computer Communication* (1975) (Rand Corp. Rep. R-1386).

[80] *See, e.g.,* "Going One Up On Voice Input," 20 *Datamation* 111 (Aug. 1974).

response systems to allow customers to obtain the status of their checking and savings accounts over the phone. The Bell System is experimenting with voice response systems. PLATO at the University of Illinois is also using a voice response system.

Within input and output device technology, therefore, major improvements in electrical technology will occur. The use of microprocessors and microcomputers in terminals, and other input and output devices will enable distributed computation to occur. The intelligent terminal will also provide the end user with a vast amount of local computational resources. Finally, commercial availability of large vocabulary speech understanding systems will not occur until the middle to latter 1980s.

Computer Systems

Overview. The electrical component and input and output device discussions have focused on the basic building blocks used to create computer systems. Currently, there are three major categories of computer systems. Supercomputers of the ILLIAC IV class are generally used for massive number processing. The medium-sized computers are used in most commercial and business applications. Finally, minicomputers have traditionally been used in industrial control applications as well as scientific areas. Due to the growth in minicomputer capacity, medium-sized general computer systems and minicomputers are merging into one class of computer. This section on computer systems will examine minicomputer and supercomputer technological developments.

Minicomputers. Early minicomputer development discussed in Chapter 1 emphasized the traditional low capabilities but low price of minicomputer systems. The term minicomputer will continue to denote a lower-priced computer system (as compared to medium-sized and supercomputers). The performance of minicomputers, however, has dramatically increased since the middle 1960s. Based on the electrical component and input and output technological forecast, the dramatic rate of minicomputer improvement is expected to continue. Originally, minicomputer costs were in the $25,000 range; however, minicomputer systems today—consisting of a full set of peripherals—now cost in the $100,000 range. As a rough comparison, the Digital Equipment Corporation PDP-11/70 minicomputer system is approximately equal to an IBM 360/50, but only costs $180,000 for a complete system with supporting peripherals.[81]

A typical minicomputer system by 1977 will be similar to the IBM System 3 Model 15, but will be equipped with 32K to 64K of RAM memory with a

---

[81] *See generally* Leavitt, "UK Test Shows Some Minis Outperform Bigger CPU's," 8 *Computerworld* 1 (Dec. 25, 1974/Jan. 1, 1975).

small mass memory of at least 512K. By 1985, a similar minicomputer will have at least 256K of RAM memory and 4000K of mass memory. Therefore, the minicomputer in the near future will be equal to or larger than many present medium-sized computers. The price of the future minicomputers will be considerably less than the present cost of $0.5 to $2.0 million for a medium-sized computer.[82]

Originally, minicomputer systems used the more powerful—but more expensive—peripheral devices designed for medium- and large-sized computer systems. Presently, however, minicomputer manufacturers are developing lower cost but lower performance peripherals that attach to minicomputer systems. The overall costs of the minicomputer system are thereby reduced.[83] These mini peripherals generally include low-cost printers, nonimpact electrostatic printers for terminals, and floppy disks for mass storage.

Minicomputer software has followed a development pattern similar to software used in large mainframe commercial computers. In the latter 1960s and early 1970s, most minicomputer software was written in assembly languages.[84] Currently, minicomputer manufacturers and users are establishing higher level languages.[85] Minicomputer manufacturers are beginning to market COBOL compilers.[86]

Minicomputers also use a new design feature called a bus system. Under a bus system, the separate parts of a minicomputer system are linked by a common datapath rather than by a continuous loop. The continuous loop requires a full cycle for an operation to be performed.[87] The bus design allows great flexibility in attaching numerous peripherals to the minicomputer system. Under the traditional computer design using a continuous loop, major changes in the control of the loop must be made to add an additional peripheral. In addition to their lower cost, minicomputers offer the end user complete

---

[82] Electronic Systems Division Air Force Systems Command, *Support of Air Force Automatic Data Processing Requirements Through the 1980's* 2-103 (1974) (Vol. 3–Technology) (Hanscom Field) (*A.D. Little Report*).

[83] *See generally* Davis, "Fresh View of Mini and Micro Computers," 13 *Computer Design* 67 (May 1974).

[84] *See* Pike, "Software Production for Minicomputers," 61 *I.E.E.E. Proceedings* 1544 (Nov. 1973).

[85] "Relations Between Users, Software Vendors Maturing," 8 *Computerworld* S-8 (Dec. 25, 1974/Jan. 1, 1975). *See generally* Holt and Lemas, "Current Minicomputer Architecture," 13 *Computer Design* 65 (Feb. 1974).

[86] Digital Equipment Corporation, *PDP-11 Computer Family–Products and Services* (June 1975) (PDP-11/70 has a COBOL compiler).

[87] *See* C. Weitzman, *Minicomputer Systems: Structure, Implementation, and Application,* 26 (1974).

security over the entire computer system as compared to purchasing computer time from a service bureau.[88]

Many firms have entered the minicomputer market. In the antitrust section of Chapter 2, the minicomputer barriers to entry were estimated at approximately five million dollars.[89] Minicomputer manufacturers are now entering the traditional large-scale, medium-sized computer market through a step up from 16 bit to 32 bit models.[90] The distribution of minicomputer costs will continue as discussed in Chapter 1. Processor costs will be the smallest element of the entire minicomputer system cost, with peripherals making up the next largest percentage of the total cost, and finally software costs being the largest part of total minicomputer system costs.[91]

Supercomputers. The continued development of microprocessors, microcomputers, and minicomputers will effectively fill the low- and middle-range computer market. At the high end of the computer market, the large computers of today will evolve into supercomputers. A supercomputer is really an entire system of peripherals and communication devices all linked to a very large central processing unit (CPU).[92]

Several computational tasks require massive amounts of computer resources. Supercomputers capable of large quantities of computation per unit of time are the only computers able to do these tasks. Examples of large computational tasks include weather analysis, atomic energy research, and integrated inventory

---

[88] *See generally* F. Gruenberger and D. Babcock, *Computing with Minicomputers* (1975); B. Soucek, *Minicomputers in Data Processing and Simulation* (1972) (Technical explanation of minicomputers).

[89] *See generally* McCartney and Wilkinson, "The Year Mini Users Shed the Security Blanket," 21 *Infosystems* 26 (Jan. 1974). IBM has entered the low end of the minicomputer market with its System/32 Model. IBM has sold more System/32 minicomputers than any other computer model. Cashman, "The IBM System/32," 21 *Datamation* 67 (Feb. 1975); McLean, "System/32 Market Prospects Seen Good," 20 *Electronic News* 26 (Jan. 20, 1975).

[90] Day, "Small Computer Makers Split On High End Market Strategy," 20 *Electronic News* 1 (April 7, 1975).

[91] D. Kenny, *Minicomputers: Low Cost Computer Power for Management* (1974); Farmer, "1974 Retrospect: Mini Advances Take Center Stage," 8 *Computerworld* 17 (Dec. 25, 1974/ Jan. 1, 1975).

[92] Interview, Donald Bitzer, Director, Computer-Based Education Research Laboratory (PLATO), University of Illinois, Urbana-Champaign (June 1975). *See generally* Koudela, "Past, Present, and Future of Minicomputers: A Scenario," 61 *I.E.E.E. Proceedings* 1526 (Nov. 1973); *Hearing on S. 1167 Before the Subcommittee on Antitrust and Monopoly of the Senate Committee on the Judiciary* 93rd Cong., 2d Sess., pt. 7, at 4947 (July 23-25, 1974) (Industrial Reorganization Act—The Computer Industry) (Prepared background material submitted by International Data Corp.).

control–accounting systems for large corporations.[93]   Supercomputers will also be used where a common resource must be shared among many users. An example of a shared resource would be an annotated index to the Library of Congress, or the National Technical Information Service (NTIS).[94] Therefore, supercomputers will be needed in areas where vast amounts of computational capabilities are required. Depending on the computational task, there are several different supercomputer designs.

Monoprocessors. A monoprocessor is a single instruction steam, single data string computer system. Many large computers today follow this design. The basic monoprocessor contains a central processing unit (CPU), random access memory (RAM), and an input/output (I/O) controller.[95] Monoprocessors have improved performance through design innovations such as concurrency in processor information, multiple independent addressable memory units, and replication of subsystems for use in modular design.

By the 1980s, most operating system software in monoprocessors will be microprogrammed. Functions that will be microprogrammed include data management operations, direct higher-order language execution, and fault detection and diagnosis procedures. By the middle of the 1980s, monoprocessors will be capable of between 100 and 500 million instructions per second (MIPS).[96] Monoprocessors will also incorporate the mass memory developments discussed in the electrical component section.

Array Processors. An array processor design is generally categorized by a single instruction stream, but multiple data streams. The ILLIAC IV computer system at NASA-Ames Research Laboratory is an array processor. Array processors have a large number of individual processing units controlled by a single control unit. Each of the processing units contains some memory and can communicate with a larger common memory. By the early 1980s, array

---

[93] Interview, Daniel Slotnick, Professor, Department of Computer Science, University of Illinois, Urbana-Champaign (June 1975). Image processing of satellite photos is another area where large computational power is needed. Interview, Robert Ray, Research Assistant Professor, Center for Advanced Computation, University of Illinois, Urbana-Champaign (June 1975).

[94] Interview, Wolfgang Poppelbaum, Professor, Department of Computer Science, University of Illinois, Urbana-Champaign (June 1975).

[95] Electronics Systems Division Air Force Systems Command, *Support of Air Force Automatic Data Processing Requirements Through the 1980's* 2-107 (1974) (Vol. 3–Technology) (Hanscom Field) (*A.D. Little Report*).

[96] R. Turn, *Computers in the 1980's* 75 (1975).

processors are expected to perform over 1000 MIPS.[97] Monoprocessor speed—
and resulting capacity—is limited by the speed of the electronic signals that
travel at the speed of light. The parallel design in array processors, however,
increases array computer capacity beyond this monoprocessor theoretical
limit. The array processors will have the largest processing capacity in MIPS,
and they will generally be used for special purpose tasks that can efficiently use
the parallel design of the numerous processing units.

Multiprocessors. Multiprocessors will be the third type of supercomputer
computer design. Major technologies employed in multiprocessors are virtual
memory systems resulting in large RAM capacity and communication network
capabilities. Data base management systems will also be used by the early 1980s
as well as distributed processing in which the multiprocessors delegate major
processing tasks to peripherals. Failsafe features, in which the entire system
does not fail but rather degrades, will also be used in the early 1980s.[98] By the
middle of the 1980s, multiprocessors will perform in the range of 100 to 500
MIPS.[99] The multiprocessor design will be the most common supercomputer
design. The array processor and the monoprocessor will also be used where
their special characteristics are most advantageous.

There are several problems in the construction of all supercomputers.[100]
The first difficulty involves overhead management. Large systems require a
great deal of processing just to manage them. In some instances, the management control function grows faster than the overall growth in capacity of the
entire computer system. Therefore, unless there are management control innovations, the marginal gain through adding additional computational power to a
computer system will be smaller than the growth in management control overhead.

Microprocessors and memory development provide tremendous design
opportunities for supercomputer builders. These developments allow the
supercomputer designer to distribute computational tasks from the central
processing unit(s) (CPU) to the peripherals. This distributed computing concept reduces the system management overhead, and thus the CPU is more

---

[97] *See* Purcell, "Control Data STAR-100 Performance Measurements," 43 *A.F.I.P.S. Pro-
ceedings* 385 (1974). *See also* Kuck, "On the Speed-Up and Cost of Parallel Computation"
(Nov. 1974) (Unpublished Paper, Department of Computer Science, University of Illinois,
Urbana-Champaign).

[98] *See* Electronics Systems Division Air Force Systems Command, *Support of Air Force
Automatic Data Processing Requirements Through the 1980's* 2-111 (1974) (Vol. 3—
Technology) (Hanscom Field) (*A.D. Little Report*).

[99] R. Turn, *Computers in the 1980's* 91 (1974).

[100] As minicomputers grow, the larger minicomputer systems will also face these problems.

efficient in processing large amounts of information.[101] The problem in construction of supercomputers, therefore, is determining the optimal composition and combination of the components.[102]

A second major problem in construction of supercomputers deals with the proper use of software. In the case of parallel or array processors, their unique design requires that special software be written to fully utilize the hardware capabilities. A third problem deals with overall system hardware reliability. Although each part in a supercomputer may have a relatively high mean time between failure (MTBF), as all the individual parts are integrated together the aggregate MTBF becomes relatively low. Therefore, exceedingly high individual component MTBFs are needed in the construction of supercomputers. Individual component design will need large amounts of redundancy. The overall system design will also need failure detection and self-repairing features, which rely on the individual component redundancy. The software reliability of the entire supercomputer is a fourth major problem. As complex systems are built, one small mistake may cause the entire system to fail. This programming error could either be unintentional or intentional. Therefore, care must be taken in the software reliability design of supercomputers.[103] Effective utilization of supercomputer potentials will, therefore, require the mastering of numerous computer design problems.

A final consideration is the intermix of minicomputers and supercomputers. In some situations, a network of minicomputers could provide the same processing power as a centralized supercomputer. For instance, a large bank with numerous branches could use one supercomputer with all branch banks communicating with it, or a network of minicomputers in which each branch bank would have a minicomputer. A communications network would link all the branch bank minicomputers together.[104] The eventual computer design will largely depend on end

---

[101] A. Zellweger, *Five-Year Computer Technology Forecast* 77 (1972) (U.S. Department of Transportation Rep. #DOT-TSC-OST-72-23). *See generally* Electronic Systems Division Air Force Systems Command, *Support of Air Force Automatic Data Processing Requirements Through the 1980's* 2-89 (1974) (Vol. 3—Technology) (Hanscom Field) (*A.D. Little Report)* (Discussion of the disaggregation of the input/output processing task into a separate function).

[102] Interview, David Kuck, Professor, Department of Computer Science, University of Illinois, Urbana-Champaign (June 1975). *See generally* Rudenberg, "Large Scale Integration: Promises Versus Accomplishments, The Dilemma of Our Industry," 35 *A.F.I.P.S. Proceedings* 359 (1969).

[103] Falk, "Computer Systems: Hardware/Software," 12 *I.E.E.E. Spectrum* 38 (Jan. 1975). *See generally* B. Boehm, *Information Processing Requirements for Future Air Force Command and Control Systems: Some Implications for Software Research and Development* (1972) (Rand Corp., Rep. No. P-4795); Bruun, "Mending the Hardware-Software Interface," 21 *Infosystems* 50 (Jan. 1974); Nissen and Wallach, "All Applications Digital Computer," *Symposium on High-Level-Language Computer Architecture* (1973) (University of Maryland, College Park) (Sponsored by A.C.M.).

[104] *See* Falk, "Analogy Forecasting II—Computers," 12 *I.E.E.E. Spectrum* 46 (April 1975).

user needs and the resulting optimal mix of distributed processing and memory capabilities.[105]

Therefore, computer systems in the forecast time frame will fill the spectrum of computational needs. The 1980 minicomputer designation will be a misnomer, because the larger 1980 minicomputers will be more powerful than the present medium-scale computers. Consequently, the minicomputer will be the mainstay of most commercial applications. At the high end of the computational spectrum, supercomputers will perform complex tasks requiring massive computational power.

Communications and Networks

Overview. This section deals with communication and networking technology. Various trends in communication technology are first examined. Emphasis is placed on wave guide developments followed by satellite technology, and local distribution communication technology, including the ALOHA system. Networking technology is then examined, and finally, the interaction of communication technology with computer technology resulting in the growth of networking is discussed.

Communications Technology. Both computer and communications technology are rapidly advancing. As an approximate comparison, the computer cost-to-performance ratio is declining faster than the communications cost-to-performance ratio.[106] This differential in cost-to-performance ratios is expected to remain throughout the forecast time frame.

Wave Guide. Wave guide technology is now in the commercial demonstration stage by the Bell System. An experimental commercial system is being constructed between White Plains, New York and New York City. Once in operation, it is expected that wave guide will have a capacity of one-half million bidirectional voice grade lines.[107] A major problem in wave guide technology is the large power requirement needed to bring the electrical signal from normal microwave

---

[105] *See generally* Withington, "Beyond 1984: A Technology Forecast," 21 *Datamation* 54 (Jan. 1975) (Until mid 1980s, federated network of dispersed minicomputers will not be capable of central control and data base management.)

[106] Interviews, P. Alsberg, Associate Director, Center for Advanced Computation, University of Illinois, Urbana-Champaign (July 1975); Abraham Covo, Electrical Systems Group—Communications Division, GTE Sylvania, Needham, Massachusetts (July 1975); Wally Ferzig, Bolt, Beranek, and Newman, Inc., Cambridge, Massachusetts (July 1975).

[107] Interview, Peter Alsberg, Associate Director, Center for Advanced Computation, University of Illinois, Urbana-Champaign (July 1975).

range down to the near optical range for transmission, and then after transmission, back to the microwave range.[108]   Assuming the White Plains to New York experiment is successful, the emergence of commercial wave guide systems will greatly aid in reducing telecommunication costs. Due to its high total cost and tremendous potential, wave guide technology can only be utilized in heavily used communication links.

Satellites. As with wave guide systems, satellite communication systems require a huge capital investment. Satellite systems heavily rely on synchronous orbit positions. With present technology, there are only one hundred synchronous orbit positions around the entire earth's equator.[109]   Synchronous satellites are positioned over 20,000 miles above the earth. As focusing techniques are improved, additional satellite positions will become available. There is a one-eighth second delay for the signal to travel between earth and the satellite. Consequently, for a conversation to be completed, a half-second delay occurs. At present prices, this half second delay is intolerable for voice communications, but is acceptable for computer interactive communications. Synchronous satellite voice communication service is inferior to either nonsynchronous or terrestrial systems, but it is also much less expensive. For the greatly reduced price, many voice long distance users would undoubtedly accept this inferior service. Although nonsynchronous satellites present problems in tracking, their closer distance to the earth reduces the delay time, and thus, they can be used for voice communications.[110]

Continuous improvements can be expected in satellite technology during the fifteen-year forecast time frame.[111]   The outcome in the competition between satellite or wave guide technology is not known at this time. Whether one becomes dominant or both are used to complement each other, the development of wave guide and satellite technology will provide large reductions in communication costs by the 1980s.

Several other competing communications technologies are also being studied. Fiber optic cables are being considered, and current estimates are that by the

[108] Interview, Wolfgang Poppelbaum, Professor, Department of Computer Science, University of Illinois, Urbana-Champaign (June 1975).

[109] Mennie, "Communications and Microwave," 12 *I.E.E.E. Spectrum* 43 (Jan. 1975). *See* Falk, "Technology Forecasting I—Communications," 12 *I.E.E.E. Spectrum* 42 (April 1975) (Major battles are expected in government hearings and judicial proceedings due to the limited available spectrum and satellite positions).

[110] Interview, Peter Alsberg, Associate Director, Center for Advanced Computation, University of Illinois, Urbana-Champaign (July 1975).

[111] Interview, James VanDermey, Director of Research, Codex, Inc., Newton, Massachusetts (July 1975). *See generally* Abramson, "Packet Switching with Satellites," 42 *A.F.I.P.S. Proceedings* 695 (1973).

early 1980s fiber optic cables will be able to carry thousands of voice grade channels.[112] Fiber optic channels are ideally suited for security applications because they cannot be passively tapped. Any taps require physically breaking into the fiber channel. Further developments in laser technology may also enable long distance communications to use lasers.

Local Distribution. The long distance costs of transmitting information will continue to decrease based on the presently developing communications technology. At the local level, a severe problem exists in the distribution of communications over relatively short distances. Local distribution costs may be as great if not greater than the long distance costs by the early 1980s. Locally, the cost of wire-based, voice grade channels is quite high. The installation cost of wire-based communications within a factory is five to six dollars a linear foot.[113]

The Aloha System. Radio packet communication technology can reduce the local communication distribution costs. Related to computers, this technology provides every terminal with a radio transmitter and receiver. Consequently, each terminal has a radio link to a computer rather than a wire link.[114] For transmission over distances outside the radio transmitter's range, repeaters are used to carry the signal from original sender to final receiver.

All terminal transmitters use the same frequency. If the message is garbled due to a simultaneous transmission from two transmitters, the transmitters retransmit until the message is received. Under a no-discipline rule, numerous simultaneous transmissions occur resulting in an 18 percent utilization rate for the radio frequency. If a listen before transmission rule is established, the radio frequency utilization rate is increased to 32 percent. On transmission back from computer to terminals, a 100 percent utilization rate can be achieved because the central computer is the only transmitter sending back to the remote terminals.[115]

The Hawaiian telecommunications system was not reliable enough for computer time sharing systems, and thus the ALOHA system was established as a substitute for wire-based local distribution. Experience from the ALOHA

---

[112] Allan, "Technology Forecasting V–Components," 12 *I.E.E.E. Spectrum* 57 (April 1975); "Fiber-optic Cable Getting Connector for Use in Field," 48 *Electronics* 29 (Aug. 21, 1975); "The Light Wave of the Future," *Business Week* 48 (Sept. 1, 1975) (No. 2396).

[113] Interview, Thomas Stone, Governmental Relations Marketing Liaison, Motorola, Inc., Washington, D.C. (July 1975).

[114] Interview, James VanDermey, Director of Research, Codex, Inc., Newton, Massachusetts (July 1975).

[115] Interview, Peter Alsberg, Associate Director, Center for Advanced Computation, University of Illinois, Urbana-Champaign (July 1975).

System is encouraging. Consequently, similar systems are used whenever the cost of additional communication equipment for local distribution is greater than installing a complementary ALOHA System.[116]

The continuing development of both long distance and local distribution communication technology will result in a continual decrease in communication costs. Today a voice grade line can generally carry 2400 baud per line.[117] In six years, a forty-to-one improvement in performance is expected.[118] In addition, by the 1980s, distance will no longer be a cost consideration. Once in the communication pipeline, the marginal addition in cost for additional miles of transmission will be negligible.[119]

Computer Networks. Network technology provides computer builders with an additional design opportunity. The trend toward distributed computation can, therefore, be carried one step further to the linkage of entire computer systems. Load sharing between computer systems will then be possible. Theories in load sharing are now being investigated in laboratories and will emerge into the commercial market in the next five to ten years.[120]

There are generally three types of computer networks.[121] Centralized networks are an outgrowth of traditional time sharing systems. In a centralized network, the central computer acts as the master, and numerous remote terminals act as slaves to the master computer. The terminals, of course, are gradually becoming more intelligent, but the centralized computer remains the master over the entire system. The second type of network is the ring-switched network. In this network, various computers are linked onto a common communication circle.

The third type of computer network is the store and forward type. In store and forward networks, all computers are linked together by a communications

---

[116] Binder *et al.,* "ALOHA Packet Broadcasting—A Retrospect," 44 *A.F.I.P.S. Proceedings* 203 (1975); Kahn, "The Organization of Computer Resources Into a Packet Radio Network," 44 *A.F.I.P.S. Proceedings* 177 (1975). The PLATO system at the University of Illinois is presently using an ALOHA-type system.

[117] *See generally* D. Davies and D. Barber, *Communication Networks for Computers* (1973) (A baud is defined as one bit per second). This 2400 baud line will support eight low-speed terminals or two high-speed terminals.

[118] Interview, Peter Alsberg, Associate Director, Center for Advanced Computation, University of Illinois, Urbana-Champaign (July 1975) (For the same cost as today's 2400 baud line, a 100K baud line will be available in six years).

[119] *See generally* Gerla and Eckl, "Moving Bits by Air, Land and Sea—Carriers, Vans and Packets," 44 *A.F.I.P.S. Proceedings* 133 (1975).

[120] Interview, Gilbert Falk, Bolt, Beranek, and Newman, Inc., Cambridge, Massachusetts (July 1975).

[121] *See generally* Frisch and Frank, "Computer Communications: How We Got Where We Are," 44 *A.F.I.P.S. Proceedings* 109 (1975).

grid. Communication occurs through a process whereby the information is stored in standardized packages (called packets) and then transmitted through the communications grid from original sender to end receiver.[122]

Packet switching technology originally developed under the Advanced Research Projects Agency (ARPA) of the Department of Defense was discussed in Chapter 1. The ARPA Network currently links several university computer centers. In addition, commercial versions of the ARPA Network technology are also being developed by several private firms.[123] The packet switching technology allows very rapid response times (in the one-second range) to communicate with remote computers as well as one-second connect times. High reliability and low error rates are also presently obtainable. In addition, user charges are now beginning to be based on the amount of information transmitted rather than on the length of connect time.[124]

The network forte will be those cases where the amount of data transferred increases at a lesser rate than the amount of computation needed to process the information once it is transferred through the computer network to a specialized computer. An example is matrix multiplication, where the amount of data increases exponentially by an order of two, but the amount of computational processing required increases by an order of three as the size of the matrix increases. In this situation, transferring the data from a general purpose computer (or in the future, a large minicomputer) to a specialized supercomputer is cost effective in cases where the processing cost is above ten to fifteen cents.[125] Therefore, networks will provide an essential function in cases where the amount of processing increases faster than the amount of data to be transferred, and where a common resource is shared between geographically dispersed end users.

Minicomputer networks are in the initial stage of establishing common communication procedures.[126] Future minicomputer networks will have failsafe capabilities in which individual minicomputers can fail, but the

[122] Chou, "Computer Communications Networks—The Parts Make Up the Whole," 44 *A.F.I.P.S. Proceedings* 128 (1975). *See generally* P. Alsberg, *et al., An Annotated Bibliography to Network Data Management and Related Literature* (1975) (Center for Advanced Computation, Urbana, Illinois).

[123] Interview, Edwin McCauley, Research Assistant Professor, Center for Advanced Computation, University of Illinois, Urbana-Champaign (June 1975). *See generally* Kershenbaum, "Tools for Planning and Designing Data Communications Networks," 43 *A.F.I.P.S. Proceedings* 583 (1974).

[124] Withington, "Beyond 1984: A Technology Forecast," 21 *Datamation* 54 (Jan. 1975).

[125] Alsberg "Distributed Processing on the ARPA Network—Measurements of the Cost Performance Tradeoffs for Numerical Tasks," *Proceedings of the Eighth Hawaiian International Conference of System Sciences* (1975).

[126] *See, e.g.,* E. Stelmach, *Introduction to Minicomputer Networks* (1974) (Digital Equipment Corporation, Maynard, Massachusetts).

network will remain operational.[127] By the early 1980s, minicomputer networks operating under a distributed computation principle will be commercially available.[128] Thus, for some applications, minicomputer networks will compete with supercomputers.

Communication technological developments will, therefore, continue, but at a slower pace than computer technological development. As computers and communication technology continue to converge, however, communication technology will play an ever-increasing role in computer development. With decreased communication costs, vast computer networks are economically viable. As network technology is further refined, distributed processing, load sharing, and unique resource sharing will become economically viable.

Software

Overview. Underlying the entire discussion of future software developments is the long-term trend toward software costs becoming an every-increasing percentage of total computer system costs.[129] Estimates of software costs as a percentage of total system costs by the middle of the 1980s range as high as 90 percent.[130] This section on software first examines several trends in software development. Software portability and language developments are briefly reviewed, and attention is then focused on structured programming developments.

Software Developments. A critical underlying factor in software production is the high cost for the first program but the near-zero marginal cost for identical copies. In addition, hardware has generally been scrapped or sold when end users purchased new hardware. Software, however, remains valuable to the end user because of the high marginal cost to develop new software that is more

---

[127] *See generally* Ornstein *et al.,* "Pluirbus, A Reliable Multiprocessor," 44 *A.F.I.P.S. Proceedings* 551 (1974); Orthner and McKeown, "A Packet Switching Network for Computers," *Fall Proceedings of COMPCON* (1975) (Washington, D.C.).

[128] Interview, Thomas Miller, Digital Equipment Corporation, Maynard, Massachusetts (July 1975).

[129] See Figure 1-6 of Chapter 1 and supporting discussion for further reference to the early stages of this long-term trend.

[130] Electronic Systems Division Air Force Systems Command, *Support of Air Force Automatic Data Processing Requirements Through the 1980's* 2-121 (1974) (Vol. 3– Technology) (Hanscom Field) (*A.D. Little Report*). The composition of this 90 percent figure varies by type of computer installation. Smaller minicomputer software costs may drop to 60-70 percent of total cost, and in very large systems software costs will be in the 85-95 percent range. Interview, J. Richard Phillips, Division of Computer Research, National Science Foundation, Washington, D.C. (July 1975).

efficient on the newly purchased hardware. In effect, the end user has a large sunk cost in software.[131] In response to this large software sunk cost, emulation programs have been written that enable the older software to operate (very inefficiently) on the newer hardware. The older software is slowly rewritten, but new software is written to utilize most efficiently the new hardware.[132]

Research is currently being conducted on methods to make software portable. For true software portability, some aspects of hardware as well as software must remain invariant between systems in order that compilers properly function on software originally written on a different machine. One of the first steps in software portability is thorough documentation.[133] Large computer system software portability may be achieved within five to eight years. However, minicomputer software portability is not expected until the middle of the 1980s.[134]

Repeatedly used software is also being implemented into hardware through the use of programmable read-only memories (PROMs). Thus, an entire payroll system with appropriate subroutines for federal, state, and local tax deductions will be implemented in PROMs.[135]

In another area, most software experts have concluded that a universal language acceptable to all software users does not exist. A fundamental conflict exists between the universal use of a single language in all applications and the efficient utilization of the language in each application.[136] Three general languages, BASIC, FORTRAN and COBOL, are widely used.[137] Modified versions of these languages as well as the development of entire new languages continue.[138]

---

[131] See Tenny, "Structured Programming in FORTRAN," 20 *Datamation* 110 (July 1974).

[132] Interview, Louis Emmons, Applied Information Development, Oakbrook, Illinois (June 1975). *See generally* W. Sharpe, *The Economics of Computers* 268 (1969). (As software ages, its reliability increases and adds reliability to the entire system. Consequently, older systems become more reliable due to the increased software reliability.)

[133] R. Keuhne, *et al., Handbook of Computer Documentation Standards* (1973).

[134] Interview, J. Richard Phillips, Division of Computer Research, National Science Foundation, Washington, D.C. (July 1975). *See also* J. Fleiff *et al., Programming for Transferability* (1974) (Technical study on software portability).

[135] See generally M. Abrams and P. Stein, *Computer Hardware and Software—An Interdisciplinary Approach* (1973).

[136] Bauer and Rosenberg, "Software—Historical Perspectives and Current Trends," 41 *A.F.I.P.S. Proceedings* 993 (1972) (Pt. 2).

[137] H. Katzan, *Introduction to Programming Languages* (1973).

[138] See, e.g., Ritchie and Thompson, "The UNIX Time Sharing System," 17 *Communications of the ACM* 32 (July 1974); Interview, Franklin Propst, Associate Director of Planning, Computer-Based Education Research Laboratory (PLATO), University of Illinois, Urbana-Champaign (July 1975) (Development of the PLATO-TUTOR Language).

There are also developments in higher level languages, which can be used by individuals not specifically trained in computer programming. Industry generally prefers manpower trained in the operation of the firm and then given supplemental training in computer programming in higher level languages.[139] The higher level languages are not as efficient in terms of hardware utilization as are assembly languages. Hardware costs, however, are continually decreasing. In economic terms, substitution is occurring between expensive programming manpower using (1) higher level languages (efficient in programmer productivity, but inefficient in hardware terms), or (2) lower level languages (i.e., assembly language, relatively inefficient in programmer productivity, but very efficient in hardware utilization). More efficient compilers are also making the use of these higher level languages more efficient in hardware terms.

Structured Programming. Until the middle of the 1960s, computer programming was generally viewed as an art rather than as an engineering science. In response to this, research began on means to apply engineering methods to software production. In Europe, Dijkstra outlined the general principles of structured programming. By the late 1960s and early 1970s, these general principles were categorized into formal structured programming procedures.[140] When software is poorly designed, the major cost in software production is not in the writing, but rather in debugging the software to make it operational.[141] Therefore, one of the goals of all structured programming procedures is to minimize the debugging effort.

Several structured programming procedures have been established.[142] Common to all structured programming procedures is the disaggregation of the programming task into several levels beginning with a macro view of the entire problem through actual code writing, and finally, the machine level execution of the software.[143] Regardless of the software engineering, the programming

---

[139] Interview, James York, Division of Industry Productivity, Bureau of Labor Statistics, U.S. Department of Labor, Washington, D.C. (July 1975).

[140] O. Dahl, E. Dijkstra, and E. Hoare, *Structured Programming* (1972).

[141] Interview, Wesley Snyder, Research Assistant Professor, Coordinated Science Laboratory, University of Illinois, Urbana-Champaign (June 1975).

[142] Baker, "Chief Programmer Management Team Management of Production and Programming," 11 *IBM Systems J.* 56 (1971). *See also* C. Irving and J. Brackett, *Automated Software Engineering Through Structured Data Management* (1974) (SOFTECH Inc., Doc. 553-37); Brattman and Court, "The Software Factory," 8 *I.E.E.E.: Computer* 28 (May 1975); Caine and Gordon, "PDL—A Tool for Software Design," 44 *A.F.I.P.S. Proceedings* 271 (1975) (Discussion of program design language—PDL).

[143] J. Richard Phillips, Division of Computer Research, National Science Foundation, Washington, D.C. (July 1975).

problem must be subdivided into its logical tasks.[144] When taken a step further, structured programming becomes a management tool in organizing an entire company.[145]

As these engineering approaches to software design evolve, software productivity will increase. Estimates range between a one-half to a three-fold improvement in software productivity by the middle of the 1980s.[146] These improvements in productivity, however, will be gradual over the fifteen-year forecast.[147]

The quality of software manpower varies widely. Structured programming procedures are most useful in large programming tasks when the quality of programming manpower varies.[148] Programmer salaries and quality of output are not linearly related. Two $10,000-a-year programmers will not produce the same quality of software that one $20,000-a-year programmer produces.[149] Therefore, the successful production of quality software relies heavily on the quality of the programming manpower.

During the forecast period, therefore, software costs as a percentage of total computer system costs will range in the 80 to 90 percent category. New techniques attempting to change programming artistry into software engineering will continue, and gradual improvement in programmer productivity will occur over the fifteen-year forecast time frame.

---

[144] Interview, James Vandormey, Director of Research, Codex, Inc., Newton, Massachusetts (July 1975).

[145] Interview, Colonel Robert O'Keefe, Information Systems Electronics Systems Division, Systems Command, U.S. Air Force, Hanscom Field, Bedford, Massachusetts (July 1975). *See also* Wilson, "CAD/CAM Breaks the Holding Pattern," 22 *Iron Age* 33 (Jan. 20, 1975).

[146] Electronics Systems Division Air Force Systems Command, *Support of Air Force Automatic Data Processing Requirements Through the 1980's* 2-137 (1974) (Vol. 3–Technology) (Hanscom Field) (*A.D. Little Report*) (Estimate of two- to three-hundred percent improvement by mid-1980's); Withington, "Beyond 1984: A Technology Forecast," 21 *Datamation* 71 (Jan. 1975) (Estimate of 50 percent or higher improvement in computer programming productivity).

[147] Interview, Edward Cohler, Computer Signal Processor, Inc., Burlington, Massachusetts (July 1975).

[148] Interview, Thomas Maggiacomo, Electrical Systems Group–Communications Division, GTE Sylvania, Needham, Massachusetts (July 1975).

[149] Interview, Donald Bitzer, Director, Computer-Based Education Research Laboratory (PLATO), University of Illinois, Urbana-Champaign (June 1975). A recent study conducted by the Arthur D. Little Co. determined that the Air Force would gain a 50 to 100 percent advantage in man hours to complete software design by subcontracting major programming tasks to properly qualified software firms. Electronics Systems Division Air Force Systems Command, *Support of Air Force Automatic Data Processing Requirements Through the 1980's* 2-165 (1974) (Vol. 3–Technology) (Hanscom Field) (*A.D. Little Report*).

Emerging Computational Patterns

Overview. Three major computing categories exist. The first class includes normal number processing as well as large number processing tasks such as weather and econometric models, and atomic energy research. The second category includes the data handling tasks such as inventory control and other data base management systems. This area is growing as commercial data base management systems are developed. The third area is nonnumeric computing and includes systems such as word processing and pattern recognition equipment.[150]

The number processing area is well established. Data handling and non-numeric computation, however, are continuing to grow. This section on emerging computational patterns first examines the development of data base management systems, followed by a discussion of several nonnumeric computer systems. Particular attention is placed on pattern recognition systems, computer aided instruction (CAI), and computer graphics.

Data Base Management. A data base is defined as "an organized set of machine readable records containing bibliographic or document-related data."[151] Emergence of data base management systems is based on several factors.[152] Large but low-cost memories are required as well as computer networks. Computer systems with large processing capabilities are also needed.[153] In Figure 3-2 the predicted mass memory performance characteristics were discussed. By the early 1980s, mass memories will be commercially available that are capable of supporting large data base management systems. Finally, data base management technology must further advance.

Several problems must be resolved in data base management theory before commercially viable data base management systems emerge. First, optimal file name and space allocation procedures must be established. Safeguards against simultaneous updating of the same file by two users must be implemented to insure that all users receive the most current information when

---

[150] Interview, Edward Romani, Office of Computing Activities, National Science Foundation, Washington, D.C. (July 1975).

[151] P. Alsberg, *Research in Network Data Management and Resource Sharing* (1975) (CAC Doc. 164 and JTSA Doc. 5510).

[152] *See generally* Blane, *et al., Annotated Bibliography of the Literature on Resource Sharing Computer Networks* (1973) (National Bureau of Standards, Information Processing Division, Computer Systems Section, Special Publication No. 384).

[153] Interview, Franklin Propst, Associate Director of Planning, Computer-Based Education Research Laboratory (PLATO), University of Illinois, Urbana-Champaign (July 1975).

accessing the data base. Data clustering techniques are needed in which an efficient retrieval system is established. Research in automatic data structure design whereby computers automatically choose an optimal data structure for incoming data must also be conducted.[154]

The establishment of several identical data bases for increased reliability presents several problems. The tradeoff between low data base system cost and high system reliability due to several identical data bases must be resolved. Once the tradeoff between costs and reliability is made, and the number of identical data bases is established, several additional difficulties are encountered. Synchronization procedures must be established to insure that all data bases possess the latest information. With separate processors servicing each data base, load sharing mechanisms are needed to transfer processing tasks from temporarily crowded processors to empty processors. Heterogeneous software and hardware systems must also be linked through the establishment of common communication protocols.[155]

Data base management systems will emerge by the early 1980s. The Department of Defense will be one of the first users of a totally integrated data base management system linking all military installations. In the commercial sector, the Fortune 500 corporations are prime targets for data base management systems.

In a related area, unique resource sharing is also growing. Private firms are currently offering on-line index searching of unique resources as the National Technical Information Services (NTIS). For instance, Lockheed Corporation now offers DIALOGUE, which has numerous indexes on-line. Cost of a typical Lockheed Dialogue service is approximately $10 per search.[156]

The emergence of these on-line data index retrieval systems in the last one to two years has been quite rapid. The main reason for this rapid emergence is the reduced storage costs of on-line information as well as the availability of computer networks which reduce communication costs. In addition, a sufficient number of machine-readable data years enabled researchers to effectively use these indexes.[157]

As the cost of computer accessed, uniquely shared resources continue to

---

[154] P. Alsberg, *Research in Network Data Management and Resource Sharing* (1975) (CAC Doc. 164 and JTSA Doc. 5510).

[155] Interview, Edwin J. McCauley, Research Assistant Professor, Center for Advanced Computation, University of Illinois, Urbana-Champaign (1975). *See also* Levin and Morgan, "Optimizing Distributed Databases—A Framework for Research," 44 *A.F.I.P.S. Proceedings* 473 (1975).

[156] Interview, Richard Caputo, Lockheed Information Systems, Washington, D.C. (July 1975).

[157] Interview, Martha Williams, Director, Information Retrieval Research Laboratory, Computer Science Laboratory, University of Illinois, Urbana-Champaign (June 1975).

decline, they will become competitive with traditional printed hard copy systems.[158] In the future, not only will the index be available for on-line searching, but the entire text will also be available for either on-line viewing or off-line printing. LEXIS, by Mead Data Central, Inc.—an on-line legal indexing and complete textual retrieval system—is presently available in a few states. By the middle to latter 1980s, the actual information will be evaluated and comparisons made between conflicting information sources. This latter service approaches artificial intelligence.[159]

Pattern Recognition. Pattern recognition includes areas as mail sorting, satellite mapping, and medical x-ray screening.[160] The development of these pattern recognition and processing techniques are now in the laboratory experimental stage.[161]

Optical character recognition (OCR) is an additional application of pattern recognition technology. In the middle of the 1960s, widespread commercial use of OCR was forecast as imminent.[162] These estimates were overly optimistic due to remote terminal development whereby the information is captured in machine-readable form at its source.[163] Consequently, OCR techniques will primarily be used in cases where the data cannot be originally captured in machine-readable form.[164] In most situations, OCR equipment will supplement other forms of data input systems.[165]

By the 1980s, low-speed optical character recognition units will sell in the $500 range. These units will have typewritten input capability. Restricted hand printed input capabilities will also be available. Handwriting input capability, however, is outside of the fifteen-year forecast period.[166] Overall, pattern recognition development will continue at an evolutionary pace, and

---

[158] *See generally* Noland, "Managing the Fourth States of EDP Growth," 52 *Harv. Bus. R.* 76 (Jan.-Feb. 1974).

[159] Interview, Edward Weiss, National Science Foundation, Office of Information Services, Washington, D.C. (July 1975).

[160] Interview, David McKeown, Department of Clinical Engineering, George Washington University, Medical Center, Washington, D.C. (July 1975).

[161] *See* R. Ray, *On the Methods for Direct Quantification of Pattern Associations* (1974) (CAC Doc. 139).

[162] *See* R. Dryer, *et al., Optical Scanning* (1966).

[163] For example, point-of-sale (POS) terminals are used rather than employing OCR techniques to read the cash register paper tape record.

[164] *See generally Computer Yearbook* (1972).

[165] *See* Yasaki, "OCR Users Study Multi-Media Methods," 20 *Datamation* 32 (Aug. 1974).

[166] Falk, "Technology Forecasting II—Computers," 12 *I.E.E.E. Spectrum* 48 (April 1975).

commercial applications are expected as the costs of processing and memory continue to decline.[167]

Word processing is another area of nonnumeric computation. Early commercial development of word processing systems is occurring in which the first draft is captured in machine-readable form and simply edited for revisions. Continued development of a totally integrated word processing system from first draft to final reader will occur as processor and terminal costs continue to decline.[168] As discussed in the input and output section, full vocabulary voice input systems will not commercially emerge until the late 1980s. Thus, the voice input intelligent terminal as part of an integrated word processing system is outside the forecast time frame.

CAI. A large domestic and international market exists for computers in computer assisted instruction (CAI).[169] As CAI developments like the University of Illinois PLATO system grow, more individuals will be interconnected by CAI terminals.[170] By the early 1980s, CAI terminal costs will be in the $400 to $700 range, and thus, available to a large number of people.[171]

Although few technical problems in the development of CAI exist, several nontechnical aspects of CAI remain unsettled. Due to the near-zero marginal cost of reproduction, a complete course developed by a well-known university may limit the demand for CAI courses produced at lesser known schools. Educational quality would not be detrimentally affected. Lesser known schools, however, might resist the diffusion of CAI courses produced at well-known schools. In addition, course ownership issues are yet to be resolved. Ownership procedures, however, will undoubtedly follow the present hard copy ownership pattern with the publisher being replaced by a university-owned CAI system.[172] As with textbook publishing, universities generally do not want to enter the commercial publishing-distributing market.

---

[167] Interview, Robert Ray, Research Assistant Professor, Center for Advanced Computation, University of Illinois, Urbana-Champaign (June 1975).

[168] "The Office of the Future," *Business Week* 48 (June 30, 1975) (No. 2387).

[169] *See generally* R. Atkinson and H. Wilson, eds., *Computer-Assisted Instruction* (1969); F. Blackwell, *The Probable State of Computer Technology By 1980, With Some Implications for Education* (1971) (Rand Corp., Rep. No. P-4693); UNESCO, *International Directory of Programmed Instruction* (1973).

[170] *See* J. Feldheisen and M. Zabo, "A Review of Developments in Computer Assisted Instruction," *The Educational Review Series* (1973) (#9—The Computer and Education); B. Luskin, *et al.*, eds., *Everything You Always Wanted to Know About CAI But Were Afraid to Ask* (1972).

[171] Interview, Daniel Alpert, Director, Center for Advanced Study, University of Illinois, Urbana-Champaign (July 1975).

[172] Interview, Edward Weiss, National Science Foundation, Office of Information Services, Washington, D.C. (July 1975).

Computer Graphics. An additional area emerging in computational patterns is the computer graphics field. The growth of computer graphics has been based on the simultaneous development of time-sharing, visual output, and graphic data processing technologies. The early development of time-sharing was discussed in Chapter 1. Today, time-sharing technology makes it economically feasible to allow single users on-line access to large computers in a real time environment. Visual output technology includes cathode ray tubes (CRTs) and plasma display devices. In the future, light emitting diodes (LEDs) and liquid crystal displays (LCDs) may provide additional visual output mediums.

The third supporting technology in computer graphics is graphic data processing. Early work on graphic data processing was completed in the late 1950s and early 1960s at the MIT Lincoln Laboratory.[173] Graphic data processing permits the user to communicate with the computer in his or her own terms by establishing a common language linking the user to the computer. People think in terms of sketches, drawings, graphs, letters, characters, and numbers, whereas computers operate in terms of bits and binary languages. Therefore, graphic data processing provides the interface between man and computer.[174]

Computer graphic applications include architectural design, engineering aids, management information systems, and art and textile design.[175] Computer graphics will become more cost effective as hardware costs continue to decline and graphic data processing technology advances. The interactive mode provides numerous opportunities for on-line problem solving. Manpower productivity is thereby increased due to improved decision making.

Within emerging computational patterns, therefore, data base management systems as well as nonnumeric computation will grow. Computer usage in CAI and computer graphics will greatly aid the teacher and worker, respectively.

Stage II—Technological Forecast: Economic Considerations

Overview. Stage II of the technological forecast will first outline the concept of technologically induced structural atomization. The overall growth cycle of the entire computer industry is then examined, followed by a discussion of the technological factors causing this trend toward structural atomization.

---

[173] *See generally* M. Masta, "What Has Computer Graphics to Offer," *Computer Graphics* 1 (1969) (R. Parslow, R. Prowse, and R. Green, eds.).

[174] *See* W. Newman and R. Sproull, *Principles of Interactive Computer Graphics* (1973).

[175] *See generally* R. Head, *Manager's Guide to Management Information Systems* (1972); J. Laurie, *Textile Graphics/Computer-Aided* (1973); M. Milne, *Computer Graphics in Architecture and Design* (1969); M. Prime, *Interactive Graphics for Computer-Aided Design* (1971).

The effect future technology will have on the barriers to entry is then considered. Brief attention is focused on the expected IBM response to this gradual trend toward structural atomization, followed by a final technological forecast scenario.

Technologically Induced Structural Atomization

Chapter 1 traced the rapid technological development of the computer industry beginning in the late 1940s to its present mature status. The industry growth rate during this thirty-year period has been very rapid. Demand for computational resources is growing in many new applications. These new applications will create many new markets. Existing firms will find it difficult to enter all these new markets. One difficulty in entering all these emerging markets is that internal corporate communication costs grow as the complexity of the corporate structure increases.[176] In addition, firms generally have a U-shaped cost of growth rate. If a firm attempts to grow too rapidly, its management services become diluted, resulting in a rapid rise in marginal cost. Therefore, a firm's most efficient growth rate is steady, but gradual. A steady but gradual growth rate insures that the marginal cost remains low.[177]

With many new markets emerging, new entrants will be attracted to these markets by the large potential profits.[178] Both vertical and horizontal dis-intergration is, therefore, occurring within the industry as computer technology opens additional markets.[179] IBM is also legally restrained from entering all these developing markets due to the antitrust constraints previously discussed in Chapter 2. Therefore, there are several economic and legal constraints slowing the entry of the existing mainframe computer manufacturers into these technologically new markets.

The growth rate of the industry combined with the rapid advances in computer technology have caused the computer industry structure to change radically over time. Based on the previous discussion of the predicted future

---

[176] See K. Arrow, *The Limits of Organization* (1974). *See also* K. Arrow, *Essays in the Theory Risk-Bearing* (1971).

[177] E. Penrose, *The Theory of the Growth of a Firm* (1959).

[178] See generally Mansfield,"Entry, the Gibrat's Law, Innovation, and the Growth of Firms," 52 *Am. Econ. Rev.* 1023 (Dec. 1962).

[179] See Stigler, "The Division of Labor is Limited by the Extent of the Market," 59 *J. Political Economy* 190 (June 1951). *See also* Kelley, "Scale Economics, Inventive Activity, and the Economics of American Population Growth," 10 *Explorations in Economic Hist.* 35 (1972); Mullen, "Functional Spin-Off; A Key to Anticipating Change in Distribution Structure," 37 *J. Marketing* 18 (July 1973); Young, "Increasing Returns and Economic Progress," 38 *Econ. J.* 527 (Dec. 1928).

technological developments as well as the economic and legal constraints on existing firms, the computer industry structure will further evolve through the forecast time frame.

Figure 3-3, Parts 1 through 4 denotes this evolving computer industry structure. Each part denotes the computer industry structure during the four decades beginning with the 1950's and ending with the predicted 1980's structure. Below each structural diagram is the approximate size of the industry during the respective time frame.

In the 1950s, a small market of end users existed; consequently, the structure of the industry was relatively simple. Independent component manufacturers supplied the basic parts to the mainframe assemblers, who then assembled, sold, and maintained their equipment. The three major firms in the 1950 period were Remington Rand (later Sperry Rand), Burroughs, and IBM. Many other firms entered the industry in the 1950's, and either failed or did not emerge as major computer manufacturers until the 1960s.

By the 1960s, the structure of the industry began to expand in all directions. First, economic factors forced mainframe assemblers to integrate vertically upstream to insure adequate control over electronic components that they were using. Wise reported that IBM's upstream integration was to insure that any trade secrets that IBM developed for use in manufacturing electronic components would remain proprietary.[180] When a firm integrates upstream, all hardware and software specifications for a new system can simultaneously be established. Consequently, the firm does not need to rely on independent electrical component manufacturers to supply components that conform to the overall system specifications.[181]

While the mainframe assemblers were vertically integrating upstream in the 1960s, independent leasing firms began to develop. These leasing firms purchased computers from the mainframe assemblers, and then leased the computers to end users at lower prices than the mainframe assembler leasing prices. In addition, independent software firms emerged and slowly grew as software costs became an ever-increasing percentage of total system costs.

In the 1970s, IBM continued to dominate the industry. Minicomputer manufacturers, however, emerged as suppliers of low price and performance computational resources. In a few instances, minicomputer manufacturers integrated upstream and to a large extent, integrated downstream into sales and maintenance. Mainframe manufacturers remained vertically integrated upstream into component manufacturers as well as downstream into sales and maintenance.

Independent leasing firms began to decline, but software firms also grew as

---

[180] Wise, "IBM's $5,000,000,000 Gamble," 74 *Fortune* 139 (Oct. 1966).

[181] Interview, James VanDermey, Director of Research, Codex, Inc., Newton, Massachusetts (July 1975).

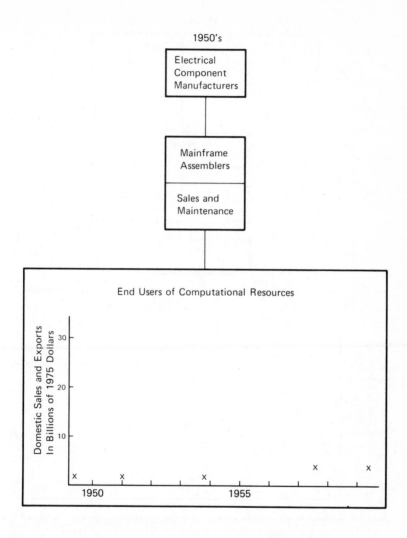

Sources: Diagram discussed in the text and the following references were consulted to estimate the annual domestic sales and exports—A. Clopper, *et al., 1985: Interindustry Forecasts of the American Economy,* E-28 (1974) (*See also* Supplement p. 66); National Planning Association, *The U.S. Economy 1973 to 1983,* S-85 (1973) (Report No. 73-r-l); U.S. Department of Commerce—Bureau of the Census, *Current Industrial Reports—Office, Computing, and Accounting Machines* (Series MA-35R (73)-1) (Table 1—Value of Shipments of Office and Computing Machines, By Class of Product: 1973 and 1972); U.S. Department of Commerce—Bureau of the Census, *1972 Census of Manufacturers* (MC 72(2)-35F) (Table 1A—General Statistics 1958 to 1972—Value of Industry Shipments); U.S. Department of Commerce—Domestic and International Business Division, *Global Market Survey—Computer Equipment* (1973).

Figure 3-3 (Part 1). Evolving Computer Industry Structure

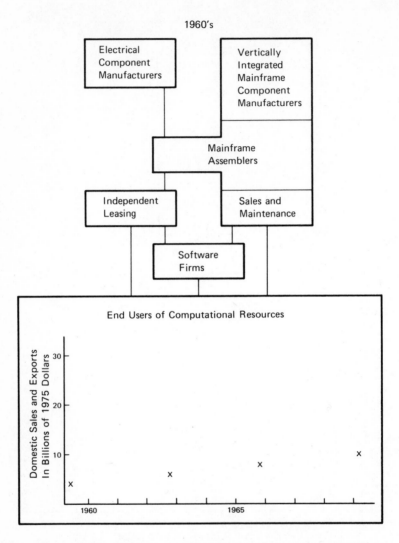

Sources: Diagram discussed in the text and the following references were consulted to
estimate the annual domestic sales and exports—A. Clopper, *et al., 1985: Interindustry
Forecasts of the American Economy,* E-28 (1974) (*See also* Supplement p. 66);
National Planning Association, *The U.S. Economy 1973 to 1983,* S-85 (1973) (Report
No. 73-r-l); U.S. Department of Commerce—Bureau of the Census, *Current Industrial
Reports—Office, Computing, and Accounting Machines* (Series MA-35R (73)-1) (Table
1—Value of Shipments of Office and Computing Machines, By Class of Product: 1973
and 1972); U.S. Department of Commerce—Bureau of the Census, *1972 Census of
Manufacturers* (MC 72(2)-35F) (Table 1A—General Statistics 1958 to 1972—Value of
Industry Shipments); U.S. Department of Commerce—Domestic and International
Business Division, *Global Market Survey—Computer Equipment* (1973).

Figure 3-3 (Part 2). Evolving Computer Industry Structure

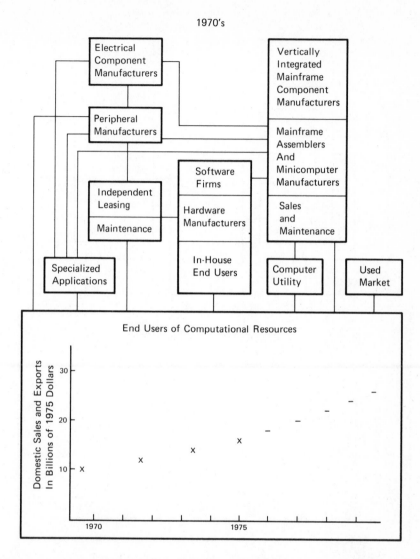

1970's

End Users of Computational Resources

Figure 3-3 (Part 3). Evolving Computer Industry Structure

Sources: Diagram discussed in the text and the following references were consulted to estimate the annual domestic sales and exports—A. Clopper, *et al., 1985: Interindustry Forecasts of the American Economy,* E-28 (1974) (*See also* Supplement p. 66); National Planning Association, *The U.S. Economy 1973 to 1983,* S-85 (1973) (Report No. 73-r-l); U.S. Department of Commerce—Bureau of the Census, *Current Industrial Reports—Office, Computing, and Accounting Machines* (Series MA-35R (73)-1) (Table 1—Value of Shipments of Office and Computing Machines, By Class of Product: 1973 and 1972); U.S. Department of Commerce—Bureau of the Census, *1972 Census of Manufacturers* (MC 72(2)-35F) (Table 1A—General Statistics 1958 to 1972—Value of Industry Shipments); U.S. Department of Commerce—Domestic and International Business Division, *Global Market Survey—Computer Equipment* (1973).

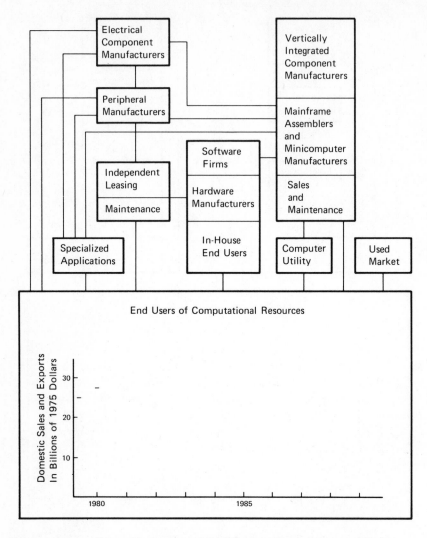

Sources: Diagram discussed in the text and the following references were consulted to
estimate the annual domestic sales and exports–A. Clopper, *et al., 1985: Interindustry
Forecasts of the American Economy,* E-28 (1974) (*See also* Supplement p. 66);
National Planning Association, *The U.S. Economy 1973 to 1983,* S-85 (1973) (Report
No. 73-r-l); U.S. Department of Commerce–Bureau of the Census, *Current Industrial
Reports–Office, Computing, and Accounting Machines* (Series MA-35R (73)-1) (Table
1–Value of Shipments of Office and Computing Machines, By Class of Product: 1973
and 1972); U.S. Department of Commerce–Bureau of the Census, *1972 Census of
Manufacturers* (MC 72(2)-35F) (Table 1A–General Statistics 1958 to 1972–Value of
Industry Shipments); U.S. Department of Commerce–Domestic and International
Business Division, *Global Market Survey–Computer Equipment* (1973).

Figure 3-3 (Part 4). Evolving Computer Industry Structure

the change in emphasis from hardware to software continued. The IBM decision to unbundle its software discussed in Chapter 2 also aided the software industry. The computer utility of selling computer time also emerged. In the latter 1950s, some end users purchased computers. When these end users purchased newer computers, some equipment was traded in, but the remaining equipment was sold to third parties. Consequently, a used computer hardware market developed in the latter 1960s and 1970s.

Peripheral manufacturers, which supplied only parts of an entire computer system, also developed in the 1970s. In some instances, the peripheral manufacturers sold directly to mainframe assemblers and minicomputer manufacturers. In other cases, they sold directly to end users. Electrical component manufacturers supplied mainframe assemblers, minicomputer manufacturers, and peripheral manufacturers. Specialized applications such as computer graphics also emerged.[182] By the middle of the 1980s the domestic and import data processing market is expected to be well over $20 billion. Prediction of future computer sales is extremely difficult. Prior to 1962, typewriters were included in the census data on computers. After 1962 computers and typewriters were separated. Ironically, as word processing becomes more automated by the use of intelligent terminals, typewriter sales may need to be reclassified back into the computer group. Various forecasts have been made, each based on constant dollars in the year of the forecast. The present forecast assumes constant 1975 dollars. In addition, it includes domestic sales and exports.

Specific dollar amounts of future computer sales based on present computer technology should not be unduly emphasized. Rather, attention should be directed toward future changes in computer technology and the resulting changes in the aggregate composition of computer sales. Minicomputers, peripherals, and software sales will increase drastically, but the medium scale market is expected to decline gradually.[183] Therefore, the estimates made in the bottom half of Figures 3-2 Parts 3 and 4 are only rough approximations of future computer industry sales.

The major addition to the 1980 computer industry structure will be the growth in minicomputer manufacturers. Electrical component manufacturers will supply large amounts of computational resources to the low end of the

---

[182] W. Sharpe, *The Economics of Computers* 186 (1969).

[183] *See* "Market Forecast 1975," 48 *Electronics* 100 (Jan. 9, 1975). (Supercomputers are expected to have an annual growth of between 5 and 9 percent, medium sized computers (.5 to 1.6 million dollars) are expected to decline approximately 6 percent, small and minicomputers in the range of .05 to .4 million dollars are expected to grow at a 13 to 14 percent rate, and finally, microcomputers are expected to grow at a whopping 50 percent annual rate. Overall, the annual industry growth rate through 1978 is predicted at 10 percent).

computational demand spectrum.[184] These electronic component manufacturers
will focus on the low end of the market because large maintenance and software
support is needed in the minicomputer systems and supercomputer systems markets.

In the 1950s, several technologically advanced firms tried to compete with
IBM and Burroughs in the business data market.[185] These firms (General Electric,
RCA, Philco) eventually withdrew from the mainframe systems market because
they did not have the business customer base as compared to the punch card base
of customers that IBM and Sperry Rand-Univac carried over from the 1940s.[186]

With the advent of large scale integration, however, electronic firms such as
Texas Instruments and National Semiconductor will be able to provide data
processing resources to a heterogeneous customer base, including such diverse
customers as the hospital industry, watch-making industry, and instrument control industry.[187] Consequently, the computer-related technology will permit the
electrical components industry to evolve into a major part of the computer
industry.

Product Cycles. By the 1980s, the computer industry sales will be well over
20 billion dollars, and gross national product (GNP) will be over 1.5 trillion
dollars. The computer industry will, therefore, comprise approximately 2 to 5
percent of the entire economy. If the late 1970s annual growth rate were to
continue through the late 1980s, the computer industry would comprise 10 to
15 percent of GNP. Consequently, a leveling in dollars sales will undoubtedly
occur by the latter 1980s. This leveling will, in effect, be the beginning of the
second stage in the industry growth cycle.[188] Although aggregate sales will level

---

[184] *See, e.g.,* Schneiderman, "Smart Cameras Clicking with the Electronic Functions," 48
Electronics 74 (Aug. 21, 1975).

[185] *See* N. Caplin, *An Introduction to Automatic Computers* 199 (1963) (2nd ed.).

[186] *See generally* Fruhan, "Pyrrhic Victories in Fights for Market Share," 50 *Harv. Bus. Rev.*
76 (Sept.-Oct. 1972); Schusell, "IBM vs. RemRand–Part 2," 11 *Datamation* 58 (June 1975)
(IBM controlled approximately 90 percent of the commercial punch card market and
Remington Rand the remaining 10 percent).

[187] *See* Hayes, "Europe's Computer Industry: Closer to the Brink," 9 *Columbia J. World
Bus.* 113 (Summer 1974). *See generally* Y. Hu, *The Impact of U.S. Investment in Europe:
A Case Study of the Automotive and Computer Industries* 80 (1973); Ball, "Computers:
Prescription for Hospitals," 21 *Datamation* 50 (Sept. 1975).

[188] *See* Vernon, "International Investment and International Trade in the Product Cycle,"
82 *Qt. J. Econ.* 190 (May 1966). *See generally* A. Groppelli, *A Growth Process in the
Computer Industry* (1970) (Ph.D. Dissertation, N.Y. University); S. Kuznets, *Secular
Movements in Production and Prices* (1930); B. Slome, *Computer Technology in Standard-
ization in the U.S. Trade and Product Abroad: A Case Study of the Vernon Product Cycle
Model* (1972) (Ph.D. Dissertation, City University of New York).

as the industry goes through a maturing second stage, technological developments will provide additional computational resources for the same price. In computational capacity, therefore, the U.S. computer industry will continue to grow, but in dollar sales the growth rate will level by the latter 1980s.[189]

The structural divisions of Figure 3-3 Part 4 will now be examined in greater detail. Particular emphasis will be placed on the computer-related electrical component industry, the peripherals and systems market (including minis and supers), computer-related communications, the software market, and finally, foreign considerations. The emphasis will be on the interaction of technology and industry structure.

Electrical Components. Between 1967 and 1972, solid state semiconductor sales doubled.[190] Through 1978, factory sales of semiconductors are expected to increase at an annual rate of 5 to 10 percent.[191] By 1978, semiconductor domestic industry sales will be $3.5 to $4.0 billion, while the world semiconductor market by 1980 is estimated at $10 billion.[192]

The RAM market by 1978 is estimated at $1.75 billion.[193] No estimates are available for the mass memory market size, because the actual capacities as well as prices of the developing mass memories are not known at this point. Mass memory technologies as discussed in the text following Figure 3-2, however, will emerge by the latter 1970s.

Specific quantities and dollar sales produced by the electronics industry for computer sources are not critically important in this technological forecast. Rather, the key factor is that computer-related technology will continue to drive the electrical component cost-to-performance ratio down. By the 1980s, electronics industry sales will level off. As sales level, however, the processing capacity of each component will continue to grow, while the price of individual components declines. Therefore, the processing capacity output of the electrical component industry will grow throughout the forecast time frame.

The electrical component industry will have a two-fold effect on the computer industry. First, by providing the building blocks at steadily decreasing

---

[189] *See generally* W. Nordhaus, *Invention, Growth and Welfare: A Theoretical Treatment of Technical Change* (1969).

[190] U.S. Department of Commerce—Bureau of the Census, *1972 Census of Manufacturers* (MC 72(2)-35F) (Table 7A Materials Consumed, By Kind: 1972 and 1967).

[191] "U.S. Markets Forecast 1975," 48 *Electronics* 100 (Jan. 9, 1975).

[192] *Hearing on S. 1167 Before the Subcommittee on Antitrust and Monopoly of the Senate Committee of the Judiciary,* 93rd Cong., 2d Sess., pt. 7, at 5436 (July 23-26, July 1974) (The Industrial Reorganization Act—The Computer Industry) (Statement by Marilyn Walter-Carlson).

[193] "SemiCon Memory Field Seen Hitting 1.75 by '78," 20 *Electronic News* 38 (Jan. 20, 1975).

prices, the computer cost-to-performance ratio will also continue to decline. Second, electrical component firms will become potential entrants to the computer industry. By the 1980s, the electrical components industry will have a large base of heterogeneous customers including diverse customers as the instrument control and digital watch industries.[194] This heterogeneous customer base will provide the electrical components industry with a continuous sales outlet independent of the traditional data processing industry. The merging of computer and electrical component technology, therefore, allows the electrical component industry to straddle two markets: electrical components and the low end of computers. Consequently, the electrical components industry will not suffer the same fate as RCA, GE, and Philco in their computer efforts because the electrical components industry will have an autonomous revenue source within the same technology.

The electrical components industry has already vertically integrated down stream into the hand held calculator, terminal, other I/O devices, and add-on memory market.[195] In most instances, the electronic components industry firms will remain weak potential entrants due to the fact that the entry into the minicomputer and supercomputer markets requires a large software effort and maintenance organization.[196] As the third party maintenance industry develops, potential entry will become more viable because a large maintenance organization will not be needed. Prices of low end minicomputers will remain closer to competitive levels due to the potential entry of electrical component manufacturers.

Peripherals and I/O Devices. This section examines the effect microprocessors and minicomputers will have on peripherals and I/O devices. The intelligent terminal and printer markets are then considered. Although overall microprocessor sales in 1973 were only $5 million, by 1975 sales were slightly under $20 million, and 1978 sales are forecast at $40 to $50 million. Microprocessor sales, therefore, will double in the next three years and will reach $100 million by the middle of the 1980s.[197] Not all microprocessors sold are used in

---

[194] *See, e.g.,* Gold, "Digital Watch Prices Due for Tumble: Benrus Chief," 20 *Electronic News* 65 (April 14, 1975); Jurgen, "Technology Forecasting IV—Instrumentation," 12 *I.E.E.E. Spectrum* 52 (April 1975); Wilson and Green, "New Markets for Control Via Microprocessors," 214 *Iron Age* 53 (July 8, 1974).

[195] Interview, George Anner, Professor, Department of Electrical Engineering, University of Illinois, Urbana-Champaign (June 1975). *See generally* "Add-On Memories," 20 *Electronic News* 1 (April 21, 1975).

[196] Interviews, John Brackett, SOFTECH, Inc., Waltham, Massachusetts (July 1975); James VanDermey, Director of Research, Codex, Inc., Newton, Massachusetts (1975).

[197] Day, "Microcomputers," 19 *Electronic News* 1 (Dec. 16, 1974).

computer-related products. A large number of microprocessors, however, are incorporated into peripherals and I/O devices.

New opportunities in computer design are available through the use of microprocessors as discussed in Stage I of the technological forecast. Microprocessors will enable computer designers to incorporate large amounts of processing power into peripherals, thereby establishing distributed processing computer systems.[198] Therefore, microprocessor usage in computers will steadily increase during the forecast time frame.

Intelligent terminals can be defined as user programmable machines. A 15 percent average annual growth through the latter 1970s is predicted in the intelligent and nonintelligent terminal market.[199] The cost-to-performance ratio of intelligent terminals will dramatically decline by the early 1980s. For example, today an intelligent terminal with 64K RAM, floppy disks containing several hundred kilobytes of secondary storage, three plasma panel visual output devices, keyboard input, and network communication interfaces costs over $80,000. By the early 1980s, an equivalent configuration will only cost between $10,000 and $20,000.[200]

With the growth in intelligent terminal communications, a major consideration will be the establishment of communication interface and protocol standards. Due to IBM's dominance, the communication standards established by IBM for its intelligent terminals will become a quasi-industry standard despite the efforts of the American National Standards Institute (ANSI). If IBM establishes a uniform communications standard, a large intelligent terminal market will exist. IBM, however, is rumored to be establishing a special communication interface and protocol standard controlled by the central computer for each customer. A separate communications standard for each customer would add some security to the end user's computer system. The large intelligent terminal market would effectively be subdivided into several distinct smaller submarkets. As a result, entry into several small submarkets would be less attractive than entry into one large intelligent terminal market. IBM would naturally be able to change its communications standards in each submarket at will.[201]

As compared to computer systems (software and hardware) the development costs of intelligent terminals are relatively low. In addition, due to their low

---

[198] *See generally* Nelson, "The Economic Implications of Microprocessors on Future Computer Technology Systems," 44 *A.F.I.P.S. Proceedings* 629 (1975).

[199] "U.S. Markets Forecast 1975," 48 *Electronics* 100 (Jan. 9, 1975). *See also* Irwin and Kosman, "Compact Computing Power for Terminals," 3 *Telesis* 239 (July and Aug. 1974).

[200] P. Alsberg, "Research in Network Data Management and Resource Sharing," 17 (1975) (CAC Doc. 164 and JTSA Doc. 5510).

[201] "Intelligent Terminals," 20 *Electronic News* 1 (March 3, 1975).

cost, many of the intelligent terminals will be purchased rather than leased. Therefore, the barriers to entry in the intelligent terminal market will be relatively low.[202] Intelligent terminals capable of producing letter perfect copy will open the entire word processing and typewriter market to intelligent terminal manufacturers. Only 3 to 4 percent of over a million active heavy-duty office typewriter stations have thus far been converted to memory typewriters similar to intelligent terminals.[203]

At present, most terminals are produced in limited quantities. The limited quantities produced result in a high average cost to pay for the design costs. The marginal manufacturing cost is low. Therefore, once terminals can be produced in large quantities, the price will drop as in the case of the original Model T automobile, and more recently the hand-held electronic calculator. Once the price of a simplified intelligent terminal drops to $300-$400, numerous businesses and many homes will undoubtedly purchase simplified intelligent terminals rather than stand-alone typewriters. Convenient but direct communication to computer systems will, therefore, become available to vast numbers of individuals.[204] By the 1980s, the cost of a key-input-visual-output terminal with academic instruction, consumer banking and shopping transaction, and entertainment capabilities will cost between $400 and $500—the present cost of a color TV.[205]

The hard copy output market by the early 1980s will have annual sales of over a half billion dollars.[206] The emphasis in the printer market will be along two divergent paths. The high-performance, but high-cost, printer market will grow. There will be some movement toward high-performance, nonimpact electronic printing. The major growth, however, will be in the low-cost, but low-performance printers used in minicomputer systems and integrated into intelligent terminals.

The card reader input market will grow very slowly due to the technological trend toward key-to-tape or key-to-disk input methods. The optical character recognition market is also expected to grow, but at a slower rate due to the trend toward capturing data in machine-readable form at its source.[207]

---

[202] See generally McLean, "Honeywell, CDC Form Peripherals Venture," 20 Electronic News 1 (April 21, 1975).

[203] Waler, "Word Processing Transforms Office Paperwork Routine," 48 Electronics 89 (June 12, 1975).

[204] Interview, Michael Faiman, Associate Professor, Department of Computer Science, University of Illinois, Urbana-Champaign (July 1975).

[205] Interview, Franklin Propst, Associate Director of Planning, Computer-Based Education Research Laborary (PLATO), University of Illinois, Urbana-Champaign (1975).

[206] Arvay, "Printers," 20 Electronic News 44 (Jan. 20, 1975).

[207] See generally "U.S. Markets Forecast 1975," 9 Electronics 100 (Jan. 9, 1975).

Large vocabulary speech input devices will not be commercially available in the latter part of the fifteen-year forecast, and thus, they are not discussed in Stage II of the technological forecast.

The peripheral and input and output markets will grow during the forecast time frame. The cost-to-performance ratio of products predominantly relying on electrical mechanical technology will only gradually decline. Those products predominantly based on electrical component technology will continue to experience a faster decline in their cost-to-performance ratios. Finally, as electrical component reliability increases, the maintenance barrier to entry will also be reduced. Electrical-mechanical products, however, will continue to require large maintenance support.

Computer Systems. Through 1978, minicomputer sales (under $50,000 per system) are estimated to increase 25 percent from $800 million in 1975 to $1 billion in 1978. Medium-size computer systems ($400,000 to $800,000) will decrease 25 percent from $1.2 billion in 1975, to $900 million in 1978. Finally, large computer systems ($1 to 3 million) will increase 20 percent from $1.7 billion in 1975 to over $2.1 billion in 1978.[208] Therefore, the general purpose computer of the 1960s and the 1970s will gradually fade and will be replaced by the versatile minicomputer and the high performance supercomputer.[209]

A broad spectrum of computational power will exist within the minicomputer market. Very powerful minicomputer systems will gradually replace the present large computer system. Prices, however, will be in the low $100,000 region. Highly reliable turnkey minicomputer systems as well as inexpensive, but high performance-no-support minicomputer systems will also be available. Finally, an original equipment manufacturer (OEM) market will exist in which the minicomputer producers simply deliver a stripped-down model for inclusion into the manufacturer's end products.[210] The traditional minicomputer market defined as machines costing under $20,000 will gradually evolve to a diverse market with systems costing as little as $5,000 to as high as $100,000 to $300,000.[211]

---

[208] "U.S. Markets Forecast 1975," 9 *Electronics* 100 (Jan. 9, 1975).

[209] Interview, J. Richard Phillips, Division of Computer Research, National Science Foundation, Washington, D.C. (July 1975).

[210] Interview, David McKeown, Department of Clinical Engineering, George Washington University Medical Center, Washington, D.C. (July 1975).

[211] Interview, Earl Haight, Digital Equipment Corporation, Maynard, Massachusetts (July 1975). The performance of minicomputer systems will dramatically increase during the forecast time frame. By 1977, a minicomputer system with 4-8K of RAMs, a 2 microsecond processing time, and 300K of mass memory will cost approximately $2,000. In 1985, a similar minicomputer system with 32-64K RAMs, 250 nanosecond processing time, and 500K of mass memory will cost $300 to $700. Electronics Systems Division Air Force Systems Command, *Support of Air Force Automatic Data Processing Requirements Through the 1980s* 2-102 (1974) (Vol. 3–Technology) (Hanscom Field) (*A.D. Little Report*).

Although today there are over 40 manufacturers of minicomputer systems, undoubtedly in the latter 1970s a shakedown will occur in which the total number of minicomputer manufacturers will decrease.[212] At the low end of the minicomputer market, the semiconductor firms will provide data processing equipment.[213] The maintenance and software support requirements of larger systems, however, will limit the entry of semiconductor firms to the low end of the minicomputer computational spectrum. Many of the present minicomputer manufacturers will grow in size. Finally, the large mainframe manufacturers will continue to enter the market.

Along with IBM's dominance, several smaller computer manufacturers are established in the traditional mainframe market[214] By the 1980s, the large mainframe market will evolve into the supercomputers, which perform large computational tasks as well as control over unique resources. Data base management systems for large corporations will be an additional application for supercomputers.[215]

Communications and Networks. Annual growth of data communications through the middle of the 1980s is estimated at 35 percent.[216] By the early 1980s, a 40 to 1 performance improvement is expected in telecommunications. In present satellite technology, satellites have 12 and 24 transponders. Each transponder has a 900 voice grade channel capacity. By the middle of the 1980s, transponders will not only have signal repeating capability, but also switching capacity. In the initial development of domestic satellite systems, each transponder will annually lease for $1.5 to $2.0 million. By the early 1980s, the annual rental cost of a transponder will decrease to the $250,000

---

[212] C. Wietzman, *Minicomputer Systems: Structure, Implementation, and Application* 329 (1974).

[213] *See generally* Herzog, "Calculator-Based Systems Challenge Minis," 46 *Machine Design* 96 (Jan. 24, 1974).

[214] The other mainframe manufacturers are Burroughs Corp., Control Data Corporation (CDC), Digital Equipment Corp. (DEC), Honeywell, and Sperry-Rand (UNIVAC).

[215] *See generally* Electronics System Division Air Force Systems Command, *Support of Air Force Automatic Data Processing Requirements Through the 1980s* 2-118 (1974) (Vol. 3–Technology) (Hanscom Field) (*A.D. Little Report*) (By 1977 a large multiprocessor computer approximately 100 times more powerful than a Burroughs 3500 will cost between $1.5 to $2.5 million dollars. By the middle of the 1980s, a large multiprocessor computer approximately 500 times more powerful than the Burroughs 3500 will cost between $1.0 to $2.0 million dollars. A Burroughs 3500 is a small computer in the middle performance range of today's minicomputers.)

[216] Withington, "Beyond 1984: A Technology Forecast," 21 *Datamation* 54 (Jan. 1975). *See generally* Electronic Systems Division Air Force Systems Command, *Support of Air Force Automatic Data Processing Requirements Through the 1980s* 3-1 (1974) (Vol. 3– Technology) (Hanscom Field) (*A.D. Little Report*).

range.[217]   Supporting earth stations in the satellite system today costs $3 to $5 million and by the early 1980s will cost in the $100,000 range. Based on these cost reductions, Withington estimated that 2400, 4800 and 50K bit per second (bps) tariffs would decline 50 percent in the next ten years.[218]

Due to the FCC open entry policy in data communications, the data communications industry structure will change during the forecast time frame. Although there are large capital entry requirements, the shift from a single monopoly in data communications to several competing firms should aid the gradual downward price trend.[219]

Software. Software costs as a percentage of total system costs will be in the 85 to 95 percent range by the early 1980s. The software industry is divisible into five parts. Network information services compose the first division and consist of time-sharing centers whereby users transmit their data needing processing to the time-sharing vendor for processing. Once processed, the final product is transmitted back to the vendee. Batch services are the second major part of the software industry. In batch services, the information is hand-carried to the vendor for processing and then hand-carried back to the vendee in finished form. Third is facilities management whereby an existing computer installation is taken over by a third party firm or an entire turnkey software system is installed and maintained by a third party software firm. Software products are the fourth part of the industry and include system and application sales. The fifth area is software services, which includes the sale of programming manpower at hourly or daily rates. The average annual growth of these five software industry parts is estimated at between 10 to 15 percent through 1980.[220]

---

[217] Electronic Systems Division Air Force Systems Command, *Support of Air Force Automatic Data Processing Requirements Through the 1980s* 3-54 (1974) (Vol. 3– Technology) (Hanscom Field) (*A.D. Little Report*).

[218] Withington, "Beyond 1984: A Technology Forecast," 21 *Datamation* 54 (Jan. 1975).

[219] *See generally* Electronics Systems Division Air Force Systems Command, *Support of Air Force Automatic Data Processing Requirements Through the 1980s* 3-16 (1974) (Vol. 3–Technology) (Hanscom Field) (*A.D. Little Report*).

[220] Roach and Jung, "Spending for Software and Service," 21 *Datamation* 53 (March 1975); *Wall Street Transcript* 39634 (Feb. 24, 1975) (Address by William R. Hoover of Computer Sciences Corporation to Los Angeles Society of Financial Analysts, Jan. 21, 1975). Definitions of the computer services industry vary widely. Bower divides the industry into the following five parts: (1) Conventional service bureaus offering customers transaction processing performed locally by using their own computer programs and batch processing techniques; (2) On-line dedicated applications: (3) Data bank reference systems operating either on- or off-line, but unlike firms in the first two sectors, provide internal information such as credit references; (4) Remote job entry firms; and (5) Timesharing firms sell time to end users on an hourly basis. Bower, "Market Changes in the Computer Services Industry," 4 *Bell J. of Econ. and Management Science* 539 (Autumn 1973).

Annual growth rates through 1978 within the five parts of the software industry will vary widely. Software services and batch services bureaus' annual growth will be 5 to 8 percent, whereas annual software products, network information services, and facilities management growth will be in the 15 to 20 percent range.

Due to the near-zero marginal cost in producing identical software packages, specialization is occurring by type of software product. Once a basic software package is developed for the first user, the modification costs for additional users is far less than the original development cost. Consequently, specialized software vendors will become committed to specific industries or cross industries such as payroll, text editing, and econometric planning.[221]

The fourth part of the software industry dealing with the sale of software is further divisible into two subparts: large integrated software systems and turnkey systems.[222] Integrated software systems from production through accounting and management will be sold to large firms such as the Fortune 500 list.[223] The other extreme of large systems will be the smaller computer systems of the turnkey nature. Each basic turnkey system will be molded to the needs of the end user, because smaller businesses do not want all the costly special options available with present commercial software systems.[224] These turnkey systems, however, will give the end user some versatility in programming.[225]

Due to the low barriers to entry, the software industry will remain competitive. With under a million dollars, a group of talented programmers can form a software firm specializing in one application area.[226] In addition, firms that have paid for a software package either through inhouse development or purchase of computer programming services from third parties can readily resell the package due to the near-zero marginal cost of selling a duplicate software package. Except for very large specialized systems such as the airline reservation programs, software package vendees can always produce their own software. Therefore, the cost of packaged software will remain well below the initial development cost.[227]

---

[221] Roach and Jung, "Spending for Software and Services," 21 *Datamation* 53 (March 1975).

[222] Interview, John Bracket, SOFTECH, Inc., Waltham, Massachusetts (July 1975).

[223] *See, e.g.,* Knight, "A Cast Study: Airlines Reservations Systems," 60 *I.E.E.E. Proceedings* 1423 (Nov. 1972).

[224] Interview, Edward Cohler, Computer Signal Processors, Inc., Burlington, Massachusetts (July 1975). *See generally* D. Spencer, *Computers in Society: The Wheres, Whys, and Hows of Computer Use* (1974).

[225] Churchman, "Functional Approach to Turn Key System Procurement," 44 *A.F.I.P.S. Proceedings* 789 (1975).

[226] Bower, "Market Changes in the Computer Services Industry," 4 *Bell J. Econ. and Management Science* 539 (Autumn 1973).

[227] *See generally* Soden, "Planning for Computer Services Spinout," 59 *Harv. Bus. Rev.* 69 (Sept.-Oct. 1972).

International Aspects. Exports of computers have grown steadily from $1.3 billion in 1972, to approximately $2.0 billion in 1975.[228] By the early 1980s, U.S. exports are estimated to be well over $3 billion annually.[229] Based on the predicted rapid advancement of U.S. computer technology, foreign competition will lag behind the U.S. in computer technology.

Several foreign countries—where labor costs are relatively low—are beginning to assemble semiconductor chips. The chip design and manufacture is performed domestically, but the assembly process of placing the silicon chips onto the integrated circuit device is highly labor intensive. Consequently, this assembly stage is being performed overseas.[230] Therefore, as long as U.S. computer technology advances, the mainstay of computer manufacturing will remain in the United States. The export of labor-intensive functions, however, will continue.

Barriers to Entry

Overview. The focus of this section is on the interaction of advancing computer technology and the barriers to entry within the computer industry. Due to the industry's short-term leasing practices, only part of the total capital needed to enter the systems market is available from the sale of lease contracts. The remaining funds must be raised as either equity or general debt capital. Modularity and standardization trends are then considered. Finally, the interaction of independent maintenance and computer technology is examined.

Capital Requirements. There are many aspects to the capital barrier to entry. Large economies to scale exist in acquiring capital. Large firms can raise many millions of dollars of debt capital, whereas smaller firms are limited to a few million.[231] In the next five years, the large systems computer industry is estimated to require over a billion dollars, while the minicomputer industry will require over $300 million of financing.[232] The reason for the $1 billion in large

---

[228] U.S. Department of Commerce—Bureau of Census, *Current Industrial Reports—Office, Computing and Accounting Machines* (SERIES NA-35R(73)-1) (Table 3, Office, Computing and Accounting Machines—Shipments, Exports, Imports, and Apparent Consumption: 1973 and 1972).

[229] C. Almon, *et al., 1985: Interindustry Forecast of the American Economy* (1974) (End Tables, p. E-28, Industry #114—Merchandise Exports in Producer Prices Millions of 1971 Dollars). *See generally* U.S. Department of Commerce—Domestic and International Business Division, *Global Market Survey—Computer Equipment* 3 (1973).

[230] Interview, George Anner, Professor, Department of Electrical Engineering, University of · Illinois, Urbana-Champaign (June 1975).

[231] *See* F. Scherer, *Industrial Market Structure and Economic Performance* 124 (1970).

[232] Potts, "Computing for Capital," 21 *Datamation* 44 (March 1975).

computers is the industry practice of leasing rather than selling computers to end users. IBM in its dominant position will more easily raise its requisite capital financing. Most minicomputers are purchased rather than leased. Despite the faster projected minicomputer growth, minicomputer manufacturers require less capital due to the selling rather than leasing practice.[233] Due to the expected continual price decrease of minicomputers, the minicomputer industry practice of selling rather than leasing will continue. By being able to sell immediately its products, a firm's balance statement shows an immediate profit, which is attractive to debt and equity investors.[234]

In the 1960s, it was estimated that $1 billion was needed to enter the entire general purpose systems market. Amdahl Corporation is presently delivering commercial computers in the large systems class. The capital backing of Amdahl Corporation was in the $100 million range.[235] If Amdahl Corporation is able to install thirty to sixty systems, then entry limited to the high end of the general purpose computer systems market may be possible with capital of $100 million.

Entry into one part of the general purpose computer systems market is not totally safe. In the 1960s, Xerox Corporation purchased Scientific Data Systems (SDS), and continued to produce the SDS SIGMA Series, a general purpose time-sharing system. In the 1960s and early 1970s, the SIGMA was competitive with other medium-sized time-sharing systems. The medium-scale time-sharing market, however, began to decline in the early 1970s. Xerox was not making a profit on the SIGMA series.[236] In addition, the SIGMA series needed a major redesign to remain competitive with new medium-sized time-sharing systems. Xerox chose not to make the requisite capital investment, and therefore, withdrew from the general purpose time-sharing market.

In the large systems market, the massive sales organization needed to insure widespread availability is an additional barrier to entry. Consequently, an entrant must plan to lose money as a sales force is built.

Standardization. Once industry standards are established, existing and new equipment could be manufactured by smaller firms to substitute or supplement the systems manufacturer's products. As computer technology continuously advances, standardization efforts constantly lag behind new products. In addition, IBM's dominance makes it naturally loath to agree to permanent industry standards, which only aid firms in competing with IBM.

---

[233] The entire DEC PDP-11 family is generally sold outright to all customers. Interview, Earl Haight, Digital Equipment Corporation, Maynard, Massachusetts (July 1975).

[234] *See* "Financial Analysis of Computer Industry Stocks," *Institutional Investor* 106 (Sept. 1974).

[235] "A Tyro Challenges IBM in Big Computers," *Business Week* (May 12, 1975).

[236] Myers, "Xerox's Frustrating Drive for Dwarfdom," 21 *Datamation* 7 (Sept. 1975).

Evolving computer technology affects standardization efforts in each segment of the computer industry. Standardization is mandatory in large scale integration (LSI) to achieve the economies of scale resulting from mass production of LSI chips. Although computer designers still favor custom built chips, a compromise solution has been reached whereby a few uniform chips are made for all parts in the computer series. Modifications are made on these basic chips for special applications.[237]

In the input and output area, standardization efforts are continuing to update the American Standard Code for Information Interchange (ASCII)—data communication standard. IBM, of course, would prefer to establish its own standard, which by virtue of its dominance would assure the IBM standard a quasi-industry-standard status. The American National Standards Institute (ANSI) will eventually establish a new industry data communication standard.[238]

In the minicomputer area, the major emphasis has been in standard bus designs in which the minicomputer processor communicates with all peripherals along a common communication path.[239] The standard bus allows great flexibility in adding peripherals to a minicomputer system.[240] With the advent of LSI, more standardization is required to obtain the resulting economies of scale from mass production of LSI chips. Therefore, hardware standardization progress will continue.[241]

Standardization efforts in software are also continuing. With the growing dominance of software costs, transferable software will lower the systems barrier by allowing firms to produce hardware that utilizes standardized software. Standardized languages and programming techniques, however, force the end user to accept inefficient use of hardware.[242]

Modularity. If standardization in various aspects of computer design were achieved, a modular computer design would be feasible. Modular construction

---

[237] *See* "A Tyro Challenges IBM in Big Computers," *Business Week* 65 (May 12, 1975).

[238] *See* Hirsch, "Does SDLC Stack the Deck for IBM," 20 *Datamation* 121 (March 1974).

[239] *See generally* Chertkow and Cady, Unified Bus Maximizes Minicomputer Flexibility," 43 *Electronics* 47 (Dec. 21, 1971); Janson, "Common Bus Structure for Minicomputers Improves I/O Flexibility," 18 *Control Engineering* 50 (Jan. 1971).

[240] *See generally* C. Weitzman, *Minicomputer Systems: Structure, Implementation and Application* 326 (1974).

[241] As computer systems become more standardized, comparisons can be made between competing systems, resulting in a more rational purchasing procedure predominantly based on price competition. *See generally* E. Joslin, *Computer Selection* (1968).

[242] Interview, John Stifle, Senior Research Engineer, Computer-Based Education Research Laboratory (PLATO), University of Illinois, Urbana-Champaign (June 1975).

of computers has a long history,[243] although developments in modularity have been relatively slow.[244] LSI technology makes modular computer design economically viable.

Modular design techniques would have several effects on the computer industry. Firms would be able to produce one or more modular parts of a total computer system, and thus, bypass the systems barrier to entry. Maintenance would also be easier under modular design, because an entire modular part can be replaced while the malfunctioning part is removed and sent back to the factory for repair. In addition, modular design allows great flexibility in adding additional capacity to a computer system in either CPU, memory, or peripherals.

Independent Maintenance. Of the total rental payment for an average computer installation, 15 to 20 percent goes to maintenance.[245] Although its initial growth was slow, the third party independent maintenance submarket now has several national firms.[246] The requirement of a large maintenance organization is still a major barrier to entry in the commercial systems market. In the minicomputer market, however, the maintenance requirements are declining. Consequently, the maintenance barrier is slightly lower than in the commercial systems market.[247]

As computer designers incorporate LSI technology into computers along modular lines, the cost of maintenance will decline. Computer system reliability will also increase in that many computer breakdowns occur at macro connections. LSI reduces the number of macro connections by placing more functions on a single chip. Due to the low marginal cost of functions on LSI chips, redundant functions can be placed on a chip to increase the overall reliability of the

[243] *See generally* W. Elliott *et al.,* "The Elliott-NRDC Computer 401–A Demonstration of Computer Engineering by Packaged Unit Construction," *Proceedings of a Symposium Held at the National Physics Laboratory, England* (March 1953).

[244] *See Hearings on Economy and Government Management–Procurement of Data Processing Equipment Before the Subcommittee on Economy in Government, Joint Economic Committee,* 91st Cong., 2nd Sess. (July 1, 1970).

[245] *See generally* H. Taylor, *Capital Budgeting Theory as Applied to the Leasing or Purchasing of Capital Assets–With Emphasis on Computer Equipment* 97 (1967) (Ph.D. Dissertation, Louisiana State University and Agriculture and Mechanical College).

[246] *See Hearings on Economy and Government Management–Procurement of Data Processing Equipment Subcommittee on Economy in Government, Joint Economic Committee* 91st Cong., 2d Sess., (July 1, 1970). *See generally* M. Mandl, *Fundamentals of Digital Computers* (1958) (Technical discussion on computer maintenance).

[247] *See generally* C. Weitzman, *Minicomputer Systems: Structure, Implementation, and Application* (1974).

chip.[248] Therefore, the maintenance barrier to entry will gradually decline as computer reliability increases through the use of LSI technology.

At the low end of the computational market, prices have been relatively low resulting in the establishment of a general industry sale rather than lease custom. As modularity developments occur, the existence of modularity will aid firms in attempting to bypass the systems market and instead enter a sub-market by selling only a part of a total computer system. Computer technology is also increasing computer reliability and ease of maintenance through modular design. Consequently, the maintenance barrier to entry is also declining. Throughout the forecast time frame, these barriers to entry are expected to decline gradually.

IBM's Response

Overview. This section of the Stage II—Technological Forecast briefly examines IBM's corporate structural changes in response to computer technological change. The product development procedures used by IBM are then reviewed. Finally, possible future IBM market strategies are discussed.

Corporate Structural Changes. IBM dominated the commercial punch card market in the late 1940s and early 1950s. This dominance in the commercial punch card market served as the springboard for IBM into the commercial computer industry in the early and middle 1950s. Based on this original commercial punch card dominance, IBM has successfully maintained its computer dominance through several computer system generations. On several occasions, IBM has been forced to revamp its entire corporate structure to keep pace with computer technological developments.[249] The international sections of IBM's corporate structure have also undergone numerous reorganizations.[250]

---

[248] *See* Electronics System Division Air Force Systems Command, *Support of Air Force Automatic Data Processing Requirements Through the 1980s* 2-107 (1974) (Vol. 3—Technology) (Hanscom Field) (*A.D. Little Report*). *See generally* B. Maguire, *Handbook of Computer Maintenance and Troubleshooting* (1974) (Technical Discussion of Computer Maintenance).

[249] *See* A. Chandler, Jr., *Strategy and Structure: Chapters in the History of the Industrial Enterprise* (1962) (Chandler's thesis is that structure follows strategy. The corporate strategy chosen by a firm determines the structure of the firm.) *See generally* W. Banks, Jr., *An Inquiry in the Growth Factors and Financial Policies of International Business Machines Corporation and Into the Possibility and Probability of the Company's Continued Dominance of the Electronic Data Processing Industry* (1968) (Ph.D. Dissertation, University of Arkansas); C. Eames, *A Computer Perspective* (1973); M. Hamid, *Price and Output Decisions in the Computer Industry* (1966) (Ph.D. Dissertation, University of Iowa); B. Randell, ed., *Origins of Digital Computers: Selected Papers* (1973).

[250] Foy, "IBM's New World Trade: The Change is Symbolic," 20 *Datamation* 105 (May 1974).

Product Development Procedures. Commercial computer product development generally occurs in three stages. Once the technical feasibility of the innovation is proven in the product development cycle discussed in Chapter 1, an initial product is developed. This initial product then is experimentally marketed. After two to three years, a reliable product appears that has most of the original problems from the initial product resolved.[251] Based on its market dominance, IBM generally introduces its products during the last stage of the product development cycle. Due to the barriers to entry, IBM can normally safely wait until a product is fully tested and through a market acceptance period before it introduces the product.[252]

The pressure from competitor's innovative products is the primary force behind IBM's new product introductions.[253] The IBM slow reaction time is due to a defect in the computer industry structure caused by IBM's dominance. The product mix of IBM equipment is presumably carefully determined to achieve maximum profits. New products, however, endanger existing product revenues, and thus, potential profits. The massive IBM leasing base also deters product introduction. Once a product is paid for after forty to fifty months (based on a forty to fifty purchase price to lease ratio), IBM is receiving pure profit (less maintenance costs of 15 to 20 percent) in keeping the product on lease. New products destroy this leasing base, and thus, IBM is naturally hesitant to introduce new products until long after other firms have introduced similar products.

By the early 1970s, the mincomputer market had fully developed, but only recently has IBM entered the minicomputer market with its SYSTEM/32 minicomputer.[254] Amdahl Corporation is beginning to market a large computer that is faster than the largest IBM/370 computer. IBM, however, will not react immediately to the Amdahl threat, due to the impact a new IBM system (competitive to the Amdahl System) would have on the existing IBM 370/168 lease base. Consequently, until Amdahl Corporation is able to sell a significant number of computers, IBM will not introduce a new model.[255] Therefore, a major result of this structural defect is the slowing of computer technology by

---

[251] Interview, Wesley Snyder, Research Assistant Professor, Coordinated Science Laboratory, University of Illinois, Urbana-Champaign (June 1975).

[252] *See* Rubin, "IBM and the Industry," 21 *Datamation* 99 (Sept. 1975) (For instance, Burroughs developed virtual memory in the 1960's, but IBM did not include the innovation into its computers until the early 1970s.

[253] *See* G. Brock, *The U.S. Computer Industry: A Study of Market Power* 103 (1975).

[254] McLean, "System/32 Market Prospects Seen Good," 20 *Electronic News* 26 (Jan. 20, 1975).

[255] *See generally* "The 470's Are Coming (But Not From IBM)," 9 *Computerworld* 1 (July 2, 1975).

IBM's natural reluctance to introduce new products, even if it presently has the products fully developed.[256]

Future IBM Market Strategies. IBM has wisely adopted several courses of action to maintain its present dominance. A massive research and development effort is needed to insure that IBM is never more than one to two years behind in all areas of computer technology.[257] Historically as well as today IBM has maintained a large research and development expenditure level.[258] IBM research and development effort has not always kept pace with technological developments in the remainder of the computer industry.[259]

IBM experienced difficulty in developing a large computer in the early 1960s. Thomas J. Watson, Jr., even made the following statement to his staff in August of 1963:

Last week CDC had a press conference during which they officially announced their 6600 system. I understand that in the laboratory developing this system there are only 34 people, "including the janitor." Of these, 14 are engineers and 4 are programmers, and only one person had a Ph.D., a relatively junior programmer. To the outsider, the laboratory appeared to be cost conscious, hard working and highly motivated.

Contrasting this modest effort with our own vast development activities, I fail to understand why we have lost our industry leadership position by letting someone else offer the world's most powerful computer. At Jenny Lake, I think top priority should be given to a discussion as to what we are doing wrong and how we should go about changing it immediately. [*United States v. IBM*, Government pretrial brief at 177 (1974).]

IBM is undoubtedly facing the general problem of diminishing corporate innovative output above corporate size of $250 million.[260] The real loss may be in the

---

[256] Once a new product is introduced, IBM uses its large market share to maintain an optimal inventory and back order mix to maximize its profits. *See generally* F. Scherer, *Industrial Market Structure and Economic Performance* 154 (1970).

[257] *See generally* Freeman, "Research and Development in Electronic Capital Goods," 34 *National Institute Economic Review* 40 (Nov. 1965) (Concept of threshold level of research and development is discussed whereby firms must maintain a minimum level of research and development expenditures to remain in the industry).

[258] *See* W. Banks, Jr., *An Inquiry Into the Growth Factors and Financial Policies of International Business Machines Corporation and Into the Possibility and Probability of the Company's Continued Dominance of the Electronic Data Processing Industry* 193 (1968) (Ph.D. Dissertation, University of Arkansas).

[259] G. Brock, *The U.S. Computer Industry: A Study of Market Power* 194 (1975) (Discussion of IBM's lagging electronic component technology in the late 1960s by one to two years).

[260] *See* F. Scherer, *Industrial Market Structure and Economic Performance* (1970).

form of managerial slack due to the lack of true competitive pressure resulting in general corporate inefficiency.[261]

IBM will be faced with a growing resale market,[262] as well as a minicomputer market that is gradually increasing its capabilities. Consequently, IBM will have fewer pricing options from its dominant market position. Several of its past successful market strategies will be even more important in the future. In the standards area, IBM will again attempt to establish its own quasi-industry data communication standards as ASCII is upgraded by the American National Standards Institute (ANSI). Although there is a trend toward distributed computation, IBM will attempt to keep critical processing functions within the CPU rather than allowing numerous processing functions to be independently performed by peripherals. Finally, within the software area, IBM will be able to control its operating system software due to its CPU dominance. The low barriers to entry in software applications will prevent IBM from dominating the applications market.[263]

IBM's corporate structure will constantly shift during the forecast time frame as computer technology evolves. Its products will continue to be introduced during the final stage of commercial product development. Continued massive research and development expenditures are expected, but slow product introductions will occur due to the large existing leasing base. The standards battle will continue with IBM continuing its attempt to establish (and thereby control) a quasi-industry standard. Finally, IBM will continue to resist the distributed computation trend to protect its CPU forte.

Technological Forecast—The Final Scenario

The scenario technological forecasting technique was chosen as the optimal forecasting procedure based on its ability to integrate scientific, economic, and legal considerations into a composite technological forecast. Within the electrical component area, the cost-to-performance ratio of electrical components is forecast to decline continually during the forecast time frame. Figure 3-1 highlighted the decreasing cost per bit trend in RAM technology. The mass memory technology illustrated in Figure 3-2 will also continuously advance. Therefore, the basic computer building block cost-to-performance ratios will steadily decline over the fifteen-year forecast time period.

---

[261] See generally Liebenstein, "Allocative Efficiency vs. 'x-Efficiency,'" 61 Am. Econ. Rev. 392 (June 1966).

[262] See generally "Patterns in Pricing Recessions Special," 20 Electronic News 16 (May 5, 1975) (Discussion of the computer resale market).

[263] See generally Bower, "Market Changes in the Computer Services Industry," 4 Bell J. of Econ. and Management Science 539 (Autumn 1973).

Within the peripheral and input and output areas, microprocessors will provide numerous new opportunities in computer design—especially in distributed computation. Therefore, the CPU will be able to specialize in its primary function of processing, leaving much of the input and output overload to peripheral devices. By the late 1970s, intelligent terminals will possess large amounts of both processing and memory capabilities. Advanced technologies, such as speech understanding, are not expected to develop within the forecast period.

Computer systems will shift in two directions. First, minicomputers will generally fill the low end of the demand for computational processing power. Microcomputers through large minicomputers will fill the needs of a wide spectrum of computational demand. Large minicomputers will replace the medium-scale commercial computers existing today. These minicomputers will be more powerful but less expensive than today's medium-scale computers. At the other end of the computational spectrum, supercomputers will emerge for those applications where large amounts of processing power are needed.

Communication technology will continue to decrease the price of the data communications. Large networks will emerge as viable methods for transporting large amounts of data between remote geographic locations. Advances in wave guide, satellite, and fiber optics will serve as the foundation for these decreases in communication costs. The FCC data communications open entry policy will also aid this price decline. Within software, development of engineering-type approaches to software design will continue. Data base management technology will evolve as well as nonnumeric computational patterns such as computer graphics.

Computer technology will, therefore, advance rather than level off as seen in Figure 1-7 of Chapter 1. Based on the continuous advancement of computer technology, the long-term trend toward structural atomization is expected to continue. This trend is caused by the interaction of scientific, economic, and legal factors. Assuming that the pending IBM case is resolved in favor of IBM, this long-term trend toward structural atomization will be relatively slow. Figure 3-3 outlined this long-term trend toward atomization. By the 1980s, the computer industry will have annual sales well over $20 billion per year. In the late 1980s, a leveling in dollar sales will occur while output of computational capacity continues to increase.

An entire spectrum of computational capabilities will be offered by numerous firms within the industry. At the low end of the computational market, electrical component manufacturers will provide much of the raw data processing capabilities at the microprocessor and microcomputer levels. These firms will have a heterogeneous customer base, and thus, will not suffer the same fate as RCA, GE, and Philco. Within the input and output area, numerous firms will be able to enter the industry due to their ability to provide products for specialized applications. In the systems market, minicomputers will expand downward and upward. Large numbers of the IBM System/32 family will be sold, but due to the relatively low barriers to entry existing within the minicomputer industry, IBM will not dominate the minicomputer industry. In the supercomputer area, IBM will face sophisticated end users who will focus on computer price and performance rather than operating systems that attempt to do everything for everyone.

The software industry will remain competitive due to the naturally low barriers to entry. Based on the long-term trend toward software becoming a large percentage of the total computer system cost, software will play a dominant role in the future computer industry. In the international area, as long as computer technology advances as discussed in Figure 1-7 of Chapter 1 the U.S. computer industry will continue to dominate the world computer market.

Barriers to entry will also begin to decline gradually over the forecast time frame. The minicomputer market sell rather than lease custom will keep the minicomputer capital barriers to entry relatively low. LSI developments will aid the trend toward standardization and modularity in computer design. Finally, due to the steady growth of independent maintenance firms, the maintenance barrier to entry will also gradually decline.

IBM will respond by attempting to slow this gradual trend toward structural atomization. Its major emphasis will be in maintaining a dual set of computer industry standards and resisting the distributed data processing trend to protect its CPU forte. The trend toward structural atomization will cause IBM's market dominance to decline gradually beginning in the latter 1980s.

4 Conclusion

This final chapter first reviews the economic origins of the computer industry and the development cycle model. The resulting policy implications of this development cycle model are then discussed. The legal environmental surrounding the computer industry is then examined. Emphasis is placed on each major legal area. Policy changes within the legal environment are considered. Within the technological area, the long-term trend toward technological induced structural atomization is reviewed. Finally, the interaction of technology and barriers to entry is considered.

Development Cycle Model

Several studies of the entire U.S. economy and technical innovation have been made.[1] No studies, however, have focused on the computer industry with the specific goal of determining the major technological growth factors of the industry.[2]

For U.S. computer industry dominance of the world computer market to continue, a governmental policy encouraging the continued advancement of computer technology must be pursued. In Chapter 1, the development cycle model of (1) a large underlying demand for computational resources, (2) early governmental funding of computer research projects to provide their technical feasibility (many times at academic institutions), and (3) commercial development was discussed. Several policy proposals can be extracted from this model. An underlying demand for computational resources must exist. As long as the computer price-to-performance ration continues to decline, traditional mechanical processing markets will open to electronic processing and new uses of computational resources will also develop. The demand for computation is very elastic. Given a large demand for computational resources, federal development projects must be aimed at specific goals, and funded for sufficient

---

[1] *See, e.g.*, U.S. Department of Commerce, Panel on Invention and Innovation, *Technological Innovation: Its Environment and Management* (1967).

[2] *See generally* B. Gilchrist and M. Wessel, *Government Regulation of the Computer Industry* (1972) (Proposed a broad study of the computer industry by a computer industry commission).

time periods.[3] The critical factor is early federal funding designed to prove the
technical feasibility of the computer innovation.[4]

The academic environment is an ideal location for proving the technical
feasibility of these projects. Not only does the academic environment insure a
free flow of information resulting from these development projects, but in
addition, universities provide the necessary manpower training facilities to insure
a continued supply of qualified computer manpower. Early federal computer
funding placed heavy emphasis on hardware development. With the continued
increased importance of software, funding should begin to shift to software
development. Due to the high percentage of overall systems cost devoted to software, even small percentage improvements in software will provide large overall
system improvements.[5]

Commercial production of computer innovations is the final stage of the
development cycle model. In this final step, governmental policy must insure
the rapid diffusion of these newly proven, technically feasible computer innovations into commercial markets. The optimal way to insure rapid diffusion of
these innovations into the market place is a governmental policy of industrial
competition.[6] Recent theoretical studies have shown that a competitive domestic market is better for long-run exports than a domestic monopoly.[7]

The Legal Environment

Antitrust policy has already affected the computer industry. The Justice Department 1969 antitrust suit strongly influenced IBM's unbundling decision in 1969.

---

[3] Interview, Weslie Snyder, Assistant Research Professor, Coordinated Science Laboratory,
University of Illinois, Urbana-Champaign (June 1975).

[4] See generally W. Gammon, Study of Opinions About the Role of the Federal Government
in Supporting Research and Development (R&D) In Computers and Information Processing
Systems (1972) (D.B.A. Dissertation, George Washington University) (Survey of 800 experts
in the computer industry concluded that the government must continue to play a large role
in the support of computer research and development); Organisation for Economic Cooperation and Development, Electronic Computers (Gaps In Technology) (1969). (Of the total
estimated world computer research and development expenditures, only 6 percent of those
expenditures occurred outside the United States).

[5] Interview, John Bracket, SOFTECH, Inc., Waltham, Massachusetts (July 1975). See generally McCall, "The Simple Economics of Inventive Contracting, 60 Am. Econ. Rev. 837
(Dec. 1970).

[6] See K. Pavitt, The Conditions for Success in Technological Innovation (1971); Avebury,
"The Economic Role of Government in Computing and Computer Development," Computing Economics—INFOTECH Information 353 (1973) (INFOTECH Information Limited,
eds.).

[7] White, "Industrial Organizations and International Trade: Some Theoretical Considerations," 64 Am. Econ. Rev. 1013 (1975).

The largest part of the computer industry, therefore, is more competitive today than in the middle of the 1960s. Naturally low barriers to entry in software also undoubtedly influenced IBM in its unbundling decision. Operating system development is inherently close to hardware design, and thus, each manufacturer will continue to dominate the operating systems used on its computers. Although large economies of scale exist in the software sale of multiple copies, due to the low barrier to entry, these large economies of scale will not enable a few firms to dominate the software industry.

Proposals for Software Protection. Any proposals to change the existing legal methods to protect computer programs must resolve a variety of difficult problems. First, there are many different types of software that need to be protected. Operating systems are very close to the manufacturer, as are compilers, both of which need legal protection. There are also application programs that are not directly tied to the manufacturer, but which are produced by numerous software firms as well as end users. If the protection scheme is to be fair, each class of software requires some type of legal protection. In addition, with the development of microprogramming, some software is hardware implemented in programmable read-only memories (PROM's). Therefore, in establishing a software protection scheme, one must not only look at the present types of software in existence, but also one must consider future software technological developments.[8]

There are also several user classes of software. Academic institutions use numerous statistical packages such as SPSS and many other types of computer programs. Finally, mainframe vendors and naturally end users compose distinct software user classes. Therefore, the view of each software user class must be considered.[9] Software also has varying shelf lives from as short as a few months to several years, as in the case of a large inventory control system.[10] Consequently, any solution to software protection must await the emergence of a concensus from these varied users of software.[11]

The eventual software protection scheme will probably follow a similar

---

[8] *See* Jones and Merwyn, "Trends in Microprogramming: A Second Reading," C-28 *I.E.E.E. Transactions on Computers* 755 (August 1974) (Technical discussion of microprogramming).

[9] Interview, Malcolm Morrison, Patent Office, U.S. Department of Commerce, Washington, D.C. (July 1975).

[10] Interview, Thomas Maggiacomo, Electrical Systems Group, Communications Division, GTE Sylvania, Needham, Massachusetts (July 1975).

[11] *See generally* Association of Independent Software Companies, "Position Paper on Legal Protection for Computer Program," (November 1968), 3 *Comp. L. Serv.* app. 4-1a (1974) (R. Bigelow, ed.).

development path taken by the present plant patent statute.[12] Problems
related to plant patents were unique, and the existing patent protection was not
sufficient. Consequently, plant patents were separated out as a unique problem.
The same situation also exists for software protection. Patent, copyright, and
trade secret protection all have various weaknesses in protecting software.
Therefore, some composite type of software protection is needed.

One year before Congress enacted the present Copyright Act,[13] the
Supreme Court in *White-Smith Music Publishing Co. v. Apollo Co.*[14] ruled that
a piano reproduction did not infringe plaintiff's copyright musical composition.
Congress then enacted the 1909 Copyright Act, but limited the copyright
owner's exclusive right to record their musical compositions by establishing a
compulsory licensing system. Under this licensing compromise, copyright
owners have the exclusive right to permit recordings of their work, but once
they permit one recording, anyone else may make a "similar use"–subject to
certain formalities and payment of two cents for each record of the work.[15]
Consequently, the 1909 Act did not provide copyright protection in sound recordings *per se*, but only in the musical composition that was the subject of the
recording.

This lack in the protection of sound recordings remained the law until the
Sound Recording Amendment of 1971 prohibited the copying of sound recordings.[16] Except for the Copyright Office procedures accepting copyrighted
computer programs, copyright software protection is in limbo between *White-
Smith* and the 1909 Copyright Act. Machine readable copies of a program may
not infringe the copyright based on *White-Smith*. In 1974, the Senate passed a
copyright revision that apparently ended the *White-Smith* problem by granting
software copyright protection.[17] The House did not act on S. 1361, but the
entire bill was reintroduced in 1975.[18]

---

[12] 35 *U.S.C.* 161 *et. seg.* (1973). *See generally* 3 *Dillers Walker Patents* sec. 189 *et. seg.* (1964,
2nd ed.); Langrock, "Plant Patents-Biological Necessities Infringement Suits," 41 *J.P. Off.
Society* 77 (1959).

[13] 17 *U.S.C.* sec. 1 *et seg.* (1973).

[14] 209 U.S. 1 (1908).

[15] *See* 2 M. Nimmer, *Nimmer on Copyright* sec. 108.41 (1974). The copyright owner must
file a "Notice of Use" and the person claiming the license must file a "Notice of Intent to
Use").

[16] 17 *U.S.C.* sec. 1 *et seg.* (1973). *See generally* Nimmer, "Photocopying and Record
Piracy: Of Dred Scott and Alice in Wonderland," 22 *U.C.L.A.L.R.* 1052 (1975).

[17] Section 102(a) of S. 1361, 93rd Cong., 2nd Sess., stated: "Copyrighted protection sub-
sists . . . in original works of authorship fixed in any tangible medium of expression . . . "
Section 106(1) stated that the copyright owner has the exclusive right "to reproduce the
copyrighted work in copies or phonographs." Copies are defined in section 101:

"Copies" are material objects, other than phonorecords, in which a work is fixed by any
method now known or later developed, and from which the work can be preceived,

Although the copyright revision law did not pass Congress, a law did pass establishing the National Commission on New Technological Uses of Copyrighted Works.[19] The Commission is to provide the President and Congress with a preliminary report within one year and a final report within three years. The purpose of the Commission is to study and compile data on the use of copyrighted works and authorships in "conjunction with automatic systems capable of storing, processing, retrieving and transferring information to make recommendations to such changes as are necessary."[20]

The World Intellectual Property Organization (WIPO) is also examining ways to protect software. In a recent meeting of nongovernmental experts on the protection of computer programs, the initial groundwork was laid for discussion of software protection schemes. Industry leaders at the advisory meeting were hesitant to deposit entire programs, but were willing to deposit descriptions of the programs for the creation of a software registry. At present, a proposal to establish a registry of computer programs has been made. In addition, there may also be developments to establish a treaty to protect computer programs as well as possible establishment of a model law for each member of WIPO to enact. To date, no definitive action has been taken, nor is any immediate action expected.[21]

These software protection proposals will undoubtedly take years before they are finalized. Thus, in the immediate future, firms will be faced with determining the best type of protection. To obtain patent protection, firms

---

reproduced, or otherwise communicated, either directly or with the aid of a machine or device, The term "copies" includes the material object, other than a phonorecord, in which the work is first fixed.

Consequently, it appears that by indirect means, *White-Smith* was reversed for all copyright protection. Section 117, however, stated:

this title does not afford to the owner of copyright in a work any greater or lesser rights with respect to the use of the work in conjunction with automatic systems capable of storing, processing, retrieving, or transferring information, or in conjunction with any similar device, machine, or process, than those afforded to works under the law, whether title 17 of the common law or statutes of a State, in effect on December 31, 1974, as held applicable and construed by a court in an action brought under this title.

Therefore, Section 117 may be read to override Sections 102(a), 106(1), and 101 and allow *White-Smith* to remain in effect for software copyrights.

[18] S. 22, 94th Cong., 1st Sess.

[19] 17 *U.S.C.* 201 (1973).

[20] The Commission has been appointed and is now beginning to work. The appropriations, however, have not passed as of July 1975. Interview, Harriett Oler, Copyright Office, Office of the Registry, Washington, D.C. (July 1975).

[21] Interview, Harriett Oler, Copyright Office, Office of the Registry, Washington, D.C. (July 1975).

will need to have software that is closely interwoven with hardware. In the copyright area, firms will need lengthy programs in which copying is easily detected. Therefore, trade secret protection will likely continue as the favored software protection procedure for private firms.

Taxation aspects of computers will also continue to be important. The major issue needing resolution is the state taxation of software. An equitable procedure must be established that allows states to tax the actual value of software.

A Modification to the Present Export Regulation Procedures. At present there is a large time delay caused by lengthy bureaucratic procedures to export computers both to friendly countries and to the communist nations.[22] Although some observers have proposed that all restrictions on the export of computers to foreign countries be removed, some regulatory policy is needed.[23] Based on the discussion of Figure 1-7 in Chapter 1, if the U.S. rate of technology continues, then an export policy based on time of first commercial use in the United States would eliminate much of the bureaucratic procedures presently used to regulate computer exports. As long as computer technology advances and the rest of the world continues to lag behind the U.S. in computer technology, it is wise for the U.S. to sell its latest computers on a regular basis.

To friendly countries, one could maintain the existing policy of selling the most recent computers once they are commercially available in the United States. Commercial availability usually takes one to two years from their first emergence as prototype computers in the United States market. Basic economic theory teaches that countries possessing comparative advantage in certain means of production should capitalize and export the products that result from those means of production.[24] Studies have shown that once computers are placed into mass production, the United States no longer has a comparative advantage in the mass production of computers.[25] In addition, it is very difficult to limit the export of computers to friendly countries. The

---

[22] *See, e.g.*, Robertson, "Export Control Office Swamped with Applications," 20 *Electronic News* (Jan. 20, 1975).

[23] *See generally* National Export Expansion Council, *A Report of the Industry Advisory Committee on Office Machines* and Computers (1972) (Department of Commerce #C 1.42/3:IN2/4).

[24] A Harman, *The International Computer Industry: Innovation and Comparative Advantage* (1971).

[25] *See* B. Slome, *Computer Technology and Standardization in U.S. Trade and Production Abroad; A Case Study of the Vernon Product Cycle Model* (1972) (Ph.D. Dissertation, City University of New York); W. Gammon, *A Study of Opinions About the Role of the Federal Government in Supporting Research and Development (R & D) in Computers and Information Processing Systems* (1972) (D.B.A. Dissertation, George Washington University) (U.S. domestic producers are higher cost producers than their international counterparts).

ramifications of such limitations are great.[26] The only restriction would be that the computers could not be reexported to the communist nations. To the communist nations, the existing export prohibition of all military computers, which can be used in missile guidance, radar systems, and other weapon systems, would continue. Then, for those general purpose business computers, a simple time period after which the computers could be sold to communist nations would be established.

From the qualitative information available, the Soviet Union and the Eastern European nations are approximately 8 to 10 years behind the U.S. in computer technology. A simple rule, which would avoid the lengthy and costly bureaucratic procedures, would be that once commercial production and sale occurred in the United States, then 8 to 10 years later the computers could be sold to the Soviet Union and the Eastern European nations. Unfortunately, our allies are generally willing to sell computers to Russia and the Eastern European nations as soon as they are commercially available in Western Europe and Japan. An optimal U.S. trading strategy, therefore, is to sell computers to Russia and the Eastern European nations approximately two to three years after the same computers are sold to our allies but before our allies are able to produce commercially the same computers for sale to Russia and the Eastern European countries.

The proposed procedure would establish clear rules as to when computers could be sold to the communist nations. One can view this plan as a dynamic model in which the United States maximizes its potential gain as long as its computer technology continues one to two steps ahead of the rest of the free world's computer technology, and three to four steps ahead of the Russian and Eastern European computer technology.

The FCC policy allowing entry into the data communications industry should continue. Several competing firms in the data communications industry will insure the fastest implementation of technological innovations.

Within the procurement area, the Federal Government should vigorously support both software and hardware standardization efforts. As in COBOL, the Federal Government is the only computer purchaser with the economic power to force standardization. The standardization efforts must be led by prominent computer specialists and supported by adequate staff. Standardization will have an immediate effect in reducing the cost of federal computer procurements, because all bidders will need to conform to the established standards, and thus, compete more on price. Standardization will have the secondary effect of aiding the trend toward modularity and permitting firms entering the industry to bypass the systems barrier by selling one or more modular parts.

---

[26] See Y. Hu, *The Impact of U.S. Investment in Europe: A Case Study of the Automotive and Computer Industries* (1973) (Discussion of the United States embargo on large computers to France resulting in the French Plan Cal).

Federal procurement purchase rather than lease policy should continue. Purchase of computers lowers the capital barrier to entry. Finally, the Federal Government should continue, where feasible, to favor the development of a viable third party maintenance industry. Bidding for federal maintenance contracts on federally purchased equipment should be open to all qualified firms.

Technological Forecast

Technologically Induced Structural Atomization. Figures 3-3 of Chapter 3 highlighted a predicted long-term trend toward structural atomization of the computer industry. This trend developed in the late 1950s and will continue through the 1980s. The full effect of this trend is not felt due to the structural defect in the industry. Based on IBM's dominance, the diffusion of computer innovations throughout the industry will continue at a slow rate. This bias against new product introductions is a natural result of IBM's large leasing base and product mix. In the case of intelligent terminals and typewriters, IBM has been very slow in the development of a fully computerized text editing system, on account of its existing huge typewriter base.

Current computer related-technological developments are the forces underlying this structural atomization trend. Both at the building block level of the electrical components as well as the design of overall computer systems, these technological developments are pushing the computer industry into many new applications. As a result, the customer base of end users is continuously expanding. There will be numerous areas, therefore, where firms can exist within the computer industry without directly competing with IBM. Numerous potential entrants to the systems market will exist in markets using the same technology. The overall systems barrier to entry will also decline by the middle to late 1980s.

A broad spectrum of computational resources from microprocessors through supercomputers will develop. At the low end of the spectrum, electronic component firms will provide microprocessors, microcomputers, and in some instances, small minicomputers. The competitive structure of the minicomputer market will remain with minicomputers expanding into the traditional mainframe medium-scale computer market.

The present software market will remain competitive. Although large economies of scale are obtainable from the sale of a duplicate software package, the cost of creating an entire application software package is not high enough to be a barrier to entry. Based on the economies of scale, however, firms are beginning to specialize within special software applications areas.

Overall, the computer industry will continue to grow during the fifteen-year forecast time frame. By the early 1980s, annual industry sales will be

well over $20 billion. Computer technology will advance throughout the fore-
cast period resulting in the continued world dominance of the U.S. computer
industry.

Appendixes

Appendix A: Structured Interview Format

I. Background Information

1. Brief introduction to the study

    (a) Historical origins
    (b) Legal environment
    (c) Technological forecast – time period 1975-1990

II. Trends in technology

1. What types of memory technology will be available from now to 1990?

    Follow-up: What about LASER, Bubble, and electron memories?

2. What role will LSI play in the next fifteen years?
3. As an input technique, when will speech understanding systems enter the commercial market?

    Follow-up: Will OCR continue to grow in importance?

4. There is much discussion in the literature concerning supers and minis, what roles will supers and minis play in the future?

    Follow-up: What about intelligent terminals?
    What effect will networking have in the interaction
    between minis and supers?
    What will be the effect of decreasing communications
    costs?
    What about satellite communication?

5. Do you foresee any major changes in software design and costs?
6. When do you expect artificial intelligence to emerge?
7. What is the most dramatic breakthrough that will occur in computer technology from now to 1990?
8. Are there any other significant technological developments that we have not discussed?

III. Economic and Legal Considerations

1. What problems exist between standardization and efficiency?

Follow-up: Any signs of future standardization efforts?

2. What role will the maintenance function play in the future industry structure?

Follow-up: Would the maintenance function be economically viable
if totally unbundled?

3. What role should the federal government play in funding new computer research and development projects as well as procurement of computer resources?
4. In the government regulation area, do you see a need to change any of the present government regulations affecting the computer industry?
5. Are there any other significant economic or legal considerations that we have not discussed?
6. Do you know of anyone in the computer industry who I could talk to?

Appendix B: Field Interviews

Alpert, Daniel, Director, Center for Advanced Study, University of Illinois, Urbana-Champaign. July 1975.

Alsberg, Peter, Associate Director, Center for Advanced Computation, University of Illinois, Urbana-Champaign. July 1975.

Anner, George, Professor, Department of Electrical Engineering, University of Illinois, Urbana-Champaign. June 1975.

Bittner, William, Captain, Judge Advocate General, Systems Command, U.S. Air Force, Hanscom Field, Bedford, Massachusetts. July 1975.

Bitzer, Donald, Director, Computer-Based Education Research Laboratory (PLATO), University of Illinois, Urbana-Champaign. June 1975.

Bracket, John, SOFTECH, Inc., Waltham, Massachusetts. July 1975.

Brichford, Maynard, Archivist, University of Illinois, Urbana-Champaign. October 1974.

Bruce, Bertram, Bolt, Beranek & Newman, Inc., Cambridge, Massachusetts. July 1975.

Caputo, Richard, Lockheed Information Systems, Washington, D.C. July 1975.

Chien, Robert, Director, Coordinated Science Laboratory, University of Illinois, Urbana-Champaign. July 1975. (Telephone interview.)

Cohler, Edward, Computer Signal Processors, Inc., Burlington, Massachusetts. July 1975.

Covo, Abraham, Electrical Systems Group—Communications Division, GTE Sylvania, Needham, Massachusetts. July 1975.

Daniels, Walter, Collins Radio Group—Rockwell International, Cedar Rapids, Iowa. July 1975.

Emmons, Lovis, Applied Information Development, Oakbrook, Illinois. June 1975.

Faiman, Michael, Associate Professor, Department of Computer Science, University of Illinois, Urbana-Champaign. July 1975.

Falk, Gilbert, Bolt, Beranek & Newman, Inc., Cambridge, Massachusetts. July 1975.

Ferzig, Walley, Bolt, Beranek & Newman, Inc., Cambridge, Massachusetts. July 1975.

Fetty, Bruce, New Ventures Group, Motorola, Inc., Phoenix, Arizona. July 1975. (Telephone interview)

Growdon, Charles, Project Manager Mid Illinois NA (Named Account) Branch, Burroughs Corporation. July 1975.

Haight, Earl, Digital Equipment Corporation, Maynard, Massachusetts. July 1975.

Huemiller, Timothy, Electrical Systems Group, Communications Division, GTE Sylvania, Needham, Massachusetts. July 1975.

Kelley, Karl, Assistant Director, Center for Advanced Computation, University of Illinois, Urbana, Illinois. June 1975.

Krone, Henry V., Assistant Director, Senior Research Engineer, Coordinated Science Laboratory, University of Illinois, Urbana-Champaign. July 1975.

Kuck, David J., Professor of Computer Science, University of Illinois, Urbana-Champaign. June 1975.

Maggiacomo, Thomas, Electrical Systems Group—Communications Division, GTE Sylvania, Needham, Massachusetts. July 1975.

McCauley, Edwin, Research Assistant Professor, Center for Advanced Computation, University of Illinois, Urbana-Champaign. June 1975.

McKeown, David, Department of Clinical Engineering, The George Washington University, Medical Center, Washington, D.C. July 1975.

Miller, Thomas, Digital Equipment Corporation, Maynard, Massachusetts. July 1975.

Morrison, Malcolm, Patent Office, U.S. Department of Commerce, Washington, D.C. July 1975.

Mullally, Donald, Director Broadcasting and Manager Radio and TV Station, University of Illinois, Urbana-Champaign. July 1975.

Muroga, Saburo, Professor, Department of Computer Science, University of Illinois, Urbana-Champaign. June 1975.

O'Keefe, Robert, Colonel, Information Systems—Electronics Systems Division, Systems Command, U.S. Air Force, Hanscom Field, Bedford, Massachusetts. July 1975.

Oler, Harriet, Copyright Office, Office of the Registry, Washington, D.C. July 1975.

Orr, John, Bell Laboratories, Holmdel, New Jersey. (On educational leave.) Attending University of Illinois, Department of Electrical Engineering, Urbana-Champaign. June 1975.

Pasta, John, National Science Foundation, Office of Computing Activities, Washington, D.C. July 1975.

Phillips, J. Richard, Division of Computer Research, National Science Foundation, Washington, D.C. July 1975.

Pollock, E.L., Research Associate, Department of Physics, University of Illinois, Urbana-Champaign. June 1975.

Poppelbaum, Wolfgang, Professor, Department of Computer Science, University of Illinois, Urbana-Champaign. June 1975.

Propst, Franklin, Associate Director of Planning, Computer-Based Education
Research Laboratory (PLATO), University of Illinois, Urbana-Champaign.
July 1975.

Ray, Robert, Research Assistant Professor, Center for Advanced Computation,
University of Illinois, Urbana-Champaign. June 1975.

Romani, Edward, Office of Computing Activities, National Science Foundation,
Washington, D.C. July 1975.

Schlosser, Stanley, Office of Legislation and International Affairs, Patent Office,
U.S. Department of Commerce, Washington, D.C. July 1975.

Slotnick, Daniel, Professor, Department of Computer Science, University of
Illinois, Urbana-Champaign. June 1975.

Snyder, Wesley, Research Assistant Professor, Coordinated Science Laboratory,
University of Illinois, Urbana-Champaign. June 1975.

Stifle, John, Senior Research Engineer, Computer-Based Educational Research
Laboratory (PLATO), University of Illinois, Urbana-Champaign. June
1975.

Stone, Thomas, Governmental Relations-Marketing Liaison, Motorola, Inc.,
Washington, D.C. July 1975.

Tenczar, Paul, Research Associate, Computer-Based Education Research Laboratory, (PLATO), University of Illinois, Urbana-Champaign. June 1975.

VanDermey, James, Director of Research, Codex, Inc., Newton, Massachusetts.
July 1975.

Weiss, Edward, National Science Foundation, Office of Information Services,
Washington, D.C. July 1975.

Williams, Martha, Director, Information Retrieval Research Laboratory,
Coordinated Science Laboratory, University of Illinois, Urbana-Champaign.
June 1975.

York, James, Division of Industry Productivity, (Formerly with Division of
Technological Studies), Bureau of Labor Statistics, U.S. Department of
Labor, Washington, D.C. July 1975.

Bibliography

Books

Abrams, M., and Stein, P., *Computer Hardware and Software: An Interdisciplinary Introduction* (1973).

Almon, C., *et al.*, *1985: Interindustry Forecast of the American Economy* (1974).

Alsberg, P., *Research in Network Data Management and Resource Sharing* (1975) (Center for Advanced Computation, University of Illinois, Doc. 164 and Joint Technical Support Activity of the Defense Communications Agency, U.S. Department of Defense Doc. 5510).

Alsberg, P., *et al.*, *An Annotated Bibliography to Network Data Management and Related Literature* (1975) (Center for Advanced Computation, University of Illinois, Urbana, Illinois).

American Bar Association, Section of Patent, Trademark and Copyright Law, *1974 Committee Report.*

Armer, P., *The Systems Gap* (1967) (Rand Corp. #PR 3641).

Armstrong, W., *Computer Leasing: Evaluating Criteria for Decision-Making* (1968) (American Mangement Association–Finance Division).

Arrow, K., *Essays in the Theory of Risk-Bearing* (1971).

———, *The Limits of Organization* (1974).

Atkinson, R., and Wilson, H., eds., *Computer-Assisted Instruction* (1969).

Atlantic Institute, *The Technology Gap–U.S. and Europe* (1970).

Auerbach Info., Inc., *Auerbach Terminal Equipment Digest* (1970).

Ayres, A., "Envelope Curve Forecasting," *Technological Forecasting for Industry and Government: Methods and Applications* (1968) (J. Bright, ed.).

Baxter, B., *Scientists Against Time* (1968).

Bekey, G., and Kapplus, W., *Hybrid Computation* (1968).

Belden, T., and Belden, M., *The Lengthening Shadow: The Life of Thomas J. Watson* (1962).

Bernacchi, R., and Larsen, G., *Data Processing Contracts and the Law* (1974).

Berstein, J., *The Analytical Engine: Computers, Past, Present, and Future* (1964).

Blackwell, F., *The Probable State of Computer Technology By 1980, With Some Implications for Education* (1971) (Rand Corp., Rep. No. P-4693).

Blane, *et al.*, *Annotated Bibliography of the Literature on Resource Sharing Computer Networks* (1973) (National Bureau of Standards, Information

Processing Division, Computer Systems Section, Special Publication No. 384).

Boehm, B., *Information Processing Requirements for Future Air Force Command and Control Systems: Some Implications for Software Research and Development* (1972) (Rand Corp., Rep. No. P-4795).

Bohlm, H., and Steinbach, K. eds., *Technological Forecasting in Practice* (1973).

Bolt, Beranek and Newman, Inc., *Natural Communications With Computers* (1974) (Report No. 2976 Vol. 1).

Bridges, H., ed., *Transistor Technology* (1958).

Brier, A., and Robinson, I., *Computers and the Social Sciences* (1974).

Brock, G., *The U.S. Computer Industry: A Study of Market Power* (1975).

Buchholz, W., *Planning a Computer System: Project STRETCH* (1962).

Cannell, C., and Kahn, R., "Interviewing," *The Handbook of Social Psychology* (1968) (2d ed., L. Lindzey and E. Aronson, eds.).

Caplin, N., *An Introduction to Automatic Computers* 199 (1963) (2d ed.).

Casey, R., *Punched Cards: Their Applications to Science and Industry* (1958).

Cavitch, *Business Organizations* (1974).

Computer Yearbook (1972).

Dahl, O., Dijkstra, E., and Hoare, E., *Structured Programming* (1972).

Davies, D., and Barber, D., *Communication Networks for Computers* (1973).

DiPaloa, R., *A Survey of Soviet Work in the Theory of Computer Programming* (1967) (Rand Corp. #5424PR).

Doncov, B., *Soviet Cybernetics Technology: Time-Sharing in the Soviet Union* (1971) (Rand Corp. #R-522PR).

Dryer, R., *et al., Optical Scanning* (1966).

Due, J., and Friedlander, A., *Government Finance: Economics of the Public Sector* (1973).

Dupree, A., *Science in the Federal Government: A History of Policies and Activities to 1940* (1957).

Eames, C., *A Computer Perspective* (1973).

Eckert, W., and Jones, R., *Faster, Faster: A Simple Description of a Giant Electronic Calculator and the Problems it Solves* (1955).

Electronics Systems Division, Air Force Systems Command, *Support of Air Force Automatic Data Processing Requirements Through the 1980's* (1974) (Hanscom Field).

Ellis, *Trade Secrets* (1953).

Feldheisen, J. and Szabo, M., "A Review of Development in Computer Assisted Instruction," *The Educational Technology Review Series* (1973) (Number 9–The Computer and Education).

Fleiff, J., *et al., Programming for Transferability* (1974).

Foy, N., *Computer Management: A Common Sense Approach* (1972).

George Washington University, Computers in Law Institute, *The Law of Software* (1968 and 1969).

Gifford, W., *Exporting: Government Assistance in Regulations* (1975) (Practicing Law Institute, Course Handbook Series #128 on Commercial Law and Practice).

Gilchrist, B., and Wessel, M., *Government Regulation of the Computer Industry* (1972).

Goldstine, A., "Report of the ENIAC," U.S. Army—Ordinance Department Contract No. W-670-ORD-4926.

Graham, *The Impact of Future Developments in Computer Technology* (June 1970) (Rand Corporation Report No. P-4401).

Gruenberger, F., *Digital Computer: The History of the JOHNNIAC* (Oct. 1968) (Rand Corporation Report Rm 5654-PR).

———, and Babcock, D., *Computing with Minicomputers* (1975).

Hattery, L., "Federal Development and Application of the Electronic Computer," *Federal Contributions to Management: Efforts on the Public and Private Sectors* (1971) (D. Brown ed.).

Head, R., *Manager's Guide to Management Information Systems* (1972).

Helmer, O., *The Delphi Method for Systematizing Judgments About the Future* (1966).

Herwald, S. "Appraising the Efforts of the Technological State of the Art on the Corporate Future," *Technological Planning on the Corporate Level* 53 (1961) (J. Bright, ed.).

Hoffman, L., "Group Problem Solving," *Advances in Experimental Social Psychology* (1965) (L. Berkowitz, ed.).

Holmes, G., and Norville, C., *The Law of Computers* (1971).

Horen, J., *Financial Management and Policy* (1971) (2d ed.).

Hu, Y., *The Impact of U.S. Investment in Europe: A Case Study of the Automotive and Computer Industries* (1973).

Husson, S., *Microprogramming: Principles and Practices* (1970).

Irving, C., and Brackett, J., *Automated Software Engineering Through Structured Data Management* (1974) (SOFTECH Inc., Doc. 553-37).

Jackson, P., Jr., *Introduction to Artificial Intelligence* (1974).

Jantsch, N., *Technological Forecasting in Perspective* (1967).

Joslin, E., *Computer Selection* (1968).

Katzan, H., *Introduction to Programming Languages* (1973).

Kenney, D., *Minicomputers: Low-Cost Power For Management* (1973).

Keuhne, R., *et al.*, *Handbook of Computer Documentation Standards* (1973).

Khambata, A., *Introduction to Large Scale Integration* (1969).

Kuznets, S., *Secular Movements in Production and Prices* (1930).

Ladas, S., *Patents, Trademarks, and Related Rights: National and International Protection* (1975).

Landauer, *Optical Logic and Optically Accessed Digital Storage* (Undated) (IBM Thomas J. Watson Research Center, Yorktown Heights, New York).

Laurie, J., *Textile Graphics: Computer-Aided* (1973).

Lee, W., ed., *The International Computer Industry* (1971).

Lein, A., Anton, P., and Duncun, J., *Technological Forecasting: Tools, Techniques, and Applications* (1968) (American Management Association Bulletin No. 115).

Lesher and Howick, *Assessing Technology Transfer* (1966) (Published by the National Aeronautical and Space Administration, Rep. #SP-5076).

Loevinger, L., "Communications Regulations," *The Law of Computers* (1971) (G. Holmes and C. Noville, eds.).

Loth, D., and Ernst, M., *The Taming of Technology* (1972).

Luskin, B., *et al.*, eds., *Everything You Always Wanted to Know About CAI But Were Afraid to Ask* (1972).

MacCaurin, W., *Invention and Innovation in the Radio Industry*, (1949).

Maginnis, J., *Fundamental ANSI COBOL Programming* (1975).

Maguire, B., *Handbook of Computer Maintenance and Troubleshooting* (1974).

Mandl, M., *Fundamentals of Digital Computers* (1958).

Mansfield, E., *The Economics of Technological Change* (1968) (1st ed.).

Martin, M., and Norman, A., *The Computerized Society; An Appraisal of the Impact of Computers on Society over the Next 15 Years.* (1970).

Martino, J., *Technological Forecasting for Decision Making* (1972).

Masta, M., "What Has Computer Graphics to Offer," *Computer Graphics* 1 (1969) (R. Parslow, R. Prowse, and R. Green, eds.).

Mathison, S., and Walker, P., *Computers and Telecommunications: Issues in Public Policy* (1970).

Michael, D., *Cybernation: The Silent Conquest* (1962).

Miller, A., *The Assault on Privacy: Computers, Databanks, and Dossiers* (1971).

Milne, M., *Computer Graphics in Architecture and Design* (1969).

Minsky, M., ed., *Semantic Information Processing* (1958).

Mishan, E., *Economics For Social Decisions: Elements of Cost-Benefit Analysis* (1973).

Morrison, P., and Morrison, E., *Charles Babbage and His Calculating Engines* (1961).

Murphy, M., "The Computer Industry Itself," *Computers and the Year 2000* 181 (1974) (Lord Avebury, ed.).

National Science Foundation, *Research and Development in Industry–Surveys of Science Resources Series* (1973) (NSP no. 73-305).

Newell, A., *et al.*, *Speech-Understanding Systems* (1971) (Carnegie-Mellon University, Pittsburgh, Pennsylvania).

Newman, W., and Sproull, R., *Principles of Interactive Computer Graphics* (1973).

Nicholson, *A Manual of Copyright Practice for Writers, Publishers, and Agents* (2d ed.) (1970).

Nimmer, *Nimmer on Copyrights* (1974).

Nordhaus, W., *Invention, Growth and Welfare A Theoretical Treatment of Technical Change* (1969).

Oppenheim, *Cases on Unfair Trade Practices* (2d ed.) (1965).

Organisation for Economic Cooperation and Development, *Electronic Computers* (Gaps in Technology) (1969).

Organisation for Economic Cooperation and Development, *Problems and Prospects of Fundamental Research in Multi-Disciplinary Fields: Computer Science* (1972).

Pasta, J., *The Role of the University in the Computer Age* (May 20, 1969) (University of Illinois, D.C.L. Rep. No. 330).

Pavitt, K., *The Conditions for Success in Technological Innovation* (1971).

Penrose, E., *The Theory of the Growth of a Firm* (1959).

Predicasts, Inc., *Basebook,* (1973).

Prime, M., *Interactive Graphics for Computer-Aided Design* (1971).

Pritchard, A., *A Guide to Computer Literature* 16 (1972) (2d ed.).

Post, E., *Finite Combinatory Process-Formulation I* (1963).

Randell, B., ed., *Origins of Digital Computers: Selected Papers* (1973).

Ray, R., *On the Methods for Direct Quantification of Pattern Associations* (1974) (Center for Advanced Computation, University of Illinois Doc. 139).

Rodgers, W., *Think: A Biography of the Watsons and IBM* (1969).

Rodriguez, F., *The Role of the Private Sector in Applying Computer Technology to the Development of Latin American Countries* (1969) (United Nations No. ED-055-601, Vol 72 #07 5B).

Rore, M., *Computers, Managers, and Society* (1969).

Scherer, F., *Industrial Market Structure and Economic Performance* (1970).

Sharpe, W., *The Economics of Computers* (1969).

Shouksmith, G., *Assessment Through Interviewing* (1968).

Smith, J., *Interviewing in Market and Social Research* (1962).

Smookler, J., *Invention and Economic Growth* (1966).

Soucek, B., *Minicomputers in Data Processing and Simulation* (1972).

Spencer, D., *Computers in Society: The Wheres, Whys, and Hows of Computer Use* (1974).

Stelmach, E., *Introduction to Mincomputer Networks* (1964) (Digital Equipment Corporation, Maynard, Massachusetts).

Stern, L., *Fundamentals of Integrated Circuits* (1968).

Streetman, B., *Solid State Electronic Devices* (1972).

Tilton, J., *International Diffusion of Technology: The Case of Semiconductors* (1971).

Time Incorporated, and the American Federation of Information Processing Societies, *A National Survey of the Public's Attitudes Towards Computers* (1971).

Turing, A., *Intelligent Machinery* (1947) (Reprinted in B. Meltzar and D. Michie, eds.).

Turn, R., *Computers in the 1980's* (1974).

Turn, R., *Computers in the 1980's: Tends in Hardware Technology* (1974) (Rand Corp. Rep. No. P-5189).

Turn, R., *The Use of Speech For Man-Computer Communication* (1975) (Rand Corp. Rep. R-1386).

Turner, *The Law of Trade Secrets* (1962).

UNESCO, *International Directory of Programmed Instruction* (1973).

United Nations Department of Economic and Social Affairs, *The Application of Technology for Development* (1973).

Univac Division—Sperry Rand Corporation, *Technology and Changes in the 1970's; A Basis for Perspective and a Better Understanding of Some of the Forces Which Influence Industrial, Economic, and Social Change in the Years Ahead* (1970).

University of Michigan, Survey Research Center, Institute for Social Research, *Interviewer's Manual* (1969).

Ware, W., *On Limits In Computing Power* (1969) (Rand Corp. Rep. No. P-4208).

Weber, S., *Large and Medium Scale Integration: Devices and Applications* (1974).

Weitzman, C., *Minicomputer Systems: Structure, Implementation and Application* (1974).

Weston, A., *Privacy and Freedom* (1967).

Wofsey, M., "The Management of Computer Systems," *Federal Contributions to Management: Effects on the Public and Private Sectors* 277 (1971) (ed. D. Brown).

Wooldridge, S., *Software Selection* 21 (1973).

Zellweger, A., *Five-Year Computer Technology Forecast* (1972) (U.S. Department of Transportation Rep. No. DOT-TSC-OST72-23).

Cases

Alfred Bell and Co. v. Catalda Fine Arts Inc., 191 F.2d 99 (2d Cir. 1951).

American Tobacco Co. v. United States, 328 U.S. 781 (1946).

Application of Benson, 441 F.2d 582 (CCPA 1971).

Application of Bernhart, 417 F.2d 1395 (CCPA 1969).

Application of Brandstadter, 484 F.2d 1395 (CCPA 1973).

Application of Doyle, 482 F.2d 1385 (CCPA 1973).

Application of Mahoney, 421 F.2d 742 (CCPA 1970).

Application of Musgrage, 431 F.2d 882 (CCPA 1970).

Application of Packet Communications Inc., 43 F.C.C.2d 922 (1973), FCC File No. P-C-8533) (Memorandum Opinion, Order and Certificate).

Application of Prater, 415 F.2d 1393 (CCPA 1969).

Applied Data Research, Inc. v. IBM, Civil No. 69-1682 (S.D.N.Y. 1969).

B. F. Goodrich Co. v. Wohlgemuth, 117 Ohio App. 493 (ct. App. 1963).

Carter v. American Tel. and Tel. Co., 250 F. Supp. 188 (N.D. Tex.), *aff'd*, 65 F.2d 456 (5th Cir. 1966).

Cincinnati Bell Foundry Co. v. Dodds, 10 Ohio Dec. Rep. 154 (Super. Ct. 1887).

Cochrane v. Diener, 94 U.S. 780 (1876).

Compco Corp. v. Day-Brite Lighting, Inc., 276 U.S. 234 (1964).

Control Data Corp. v. International Business Machines Corp., Civil No. 3-68-312 (D. Minn. 1968).

Crozier v. Crupp, 224 U.S. 290 (1912).

Dann v. Johnson, _____ U.S. _____, 44 *U.S.L.W.* 4463 (1976).

DuPont Powder Co. v. Masland, 244 U.S. 100 (1917).

Forro Precision, Inc. v. IBM, 697 *B.N.A.-A.T.R.R.* A-10 (Jan. 21, 1975).

General Aniline and Film Corp. v. Frantz, 50 Misc. 2d 944, 274 N.Y.S. 2d 634, 151 U.S.P.Q. 136 (N.Y. Sup. Ct. 1966).

Goldstein v. California, 412 U.S. 546 (1973).

Gottschalk v. Benson, 409 U.S. 63 (1972).

Hamilton National Bank v. Belt, 210 F.2d 706 (D.C. Cir. 1953).

Hancock v. Texas, 402 S.W. 2d 906 (Texas Crim. App. 1966), 379 F.2d 552 (5th Cir. 1967).

Honeywell v. Sperry Rand Corp., Civil No. 4-67-138 (D. Minn., 1973). [Reprinted in *Hearings on S. 1167 Before the Subcommittee on Antitrust and Monopoly of the Senate Committee on the Judiciary,* 93rd Cong., 2d Sess., pt. 7, at 5794 (July 23-26, 1974) (The Industrial Reorganization Act–The Computer Industry).]

Hush-a-Phone Corp. v. American Tel. and Tel. Co., 20 F.C.C. 391, 420 (1955).

In re Allocation of Frequencies in the Banks Above 890 Mc., *petition for reconsideration denied,* 29 F.C.C. 825 (1960).

In re American Tel. and Tel. Co., 13 F.C.C.2d 430 (1967).

In re Application of Microwave Communication Inc. For Construction Permits to Establish New Facilities in the Domestic Public Point-to-Point Microwave Radio Service, 18 F.C.C.2d 979 (1967).

In re Establishment of Policies and Procedures for Consideration of Application to Provide Specialized Common Carrier Service in the Domestic Public Point-to-Point Microwave Radio Service and Proposed Amendments to Parts 21, 43 and 61 of the Commission's Rules, 24 F.C.C.2d 318 (1970).

In re Regulatory and Policy Problems Presented by the Interdependence of Computer and Communication Services and Facilities, 7 F.C.C.2d 11, 17-18 (1967).

In re Western Union Tel. Co., 11 F.C.C.2d 1 (1967).

Irizarry y Puente v. Harvard College, 248 F.2d 799, (1st Cir.) *cert. denied,* 356 U.S. 947 (1957).

Kaumagraph Co. v. Stampagraph Co., 235 N.Y. 1 (1923).

Kewanee Oil Company v. Bicron Corporation, 416 U.S. 470 (1974).

Mackay Co. v. Radio Corp., 306 U.S. 86 (1938).

MAI Equipment Corp. v. Courterfield, 3 C.C.H. State Tax Rep., par. 200-433, at 10 (Ohio 1971).

National Association of Regulatory Utility Commissioners and the Washington Utilities and Transportation Commission v. Federal Communications Commission, 513 F.2d 1142 (9th Cir. 1975).

National Tube Co. v. Eastern Tube Co., 3 Ohio Ct. C. Rep. N.S. 459 (Cir. Ct. 1902), *aff'd.,* 69 Ohio St. 560, 70 N.E. 1127 (1903).

Oil Co. v. Bicron Corp., 416 U.S. 470 (1974).

O'Reilly v. Morse, 15 How. (56 U.S.) 62 (1853).

Phonetele, Inc. v. General Tel. of California, 3 Comp. L. Rep. 1192 (1972).

Quest Electronics Corp., Comp. Gen. B-163200 (March 12, 1968).

Schulenburg v. Signatrol, Inc., 33 Ill. 2d 379 (1965). *cert. denied,* 383 U.S. 959 (1966).

Standard Oil Co. v. United States, 221 U.S. 1 (1911).

Telex Corp. v. IBM Corp., 367 F. Supp. 258 (Okla. 1973), 510 F.2d 894 (10th

Cir.), *cert. dismissed,* ___ U.S. ___ , 96 5.Ct. 8 (1975).

United Software Corp. v. Sperry Rand Corp., Civil No. 74-1214 (E.D. Pa. 1974), 691 *B.N.A.-A.T.R.R.* A-20 (Dec. 3, 1974).

United States v. American Radiator and Standard Sanitary Corp. 433 F.2d 174 (3d Cir. 1970).

United States v. Bottone, 365 F.2d 389 (2d Cir. 1966), *cert. denied,* 385 U.S. 974 (1966).

United States v. DuPont Nemours Co., 351 U.S. 337 (1956).

United States v. Gerald Electronics Corp., 365 U.S. 567 (1961).

United States v. Greenwald, 479 F.2d 320 (6th Cir.), *cert. denied,* 414 U.S. 854 (1973).

United States v. IBM, Government pretrial brief at 117 (1974).

United States v. IBM, 1956 CCH Trade Cas. par. 68,256 (S.D.N.Y. 1956) *amended,* Civil No. 72-344 (S.D.N.Y. 1963 and 1970).

United States v. International Business Machines Corp., Civil Action No. 69-200 (S.D.N.Y. 1969).

United States v. International Business Machines Corp. 13 F. Supp. 11 (S.D.N.Y. 1935), *aff'd* 298 U.S. 131 (1936).

United States v. Lester, 282 F.2d 750 (3rd Cir. 1960), *cert. denied,* 364 U.S. 937 (1961).

United States v. The Southwestern Cable Co., 392 U.S. 157 (1968).

United States v. United Shoe Machinery Corp., 110 F. Supp. 295 (Mass. 1953), *aff'd per curian,* 347 U.S. 521 (1954).

United States v. Western Elec. Co., 1956 *C.C.H.–Trade Cas.* par. 71,134 (D.N.J. 1956).

Wesley-Jessen Inc. v. Reynolds, 182 *B.N.A. Pat., Trademark and Copyright J.,* A-2 (June 13, 1974).

White v. Kimmell, 193 F.2d 744 (9th Cir. 1952).

Williams and Wilkins v. United States, 420 U.S. 376 (1975).

W.R. Grace & Co. v. Hargadine, 392 F.2d 9 (6th Cir. 1968).

Dissertations

Banks, W., Jr., *An Inquiry Into the Growth Factors and Financial Policies of International Business Machines Corporation and into the Possibility and Probability of the Company's Continued Dominance of the Electronic Data Processing Industry* (1968) (Ph.D. Dissertation, University of Arkansas).

Billings, T., and Hogam, R., *A Study of the Computer Manufacturing Industry in the U.S.* (1970) (Masters Thesis, Naval Post Graduate School, Monterey, California).

Chandler, A., Jr., *Strategy and Structure: Chapters in the History of the Industrial Enterprise* (1962).

Gammon, W., *Study of Opinions About the Role of the Federal Government in Supporting Research and Development (R&D) in Computers and Information Processing Systems* (1972) (D.B.A. Dissertation, George Washington University).

Gropelli, A., *The Growth Process in the Computer Industry* (1970) (Ph.D. Dissertation, New York University).

Hamid, M., *Price and Output Decisions in the Computer Industry* (1966) (Ph.D. Dissertation, University of Iowa).

Kleiman, D., *The Integrated Circuit: A Case Study of Product Innovation in the Electronics Industry* (1966) (D.D.A. Dissertation, George Washington University).

Phillips, J., *Patterns of Price in Competition in the Computer Industry* (1971) (Ph.D. Dissertation, University of Illinois at Urbana-Champaign).

Riley, R., *A Case Study of a Differentiated Oligopoly: The Computer Time Sharing Industry* (1970) (Ph.D. Dissertation, University of Cincinnati).

Rock, M., *A Survey of MOS Devices and Processing* (1974) (Masters Thesis, University of Illinois).

Shuster, E., *Selective Demand Determinants in the Computer Acquisition Process,* (1969). (Ph.D. Dissertation, American University).

Slome, B., *Computer Technology and Standardization in U.S. Trade and Production Abroad: A Case Study of the Vernon Product Cycle Model* (1972) (Ph.D. Dissertation, City University of New York).

Sood, J., *A Study of the International Computer Industry and A Projection of the Effect of the American Computer Industry on the United States Balance of Payments from 1969 to 1975* (1971). (D.B.A. Dissertation, The George Washington University).

Taylor, D., *Capital Budgeting Theory as Applied to the Leasing or Purchasing of Capital Assets–With Emphasis on Computer Equipment* (1967) (Ph.D. Dissertation, Louisiana State University and Agriculture and Mechanical College).

Government Documents

Commission on Patent System, *The 1966 Report of the President's Commission on the Patent System* (reprinted in S. Doc. No. 5 90th Cong., 1st Sess. at 21).

Bryant and Mather, "Property Taxation of Computer Software," 18 *N.Y.L. Forum* 59 (1972).

Caine and Gordon, "PDL–A Tool for Software Design," 44 *A.F.I.P.S. Proceedings* 271 (1975).

Chertkow and Cady, "Unified Bus Maximizes Minicomputer Flexibility," 43 *Electronics* 47 (Dec. 21, 1971).

Chien and Snyder, "Hardware for Visual Image Processing," CAS-22 *I.E.E.E. Transactions on Circuits and Systems* 22 (June 1975).

Chou, "Computer Communications Networks–The Parts Make Up the Whole," 44 *A.F.I.P.S. Proceedings* 128 (1975).

———, "Technological Change and the Demand For Computers," 57 *Am. Econ. Rev.* 1117-1130 (Dec. 1967).

Churchman, "Functional Approach to Turn Key System Procurement," 44 *A.F.I.P.S. Proceedings* 789 (1975).

"Computer Leasing Today–Interview With J.N. Randolph," 42 *Financial Executive* 50 (May 1974).

"Computer Services in the Federal Regulation of Communications," 116 *U. Pa. L. Rev.* 328 (1967).

Cook, *et al.*, "An Overview of the 1974 COBOL Standard," 44 *A.F.I.P.S. Proceedings* 301 (1975).

Cunningham, "The Need for ADP Standards in the Federal Community," 15 *Datamation* 28 (Feb. 1969).

Curtis, "Theft of Secrets Continue," 48 *Electronics* 63 (May 15, 1975).

Davis, "Fresh View of Mini and Micro Computers," 13 *Computer Design* 67 (May 1974).

Davison, "Export Controls on Computers," 4 *Comp. L. Serv.* sec. 9-3, art. 2 (1974) (R. Bigelow, ed.).

Day, "Microcomputers," 19 *Electronic News* 1 (Dec. 16, 1974).

Day, "Small Computer Makers Split On High End Market Strategy," 20 *Electronic News* 1 (April 7, 1975).

Denison, "Source of Economic Growth in the United States," *Committee for Economic Development* (1962).

Desmonde and Berkling, "The ZUSE Z 3," 12 *Datamation* 30 (Sept. 1966).

Dobyns and Block "Adequate Disclosure of Computers and Programs in Patent Specifications," 56 *J. Pat. Office Society* 574 (1974).

Doerfer, "The Limits on Trade Secret Law Imposed by Federal Patent and Antitrust Supremacy," 80 *Harv. L. Rev.* 1432 (1967).

Dunn, "Policy Issues Presented by the Interdependence of Computer and Communications Services," 34 *Law and Contemp. Prob.* 369 (1969).

Dunwell, "Design Objectives for the IBM Computer," *Proceedings of the*

Eastern Joint Computer Conference 20 (Dec. 1956).

Eckert, "UNIVAC–LRAC, The Next Step in Computer Design," *Proceedings of the Eastern Joint Computer Conference* 16 (Dec. 1956).

Electronics Newsletter, *Electronics* 25 (June 26, 1975).

Elliott, W., *et al.*, "The Elliott-NRDC Computer 401–A Demonstration of Computer Engineering by Packaged Unit Construction," *Proceedings of a Symposium Held at the National Physics Laboratory, England* (March 1953).

"Eniac In Court: What Might Have Happened," 19 *Datamation* 119 (June 1973).

Erickson, "Regulation of Computer Communication," 7 *Harv. J. Leg.* 208 (1970).

Ershov, "A History of Computing in the U.S.S.R.," 21 *Datamation* 80 (Sept. 1975).

Evans, "Satellite Communications–The Legal Gap," 11 *Jurimetrics* J. 92 (Dec. 1972).

———— , "Computer Program Classification: A Limitation on Program Patentability as a Process," 53 *Or. L. R.* 501 (1974).

Falk and Popper, "Computer Programs and Nonstatutory Subject Matter in Canada," 4 *Comp. L. Serv.* sec. 9-4, art. 2 (1975) (R. Bigelow, ed.).

Falk, "Computer Systems: Hardware/Software," 12 *I.E.E.E. Spectrum* 38 (Jan. 1975).

———— , "Technological Forecasting II–Computers," 12 *I.E.E.E. Spectrum* 48 (April 1975).

Farmer, "1974 Retrospect: Mini Advances Take Center Stage," 8 *Computerworld* 17 (Dec. 25, 1974/Jan. 1, 1975).

"Fiber-optic Cable Getting Connector for Use in Field," 48 *Electronics* 29 (Aug. 21, 1975).

"Financial Analysis of Computer Industry Stocks," *Institutional Investor* 106 (Sept. 1974).

Flyer and Buell, "Tax Free Transfers of Computer Software to Foreign Corps: An Up-to-date Analysis," 41 *J. Tax.* 26 (July 1974).

Forest, "How to Build a Computer Industry: Is the Issue as Critical as Oil?" 21 *Datamation* 98 (1975).

Foy, "IBM's New World Trade: The Change is Symbolic," 20 *Datamation* 105 (May 1974).

Frank, "DDS Users in 19 Cities to Pay More," 8 *Computerworld* 1 (Dec. 25, 1974/Jan. 1, 1975).

———— , "FCC Restricts IBM's Satellite," 9 *Computerworld* 1 (Feb. 5, 1975).

———— , "Firm Testing Datran's Digital Dial-up Service," 8 *Computerworld* 15 (Dec. 25, 1974/Jan. 1, 1975).

Freeman, C., "Research and Development in Electronic Capital Goods," 34 *National Institute–Economic Review* 40 (Nov. 1965).

French, "Should DP Firms Trade with the East?" 8 *Computerworld* 1 (May 8, 1975).

Frisch and Frank, "Computer Communications: How We Got Where We Are," 44 *A.F.I.P.S. Proceedings* 109 (1975).

Fruhan, "Pyrrhic Victories in Fights for Market Share," 50 *Har. Bus. Rev.* 76 (Sept.-Oct. 1972).

Fueche, "Second-Generation Computers Live Again–In the Resale Market," 16 *Computers and Automation* 24 (Sept. 1967).

Galbi, "Copyright and Unfair Competition Law As Applied to the Protection of Computer Programming," 3 *Comp. L. Serv.* sec. 4-3, art. 1 (1975) (R. Bigelow, ed.).

–––––– , "Proposal for New Legislation to Protect Computer Programming," 17 *Bull. Copyright Soc'y.* 280 (1970).

Gardner, "Common Market May Step Up Probe of IBM's Dominance," 20 *Datamation* 54 (August 1974).

–––––– , "Leasing: A Phenomenon that Drains the Balance Sheets of All But IBM," 21 *Datamation* 78 (July 1975).

–––––– , "Will the Inventor of the First Digital Computer Please Stand Up," 20 *Datamation* 84 (Feb. 1974).

Gerla and Eckl, "Moving Bits by Air, Land and Sea–Carriers, Vans and Packets," 44 *A.F.I.P.S. Proceedings* 133 (1975).

Gibson, C.G., and Wilkinson, Should the Two Mix," 21 *Infosystems,* 28 (May 1974).

Gillies, Hoffman and Nelson, "Holographic Memories–Fantasy or Reality," 44 *A.F.I.P.S. Proceedings* 529 (1975).

Glauthier, "Computer Time-Sharing: Its Origin and Development," 16 *Computers and Automation* 23 (Oct. 1967).

"Going One Up On Voice Input," 20 *Datamation* 111 (Aug. 1974).

Gold, "Digital Watch Prices Due for Tumble: Benrus Chief," 20 *Electronic News* 65 (April 14, 1975).

Gordon and Becker, "The Cross Impact Approach to Technological Assessment," 15 *Research Management* 73 (July 1972).

Gosling, "Pre-History of the Transistor," 43 *Radio and Electronic Engineer* 10 (Jan.-Feb. 1973).

Gottlieb, Dalfen and Katz, "Transborder Transfer of Information by Communications and Computer Systems: Issues and Approaches to Guiding Principles," 68 *AM. J. International Law* 227 (April 1974).

Graham, "The Parallel and the Pipeline Computers," 16 *Datamation* 68 (April 1970).

Greenblott and Hsiao, "Where is Technology Taking Us in Data Processing Systems," 44 *A.F.I.P.S. Proceedings* 523 (1975).

Gross, "World Computer Market," 9 *Columbia J. World Bus.* 13 (March 1974).

Grove, "Information Processing Standardization: An Evaluation," 29 *Datamation* 47 (Feb. 1969).

Gruenberger, "Are Small, Free Standing Computers Here to Stay," 13 *Datamation* 67 (April 1966).

Gustafson, "Computers—Lease or Buy?" 41 *Financial Executive* 64 (July 1973).

Guttentage, "Prospects for New Tax Legislation Affecting Exports," *Exporting Governmental Assistance and Regulation* (1975) (Randall, Chairman, Practicing Law Institute, Commercial Law and Practice Handbook Series, No. 128).

Hacker, "For Printers Everywhere Computer Countdown is Now," *Printing Impressions* 20 (Feb. 1974).

Hammer, "IBM—Tighter Reins on Trade Secrets; Pledges Fight on Lawsuits," *New York Times* 57 (April 30, 1974).

Harvard University, "Symposium on Large-Scale Digital Calculating Machines," 16 *Annals of the Computation Laboratory* (1974) and 26 *Annals of the Computation Laboratory* (1949).

Hayes, "Europe's Computer Industry: Closer to the Brink," 9 *Columbia J. World Bus.* 113 (Summer 1974).

_____ , "Western Europe: Problems of Computer Industry Government Subsidizations," 9 *Columbia J. of World Bus.* 113 (Summer 1974).

Head and Linilk, "Software Package Acquisition," 14 *Datamation* 24 (Oct. 1968).

Heiborn, "The Art of Leasing Computers," 16 *Computers and Automation* 42 (Jan. 1967).

Herzog, "Calculator-Based Systems Challenge Minis," 46 *Machine Design* 96 (Jan. 24, 1974).

Himsworth, "Funding Cash for Communications," 21 *Datamation* 49 (March 1975).

Hinrichs, "Proprietary Data and Trade Secrets Under Department of Defense Contracts," 36 *Mil. L. Rev.* 61 (1967).

Hirsch, "Does SDLS Stack the Deck for IBM," 20 *Datamation* 121 (March 1974).

_____ , "The United States Electronics Industry in International Trade," *National Institute Economic Review* 92 (Nov. 1965) (No. 34).

Hirschel, Arnold, Neil, "The Allocation of Computer Time by University Computer Centers," 41 *J. Bus.* 383 (July 1968).

Hittinger and Sparks, "Microelectronics," 215 *Scientific American* 56 (Nov. 1965).

Hobbs and McLaughlin, "Minicomputer Survey," 20 *Datamation* 50 (July 1974).

Hockman and Hogman, "Technological Advances in Large-Scale Integration," 7 *I.E.E.E. Spectrum* 50 (May 1970).

Hogarth, "Transistor—Its Invention and Current Prospects," 4 *Physics in Technology* 173 (1973).

Holn and Jones, "Control Data STAR 100 Paging Station," 42 *A.F.I.P.S. Proceedings* 421 (1973).

Holt and Lemas, "Current Minicomputer Architecture," 13 *Computer Design* 65 (Feb. 1974).

Hopper, "Standardization and the Future of Computers," 8 *Data Management* 32 (April 1970).

Houser and Frahn, "Technology, Trade and the Law: A Preliminary Exploration," 6 *Law and Policy in Int. Bus.* 85 (1974).

"How the Judge Looked at the IBM-Sperry Rand ENIAC Part," 20 *Datamation* 78 (Jan. 1974).

Janson, "Common Bus Structure for Minicomputers Improves I/O Flexibility," 18 *Control Engineering* 50 (Jan. 1971).

Jones, L. and Merwin, R., "Trends in Microprogramming: A Second Reading," 23 *I.E.E.E. Transactions on Computers* 755 (Aug. 1974).

Jurgen, "Technology Forecasting IV—Instrumentation," 12 *I.E.E.E. Spectrum* 52 (April 1975).

Kaenel, "Mini Computers: A Profile of Tomorrow's Component," 18 *I.E.E.E. Transactions on Audio and Electroacoustics* 354 (Dec. 1970).

Kahn, "The Organization of Computer Resources Into a Packet Radio Network," 44 *A.F.I.P.S. Proceedings* 177 (1975).

Kamien and Schwartz, "Market Structure and Innovation: A Survey," 13 *J. of Econ. Lit.* 1 (March 1975).

Kamrany, "Technology: Measuring the Socioeconomic Impact of Manufacturing Automation," *Socio-Econ Planning Sciences* 281 (Oct. 1974).

Kaul, "And Now State Protection of Intellectual Property?" 60 *A.B.A.J.* 198 (Feb. 1974).

Keefe, "Not all Quiet on the IBM Antitrust Front," 60 *A.B.A.J.* 850 (July 1974).

Kelley, "Scale Economics, Inventive Activity, and the Economics of American Population Growth," 10 *Explorations in Economic Hist.* 35 (1972).

Kershenbaum, "Tools for Planning and Designing Data Communication Networks," 43 *A.F.I.P.S. Proceedings* 583 (1974).

Keyes, "Physical Limits in Digital Electronics," 63 *I.E.E.E. Proceedings* 740 (May 1975).

Klein, "The Technical Trade Secret Quadrangle: A Survey," 55 *Nw. U. L. Rev.* 437 (1960).

Knight, "A Case Study: Airlines Reservations Systems," 60 *I.E.E.E. Proceedings* 1423 (Nov. 1972).

_____ , "Evolving Computer Performance", 14 *Datamation* 42 (Jan. 1968).

Kostos, "Unauthorized Use of Technical Data in Government Contracts: Remedies of the Data Owner," 6 *Boston Coll. Ind. and Com. L.R.* 753 (1965).

Koudela, "Past, Present, and Future of Minicomputers: A Scenario," 61 *I.E.E.E. Proceedings* 1526 (Nov. 1973).

Langrock, "Plant Patents-Biological Necessities Infringement Suits," 41 *J.P. Off. Society* 77 (1959).

Laven, "Time Sharing Grows Up," 22 *Infosystems* 32 (Feb. 1975).

Leavitt, "UK Test Shows Some Minis Outperform Bigger CPU's," 8 *Computerworld* 1 (Dec. 25, 1974/Jan. 1, 1975).

Lien, Anton, and Duncan, "Technological Forecasting: Tool, Techniques, and Applications," *American Management Association—Management Bulletin* No. 115 (1968).

Levin and Morgan, "Optimizing Distributed Databases—A Framework for Research," 44 *A.F.I.P.S. Proceedings* 473 (1975).

Levy, "Computer Programs in Government Procurement," 10 *Will. and Mary L.R.* 658 (1969).

Liebenstein, "Allocative Efficiency vs. 'X-Efficiency,'" 61 *Am. Econ. Rev.* 392 (June 1966).

Lundell, "IBM/CDC Pact: 'No user disruption,'" 7 *Computer World* 1 (January 24, 1973).

Maltson, "Soviet Integrated Circuit Technology," 6 *I.E.E.E. Intercon Technical Papers 30/5* (March 26-30, 1973).

Mauchly, "Mauchly on the Trial of Building of ENIAC," 12 *I.E.E.E. Spectrum* 70 (April 1975).

McCartney and Wilkinson, "The Year Mini Users Shed the Security Blanket," 21 *Infosystems* 26 (Jan. 1974).

McLean, "Honeywell, CDC Form Peripherals Venture," 20 *Electronic News* 1 (April 21, 1975).

McDermott, "Take-Your-Pick Software is Making the Mini Mighty, But Watch Out—It Costs," 22 *Electronic Design* 78 (April 1974).

McGovern, "The Computer Field and the IBM 360," 16 *Computers and Automation* 16 (Jan. 1967).

_____ , "World Computer Market," 6 *I.E.E.E. Intercon Technical Paper* 2511 (March 26-30, 1973).

McGugan and Caves, "Integration and Competition in the Equipment Leasing Industry," 47 *J. Bus.* 382 (July 1974).

McIntyre, "An Introduction to ILLIAC IV Computer," 16 *Datamation* 60 (April 1970).

McLaughlin, "Monopoly is Not a Game," 19 *Datamation* 75 (Sept. 1973).

McLean, "System/32 Market Prospects Seen Good," 20 *Electronic News* 26 (Jan. 20, 1975).

"Memorex, IBM Ends Squabble Involving Trade Secret Suits," 6 *Computer World* 29 (Jan. 26, 1972).

Mennie, "Communications and Microwave," 12 *I.E.E.E. Spectrum* 43 (Jan. 1975).

McCall, "The Simple Economics of Inventive Contracting," 60 *Am. Econ. Rev.* 837 (Dec. 1970).

Moorhead, "Limiting Liability in an Electronic Data Processing Service Contract," 4 *Rutgers J. Computers and Law* 141 (1974).

Mullen, "Functional Spin-Off; A Key to Anticipating Change in Distribution Structure," 37 *J. Marketing* 18 (July 1973).

Myers, "Software and Taxes: A Basic Question," 14 *Datamation* 34 (July 1972).

_____ , "Xerox's Frustrating Drive for Dwarfdom," 21 *Datamation* 7 (Sept. 1975).

"Nanoseconds, Megabytes, Antitrust," 706 *B.N.A.-A.T.R.R.* B-1 (March 25, 1975).

"NBS Plans to Clarify a Rule on ASCII Use," 20 *Electronic News* 31 (Jan. 20, 1975).

Nelson, "The Economic Implications of Microprocessors on Future Computer Technology Systems," 44 *A.F.I.P.S. Proceedings* 629 (1975).

Nelson, R., "The Link Between Science and Invention: The Case of the Transistor," *The Rate and Direction of Inventive Activity: Economic and Social Factors* 549 (1962) (National Bureau of Economic Research).

Nimmer, "Photocopying and Record Piracy: Of Dred Scott and Alice in Wonderland," 22 *U.C.L.A.L.R.* 1052 (1975).

Nissen and Wallach, "All Applications Digital Computer," *Symposium on High-Level-Language Computer Architecture* (1973) (University of Maryland, College Park) (Sponsored by A.C.M.).

Noland, "Managing the Fourth States of EDP Growth," 52 *Harv. Bus. R.* 76 (Jan.-Feb. 1974).

Note, "Accommodation of Federal Patents and the State Interest in Trade Secrets," 16 *Will. and Mary L. Rev.* 171 (1974).

Opler, "Fourth Generation Software," 13 *Datamation* 22 (Jan. 1967).

Ornstein, *et al.*, "Pluribus, A Reliable Multiprocessor," 44 *A.F.I.P.S. Proceedings* 551 (1974).

Orthner and McKeown, "A Packet Switching Network for Computers," *Fall Proceedings of COMPCON* (1975) (Washington, D.C.).

Pantages, "An Introduction to Leasing," 14 *Datamation* 26 (August 1968).

"Patterns in Pricing Recessions Special," 20 *Electronic News* 16 (May 5, 1975).

Phillip, "Economic Development in the Use of Computers," 2 *Management Informatics* 265 (1973).

Pike, "Software Production for Minicomputers," 61 *I.E.E.E. Proceedings* 1544 (Nov. 1973).

Potts, "Computing for Capital," 21 *Datamation* 44 (March 1975).

Powell, "Satellites, Sovereignity and Speculation," 22 *Fed. Comm. Bar J.* 218 (1968).

Prasinos, "Worldwide Protection of Computer Programs by Copyright," 4 *Rutgers J. Comp. and Law* 42 (1974).

Purcell, "Control Data STAR-100 Performance Measurements," 43 *A.F.I.P.S. Proceedings* 385 (1974).

Ramamoorthy and Shankar, "Automatic Testing for the Correctness and Equivalence of Loop Free Microprograms," C-23 *I.E.E.E. Transactions on Computers* 37 (Aug. 1974).

"Relations Between Users, Software Vendors Maturing," 8 *Computerworld* S-8 (Dec. 25, 1974/Jan. 1, 1975).

Ridloff, "Procurement of Computers and Computer Services," 17 *Practical Lawyer* 73 (1971).

Riley, ed., *Electronic Computer Memory Technology* (1971).

Ritchie and Thompson, "The UNIX Time Sharing System," 17 *Communications of the ACM* 32 (July 1974).

Roach and Jung, "Spending for Software and Service," 21 *Datamation* 53 (March 1975).

Rosen, "Electronic Computers: A Historical Survey," 1 *Computing Surveys* 13 (March 1969).

Rosenberg, "Factors Affecting the Diffusion of Technology," 10 *Explorations in Economic History* 3 (1972).

_____ , "Science Invention and Economic Growth," 84 *Econ. J.* 90 (Mar. 1974).

_____ , "Technical Change in the Machine Tool Industry, 1840-1910," 23 *J. Econ. Hist.* 414 (Dec. 1963).

_____ , "The Direction of Technological Change: Inducement Mechanisms and Focusing Devices," 18 *Economic Development and Cultural Change* 22 (Oct. 1969).

Rubin, "IBM and the Industry," 21 *Datamation* 99 (Sept. 1975).

Rudenberg, "Large Scale Integration: Promises versus Accomplishments, A

Dilemma of Our Industry," 35 *A.F.I.P.S. Proceedings* 359 (1969) (Fall
Joint Computer Conference).

"Rumors and Raw Random Data," 16 *Datamation* 18 (Nov. 15, 1970).

Saragovitcz, "Patents-Trade Secrets—Technical Data Use and Misuse by the U.S.
Government," 15 *Vill L. Rev.* 331 (1970).

Scaletta and Walsh, "Comparison of Provisions in Government Computer
Purchase Contracts and the Standard Commercial Purchase Contracts," 10
Data Management 14 (Dec. 1972).

Schlesinger, "Federal Communications Commission—Review of Regulations
Relating to Provisions of Data Processing Services by Communications
Common Carriers," 15 *Bost. Coll. Ind. Comm. L. R.* 162 (1973).

Schneiderman, "Smart Cameras Clicking with the Electronic Functions," 48
Electronics 74 (Aug. 21. 1975).

Schusell, "IBM vs. RemRand—Part 2," 11 *Datamation* 58 (June 1975).

"SemiCon Memory Field Seen Hitting 1.75 by '78," 20 *Electronic News* 38
(Jan. 20, 1975).

Serrel, *et al.,* "The Evolution of Computing Machinery and Systems," 49
Proceedings of the Institute of Radio Engineers 1039 (1961).

"Seymour Cray's Cray-I Super Computer: Almost Five Times Faster Than a
7600," 21 *Datamation* 71 (July 1975).

Shortland, "Developments in European Mini-Computer Technology," 86
*Bulletin Scientifique del 'Association des Ingenieurs Electriciens Sortis
de l'Institut Electrotechnique Montefiore* 27 (Jan. 1973) (*Bull. Sci.
A.I.M.*).

Slotnick, "The Fastest Computer," 224 *Scientific American* 76 (Feb. 1971).

Smith, "Unidata Starts Long Climb Upward," 47 *Electronics* 1 (March 7,
1974).

Soden, "Planning for Computer Services Spinout," 59 *Hav. Bus. Rev.* 69
(Sept.-Oct. 1972).

"Software, Statutes, and Stare Decisis," 13 *How. L.J.* 420 (1967).

Solow, "Technical Change and the Aggregate Production Function," 39 *Rev.
Econ. Stat.* 312 (Aug. 1957).

"Soviet Union: The Computer Gap," 39 *Electronics* 187 (Jan. 24, 1966).

Steel, "Artificial Intelligence Research—Retrospect and Prospects," 16
Computers and Automation 22 (Jan. 1967).

———, "Standards for Computers and Information Processing," 8 *Advances
In Computers* 103 (1967).

Stern, "A Reexamination of Preemption of State Trade Secret Law After
Kewanee," 42 *Geo. Wash. L.R.* 927 (1974).

Stibitz, "The Relay Computers at Bell Labs," 35 *Datamation* 44 (April 1967).

Stigler, "The Division of Labor is Limited by the Extent of the Market," 59 *J. Political Economy* 190 (June 1951).

Strachey, "Time Sharing In Large Fast Computers," *First International Conference on Information Processing* 1 (June 1959) (Paris)

Stringer, "Microprogramming and the Choice of Order Code," *Automatic Digital Computation Proceedings of a Symposium held at the National Physical Laboratory* 71 (March 25-28, 1953) (No. 10).

Szuprowicz, "Soviet Bloc's RIAD Computer System," 19 *Datamation* 80 (Sep. 1973).

———, "Informationalization of Japan," 15 *Angewandie Informatik–Applied Informatics* 317 (Aug. 1973).

Taub, "Federal Communications Commission Regulation of Domestic Computer Communications: A Competitive Reformation," 22 *Buffalo L. Rev.* 947 (1973).

"Technological Piracy in Reprographic Revolution," 36 *Univ. Pitt. L. Rev.* 153 (1974).

"Telex v. IBM: Monopoly Pricing Under Section 2 of the Sherman" Act, 84 *Yale Law J.* 558 (1975).

"Telex v. IBM: Implications for the Businessman and the Computer Manufacturer," 60 *Virg. L. Rev.* 884 (1974).

Tenny, "Structured Programming in FORTRAN," 20 *Datamation* 110 (July 1974).

"The FCC Computer Inquiry: Interfaces of Competition and Regulated Markets," 71 *Mich. L. Rev.* 172 (1972).

"The 470's Are Coming (But Not From IBM)," 9 *Computerworld* 1 (July 2, 1975).

"The H.P. Model 2640A," 26 *Hewlett-Packard J.* (June 1975).

"The Light Wave of the Future," *Business Week* 48 (Sept. 1, 1975) (No. 2396).

"The Office of the Future," *Business Week* 48 (June 30, 1975) (No. 2387).

"The Shrinking of Stretch," 7 *Datamation* 17 (June 1961).

Thornton, "Parallel Operation In the Control Data 6600," 26 *A.F.I.P.S. Proceedings* 33 (1964) (Part II).

Threewitt, "The Microprocessor Rationale," 44 *A.F.I.P.S. Proceedings* 20 (1975).

Tolta, "IBM Reliability Experience With Hybrid Microcircuits," *I.E.E.E. International Reliability Physics Symposium-11th Annual Proceedings* 92 (March 1973).

Tom Disco (No. B-181956, Feb. 13, 1975), 570 *B.N.A.–Fed. Cont. Rep.* A-17 (March 3, 1975).

"Unauthorized Use of Proprietary Information by the Government: A Mixed

Bag of Remedies" 512 *B.N.A.-Fed. Contract Rep.* K-1 (July 1, 1974).

"U.S. Markets Forecast 1975," 48 *Electronics* 100 (Jan. 9, 1975).

Uselding, "Factor Substitution and Labor Productivity Growth in American Manufacturing 1839-1899," 32 *J. Econ. Hist* 670 (1972).

Vacroux, "Microcomputers," 232 *Scientific American* 32 (May 1975).

Vernon, "International Investment and International Trade in the Product Cycle," 82 *Qt. J. Econ.* 190 (May 1966).

vonNeumann, Burks, and Goldstine "Preliminary Discussion of the Logical Design of an Electronic Computing Instrument," 8 *Datamation* 24 (Sept. 1962).

Waler, "Word Processing Transforms Office Paperwork Routine," 48 *Electronics* 89 (June 12, 1975).

Walker, Mathison, and Jones, "Data Transmission and the Foreign Attachment Rule," 16 *Datamation* 60 (Feb. 1969).

Weiner, "How the Transistor Emerged," 10 *I.E.E.E. Spectrum* 24 (Jan. 1973).

Wessel, "Legal Protection of Computer Programs," 43 *Har. Bus. Rev.* 97 (March-April 1965).

_____ , "The Real Meaning of Telex," 21 *Datamation* 52 (July 1975).

_____ , "Third Party Maintenance for Those Above and Beyond Unbundling," 16 *Datamation* 177 (June 1970).

White, "Industrial Organizations and International Trade: Some Theoretical Considerations," 64 *Am. Econ. Rev.* 1013 (1975).

White, "Software Standards," *Digital Equipment Computer Users Society (DECUS)* 338 (Nov. 28-30, 1973).

Wilkes, "The Best Way to Design an Automatic Calculating Machine," *Manchester University Computer Inaugural Conference* 16 (1951).

Williams, "FCC Defines Its Impact Into Interconnect Impact," 20 *Electronic News* 38 (Jan. 22, 1975).

Wilson, "CAD/CAM Breaks the Holding Pattern," 22 *Iron Age* 33 (Jan. 20, 1975).

_____ and Green, "New Markets for Control Via Microprocessors," 214 *Iron Age* 53 (July 8, 1974).

Wise, "IBM's $5,000,000,000 Gamble," 74 *Fortune* 118 (Sept. 1966).

Withington, "Beyond 1984: A Technology Forecast," 21 *Datamation* 54 (Jan. 1975).

_____ , "The Next (and Last) Generation," 18 *Datamation* 71 (May 1972).

Wofsey, "Contracting for Software," 2 *Comp. L. Serv.* sec. 3-3, art. 2 (1975).

Woodcock, "Mental Steps and Computer Programs," 52 *J. Pat. Off. Soc'y.* 275 (1970).

Yasaki, "Japanese Slash AC Project Funds," 20 *Datamation* 111 (Aug. 1974).

_____ , "OCR Users Study Multi-Media Methods," 20 *Datamation* 32 (Aug. 1974).

Young, "Increasing Returns and Economic Progress," 38 *Econ. J.* 527 (Dec. 1928).

Statutes

10 *U.S.C.* sec. 2314 and 2315 (1973).

12 *U.S.C.* sec. 635 (1973).

15 *U.S.C.* sec. 1 (1973).

15 *U.S.C.* sec. 2 (1973).

15 *U.S.C.* sec. 18 (1973).

17 *U.S.C.* sec. 1 *et seg.* (1973).

18 *U.S.C.* sec. 1905 (1973).

28 *U.S.C.* sec. 1494 (1973).

35 *U.S.C.* sec. 151 (1973).

35 *U.S.C.* sec. 161 *et seg.* (1973).

40 *U.S.C.* sec. 759 (1973).

41 *U.S.C.* sec. 10(a) (1973).

47 *U.S.C.* sec. 151 (1973).

47 *U.S.C.* sec. 701 (a) (1973).

58 app. *U.S.C.* sec. 2402 (1973).

Index

199

About the Author

John T. Soma received the B.A. in Economics and Political Science from Augustana College, Rock Island, Illinois in 1970. In 1973 he received the J.D. from the University of Illinois, College of Law as well as the M.A. in Economics at the University of Illinois. In 1975 he received the Ph.D. in Economics at the University of Illinois. He is a member of the Illinois Bar.

His publications include "Enforcement Under the Illinois Antitrust Act," 5 *Loyola University of Chicago Law Journal* 25-44 (1974); "Functional Discounts: A Legal-Economic Concept Permitting New Experiments in Distribution Systems," 14 *Santa Clara Lawyer* 211-245 (1974); and "A Method for Analyzing, Detecting, and Correcting Multicollinearity," Center for Advanced Computation, University of Illinois, Urbana-Champaign, Document No. 118 (1974) (With Morris M. Kleiner).